# FINDING THE NEWS

# FROM OUR OWN CORRESPONDENT

John Maxwell Hamilton, *Series Editor*

# FINDING THE NEWS

**ADVENTURES OF A YOUNG REPORTER**

## PETER COPELAND

LOUISIANA STATE UNIVERSITY PRESS —— BATON ROUGE

Published by Louisiana State University Press
Copyright © 2019 by Peter Copeland
All rights reserved
Manufactured in the United States of America
First printing

Designer: Barbara Neely Bourgoyne
Typeface: Sentinel
Printer and binder: Sheridan Books

Library of Congress Cataloging-in-Publication Data
Names: Copeland, Peter, 1957– author.
Title: Finding the news : adventures of a young reporter / Peter Copeland.
Description: Baton Rouge : Louisiana State University Press, [2019] | Series: From our own
    correspondent | Includes index.
Identifiers: LCCN 2019009871 | ISBN 978-0-8071-7192-9 (cloth : alk. paper) | ISBN 978-0-
    8071-7250-6 (pdf) | ISBN 978-0-8071-7251-3 (epub)
Subjects: LCSH: Copeland, Peter, 1957– | Journalists—United States—Biography.
Classification: LCC PN4874.C686 A3 2019 | DDC 070.92 [B]—dc23
LC record available at https://lccn.loc.gov/2019009871

*To my mother, and to Maru*

# CONTENTS

----

*Illustrations appear after page 132*

# FOREWORD

_____

WANTED: Individuals willing to live out of a suitcase, sleep on the desert sand next to an army tank, look for scorpions in their boots when they wake up, go without a warm bath for days, worry about death threats from Latin American drug cartels, and day-in and day-out act as the faithful eyes and ears of their newspaper readers back home.

George Seldes spoke of foreign correspondents as the "nobility of American journalism." And rightly so. Given their distance from editors at home, correspondents have the most freedom of any kind of reporters. They hobnob with foreign leaders. They dine on exotic food. They cover news that can be the most perplexing and often is the most vital. Understanding what people abroad are doing and thinking is essential to anticipating threats to our national security.

Foreign reporting is also the most difficult. Correspondents cover economics and politics, culture and sports, the environment and immigration, epidemics and religion. They combine, in effect, the news beats of dozens of reporters in a domestic newsroom, but on a greater scale. They cover at least an entire country and often a vast region. When a crisis erupts, they hop planes to places they may have never seen before. When they land, they do not enjoy the legal protections that their home country assures them. In war, they can be killed as easily as any soldier.

For all of these reasons, correspondents have written thrilling, memorable books over the ages about their experiences. Peter Copeland's is no exception.

Readers will feel the frustration that comes with trying to penetrate foreign lands, the challenges of making stories relevant and meaningful for readers, and the exhilaration and raw fear of covering news in dangerous places. Copeland is a deft storyteller.

But this book has attributes not typical of correspondents' memoirs. This is what makes reading it unusually satisfying.

First, Copeland exemplifies a quality that is essential to the success of any correspondent, empathy. He has the ability to put himself in the place of the people he covered. While other (but not all) correspondents do this, he vividly shows the challenges and satisfaction of connecting with people and understanding the circumstances in which they live and act.

This approach is much in keeping with the traditions of the E. W. Scripps Company, formerly known as the newspaper group Scripps Howard. The newspapers never sent large numbers of reporters abroad, partly because until 1982 the company owned United Press International (UPI), which had a large overseas presence. Copeland was the only one from the newspapers permanently abroad when he was sent to Mexico City in 1984. A single correspondent in Europe was added later. But the company always covered wars, and its notable specialty has been its focus on people. In World War II, long before the military invented the term *embedded reporting,* Ernie Pyle was in the mud with soldiers and Marines, poignantly reporting their experiences and feelings. He was killed by enemy machine-gun fire on the Pacific island of Ie Shima. Scripps Howard's Raymond Clapper, one of the best reporters and commentators of his age, also died in the Pacific Theater. Jim Lucas, a former Marine who covered that war and subsequent ones in Korea and Vietnam, won a Pulitzer Prize for his boots-on-the-ground reporting.

Second, Copeland's autobiography is an object lesson in fidelity to professional norms. As he points out frequently in these pages, he was concerned with facts, not judging, in assignments that ranged from night police reporting in Chicago to overseas postings and Washington, DC. His job was to record the news, not shape it. While this was once taken for granted, it is less so today. Changes in news media in recent years have opened the door wider to opinion and commentary. Copeland reminds us of the value of accurately and fairly telling what happened.

Finally, and related to the first two points, Copeland's memoir is unsurpassed in showing how reporting is done at home and abroad. This nuts-and-bolts aspect of the book is in no way a dry how-to manual. In a lively manner, Copeland explains what goes into good reporting. Of course, the filing of news stories from overseas has changed since Copeland's time—which, by the way, makes his book a valuable reference for historians and others who want to know how things were done at that time. But technology—the essential determinant of the speed with which news can be transmitted—is only one part of foreign correspondence. Doing the heavy-lift of reporting to acquire a meaningful story is quite another. Every would-be journalist can profitably read this book for that reason alone.

No students of journalism can fail to learn from and be inspired by this book, even if they want to remain domestic reporters. Peter Copeland celebrates journalism's high calling, essential in a democracy, of serving readers—even when it means having to watch out for scorpions in your boots.

John Maxwell Hamilton
Washington, DC

# ACKNOWLEDGMENTS

———

Writing can feel like a solitary pursuit, but publishing a book requires a lot of help. I'm grateful to friends and family, especially my wife, Maru, who kept up my spirits and checked my facts.

Veteran newsman and friend George Hager, who has been backing me up since we covered Central America thirty-five years ago, was a generous and enthusiastic advisor.

Because of constructive feedback from early readers, especially Stephen Baker, I expanded the book from stories about covering the news to include the lessons I learned about journalism. I was trained by many great reporters and editors, and it is in honor of them that I humbly pass along their wisdom to future generations of young journalists.

Other early readers who made important suggestions and fixes include Zita Arocha, Matt Casey, Julie Castiglia, Luis Ferré Sadurní, Bart Gellman, Harry Moskos, Amie Parnes, Ruben Ramirez, Theo Stamos, and my first city editor, Paul Zimbrakos.

Kathleen Dragan edited the first draft with the perfect mix of encouragement and course correction.

At LSU Press, I enjoyed working with editor in chief Rand Dotson, senior editor Neal Novak, and copy editor Gary Von Euer. Journalist and scholar Jack Hamilton guided me through the process and improved the book.

I received needed guidance about book publishing, and how to make my story relevant to today's journalists and readers, from Battinto Batts,

Monica Bhide, Mary Kay Blake, Rich Boehne, Bruce Brown, Chris Callahan, Liz Carter, Roy Peter Clark, Isabella Copeland, Lucas Copeland, Trevor Corning, Ken Doctor, Peter Fritzell, Dave Giles, Josh Griffith, Ray Hanania, Sandy Johnson, Paul Mahon, Bruce Sanford, Bob Stewart, Mark Tomasik, Marvin West, and the outstanding students of the Foreign Correspondence course at Ohio University.

Photos were generously shared by Frank Aukofer, Michael Haederle, John Hopper, David Lawhorn, Ruben Ramirez, and Kirk Spitzer.

Lauren Francis-Sharma and colleagues at the DC Writers Room provided a productive and friendly place to work.

Thank you to *Washington City Paper,* which printed some of my Gulf War stories, edited by the inimitable Jack Shafer.

Finally, and most warmly, thank you to the Scripps and Howard families and everyone at the E. W. Scripps Company for always supporting me, for sending me around the world to cover the news, and for permission to reprint my experiences.

# FINDING THE NEWS

# 1

## SIRENS IN THE LOOP

—— ON GETTING IT FIRST ——

I walked through a badly burned apartment on Chicago's Far North Side, trailing a beautiful woman, on my fourth day of training. The woman was Theo Stamos, a young but experienced reporter, who had been assigned to teach me the basics. I stood alongside and listened while she called in a story on a fire that had gutted the apartment and killed an older woman and her young granddaughter. The apartment had been destroyed, but the rest of the building seemed fine, except for the bitter smell of smoke.

After Theo finished filing her story, we left the building and stood out front on the sidewalk. Theo said my training was complete, so I should head back to the office downtown. I was now, officially at least, a reporter.

The City News Bureau of Chicago did not allow reporters to spend money on frivolities such as taxis, and the job didn't pay enough for me to own a car, so I went looking for a bus down North Sheridan Road to the Loop. The day was cold and clear, February 7, 1980, and I was on my own for the first time as a reporter. I was twenty-two years old, dressed in a new three-piece suit under a buttery camelhair overcoat, and I had a fresh haircut. I liked the job so far, but there was a lot to absorb. Theo had taken me to press conferences, police stations, and crime scenes. I watched her navigate the city, come up with stories, and work with people back at the office. She was poised, smart, and determined.

I did not know what I was doing.

The sky was gray, and the tall buildings stood out in the crisp air; everything was sharply delineated, the colors bright. To the west I noticed a white cloud of smoke rising silently from behind the distant buildings. The cloud was getting bigger and turning black at the bottom. Fire. Big fire. As instructed by Theo, I had memorized the phone number of the office and carried a pocketful of change. I found a pay phone, dropped in some coins, and dialed. The operator answered quickly: "City News."

"This is Copeland," I said. "I'm on the North Side and I see smoke. Is there a fire in Uptown?" The plastic receiver felt cold against my ear. In the background, I heard scratchy voices over police and fire radios. Manual typewriters clacked and dinged.

"Hang on."

The smoke was thickening. It looked like it was just a few blocks away, but I couldn't be sure. Nobody around me seemed to notice. People were walking by on the sidewalk, hunched from the cold, eyes on the ground. Cars went up and down the street. I didn't hear any sirens.

"There's a fire coming in on Winthrop. Head over there now."

I ran toward the smoke. Soon my chest ached from the big gulps of cold air. My clunky dress shoes, only a week old, felt like blocks of frozen wood. Faint sirens coming from different directions grew louder as police and firefighters raced toward the cloud of smoke. I swallowed hard and breathed through my nose to keep my lungs from freezing.

I turned a corner and there it was: set back from the street was a large apartment building, four stories tall and half a block long. The lawn in front was covered by snow, but the sidewalks were clear. Cars were parked up and down the street.

Smoke was coming off the top of the building in a thick, steady cloud. Flames licked out from the upper windows and curled toward the roof. People near me, still a safe distance from the fire, were watching and pointing at the building. I looked up where they were pointing and saw men and women leaning far out the upper-floor windows, gasping for air and pushing their bodies away from the heat. Other people had jumped to the ground and were pulling themselves through the snow toward us. Babies and little children, shrieking like birds, were dropped from shattered windows to waiting arms below.

I could feel the heat of the fire on my face. The smell was burning wood and melting plastic. People screamed and the flames cracked and popped. I didn't think; I didn't hesitate. I ran toward the burning building. I pulled the stiff reporter's notebook from my overcoat pocket. The air was so frigid that I had to rub the tip of the pen across the paper to get the ink flowing.

My hands were steady and I no longer felt the cold. I scribbled notes about the people in the windows and the ones who had jumped, their legs twisted or broken, using their arms to pull themselves across the snowy ground. I wrote about the neighbors watching and trying to help. Not full sentences but words, phrases, impressions, down the narrow page of the notebook.

Fire engines with lights flashing pulled up fast and loud and clogged the street, so packed together, nose to tail, that they couldn't move back or forward. An old car with faded paint was blocking a fire hydrant. Move that car, someone shouted. A firefighter took a long iron rod off a truck and speared it through the driver's side window of the car, shattering the glass. He and another firefighter, their faces red from the cold and exertion, rammed the pole across the front seat and crashed it through the passenger side window like a shish kebab. Then they heaved on the bar to move the car enough to connect a hose to the hydrant.

A phone. I needed a phone. I had enough coins, but there was no pay phone in sight. The story didn't matter if you couldn't file, Theo said. You've got to be first. You've got to beat everybody. Call the office. File. Weaving through the fire trucks and the thick men in rough, heavy coats, I ran across the street and pulled open the glass door of an apartment complex facing the burning building.

I banged on doors until a lady opened, shyly, bowing her head toward me and stepping backward into the room. The way she looked at me, I sensed she did not speak much English. Phone, I said, making a calling gesture with my thumb and pinkie up to my ear. I have to make a call. She backed further into the room and I followed, spotting a phone on a table.

I dialed the office.

"City News."

"This is Copeland," I said. "I'm at the fire on Winthrop."

"Hang on. I'm going to give you to a rewrite."

A woman picked up the phone. "What have you got?"

"There are people throwing babies out the window! They're dragging themselves through the snow. A guy broke his legs jumping. The thing is burning like crazy." I was breathing hard again.

"How many trucks and how many pumpers?"

What?

"How many trucks? How many pumpers? How many responding?"

People are jumping out of the building, I repeated. Did she not hear me?

There were typing sounds in the background. I looked out the picture window and could see the burning building. The scene was oddly quiet now because I was inside.

"Count the trucks," she said. "The trucks are the ones with ladders. The pumpers are the ones with hoses. Tell me how many there are, and I can tell you how many firemen responded."

I could do that. I walked around the living room to get a better view and counted the trucks and "pumpers." I gave her the numbers.

What's the address? she asked. What time did it start?

I looked at my notebook, but the time wasn't there. Nor had I thought to write down something as obvious as the address. I don't know, I said, it started a few minutes ago.

Number of injured?

I don't know.

Where did it start?

Upper floors maybe. I don't know.

Where are the injured going?

The hospital, I suppose.

Yes, but which hospital?

I'm not sure.

Confirm the building address.

I wrote down her questions.

You need to find the chief and get the answers, she said. Call me back in five minutes. My name is Holley. The chief will be wearing a white helmet.

I held up one finger and told the lady I would be right back. She bowed again. I ran out of the building and into the chaos across the street, scanning the helmets until I saw an older man standing by himself, wearing a white helmet. Bingo. His heavy coat and boots were worn and dirty. His face was lined and grim. The burden of command.

My notebook out, my pen ready, I said, "Chief, what have we got here?"

He looked at me with a glare that smacked me back a step. Then his faced softened, a little. "Son," he said, as if to a small child, "I'm not the chief. I'm the chaplain."

What about the white hat? I looked at his white helmet again, which also helped me avoid his eyes, and I noticed the shield with a red cross.

"The chief is over there," he said, pointing me toward an even bigger, more serious guy in a similar heavy jacket. And an all-white hat.

I strolled over, more confident now that I had found my man.

"Chief, what have you got here?"

If the chaplain had looked at me with condescension and pity, the chief's face was pure contempt, unleavened by any compassion.

"What the fuck do you think I've got here?" His voice rose above the noise of the trucks and the fire and the people yelling. "I've got a building fully engaged and a bunch of my men inside. Now get the fuck out of here!"

I slinked away from the chief, pretending to check my notebook and hoping to find instructions for what to do next. My face was burning with shame and frustration. The cold made my eyes water. I couldn't read my own scratches on the page.

A TV crew piled out of a van and clambered toward the chief in a noisy cluster of gear, the camera rolling and a long foam-covered microphone aimed like a lance at the chief's head. The blow-dried reporter, dropping into his on-air voice, fired off questions. With the camera rolling, the chief turned all professional and calmly described the situation. I wrote down everything he said. The reporter got in a series of questions before the chief excused himself and pulled away to fight the fire. The questions the TV reporter asked were the ones in my notebook that Holley had told me to ask, in almost the same order.

I ran back across the street and pounded on the shy lady's door. She opened, bowing again, and stepped back, and I nearly ran her over to get to the phone. I clumsily dialed, my fingers swollen with cold. "Let me talk to Holley."

Holley walked me through the questions, interviewing me about the details and going back over things that weren't clear. She didn't assume anything and didn't allow me to presume I knew something when I did not. Only when we both were sure of a detail did she take it down. I heard the THWUK THWUK of her typing. Anything else? I flipped through the pages of the notebook, but that was it. I had told her everything I had written down.

"Go," she said. "Get more."

Back in front of the burning apartments, I saw a young African American man and introduced myself. I had noticed him when I arrived, so I asked when he first spotted the fire. I was trying to answer Holley's questions about where and when the fire had started. That would be a scoop if I could figure out the cause of the fire. He told me he was painting one of the apartments when he heard screaming and ran outside. That's when he saw the building was on fire. I tried to write down everything the young man said.

Then he mentioned he had caught a baby dropped from an upper floor.

Excuse me? I looked up from my notebook. Holley had not asked for that, but even I knew it was good stuff. I pressed for details.

He looked about my age. He was very matter-of-fact about catching the baby, who actually was a twenty-month-old boy, and pretty big.

Somebody dropped it, I caught it, he said. "Easy, man. No problem."

This is great, I said. Really great. What's your name?

He pronounced it, "Suh-BEE."

What's your first name?

"That is my first name, man."

I checked the spelling with him and asked for his last name and middle initial. There probably weren't many "Sabbes," but I had been instructed that a name, even an unusual one, was not complete without a middle initial.

My notebook filled up with more quotes from residents and witnesses, more details from the chief. I didn't ask him anything myself, but now many other reporters were shouting questions. All I had to do was write down the answers.

The fire was coming under control, and some of the firefighters were cleaning their gear and putting hoses back on the pumpers. Nobody claimed the car that had been smashed and muscled away from the hydrant. Groups of reporters interviewed people on camera, with white lights shining like little stars on the snow.

When I returned to the office my new clothes reeked of smoke, and my good shoes were soaked. I was cold and exhilarated. I met Holley Gilbert in person for the first time at her desk. I looked down and saw the stacks of carbon paper where she had written the story. The sheets of paper were stuck together and backed with ink, so typing on them made several copies at once. On top of each page were the words "Copeland to Gilbert."

She had taken my jumble of impressions and formed a clear, concise picture of the fire. She had guided me to see what others did not notice, made me check everything twice, and then crafted the chaos I witnessed into a news story. I got my first—and I would learn later, rare—attaboy from Paul Zimbrakos, the editor. There were jokes about the new guy getting his baptism by fire.

Then over the noise of the police and fire radios, above all the typewriters and the Teletype machines, and the yelling back and forth between reporters and editors, I heard the clear voice of an announcer on an all-news radio station. He was reading a story about the fire, and it was my story. I heard my own words coming over the air and through the radio. Right back to me. It was thrilling, a rush, the best attaboy ever. This was what I wanted to do with my life.

---

I spent the next thirty years chasing stories. Over time, I got better at covering the news, but it was a craft you never stopped learning. The basics were pounded into me in my first job: be fast, be accurate, be fair. We reported real news based on verified facts. At my first job I also learned how to operate the technology used to cover the news and share it with our audience, an aptitude that would be useful years later when the internet changed the business of news.

One thing that never changed during my career was the importance of journalism to democracy and to our future. Although many will disagree, I believe our core journalism values have not changed, either. We might lose sight of them, but those traditional values are the engines that power good journalism today, whatever the type of media or latest technology.

I was raised in an old-school news culture that had clear expectations and standards of behavior, so clear they didn't need to be written down or recited. The burden was on me and other young reporters to learn the rules, to ask, to watch, and then to get our own stories. We were called "cub" reporters because we were just starting, but we were given a lot of responsibility early and were expected to grow into our jobs. We were learning, so we made mistakes, and the humiliation we felt made us less likely to repeat them.

This is the story of my time as a cub reporter, which, like during kindergarten, is when you learn everything that matters. The most important lessons were not about reporting techniques, or writing skills, or the latest technology, but about the values that underlie the work. Later I would become an editor, a Washington bureau chief and news executive, but the time when I absorbed the most fundamental and enduring lessons, and had the most outrageous fun and adventure, was chasing cops, criminals, soldiers, and dictators around the world.

The lessons I learned—the journalism values—are more relevant today than ever before, especially as media technologies evolve. If we adhere to those solid values of speed, accuracy, and fairness, we can stay true to our mission and earn the trust of our audience, even those who accuse us of manufacturing "fake news."

The story of my career appears to be a logical, steady progression toward better assignments, but at the time I felt no such sense of order or direction. Often I felt fear and anxiety over what would become of me, or I was swept along by forces I did not control or even see. Every time I visited a strange country or was given a fresh beat, it felt like starting something new, in ways that were both exhilarating and terrifying.

I had no idea I would love covering the news until I did it for a living. Nor did I realize the work would give me a profound sense of purpose and belonging, things I didn't even know I craved. Growing up, I wasn't one of those kids with a "passion" for journalism, or for anything. How my career developed is still kind of a mystery, even to me.

Along the way, and far from home, I fell in love with a girl. That story remains just as mysterious, especially to me.

All I can tell you now is what happened at the time, based on my memories, the journals I kept, and the thousands of stories I wrote from dozens of countries on five continents. During an era when newspapers ruled the earth, I was trained by some of the great characters in a wild and quirky business, and they pushed me forward, often when I was afraid to go.

———

In the beginning, I was petrified. Riding up the elevator for my first shift at my first job, dressed in my grownup clothes, I felt a woman staring at me. She was about my age, but a little stern. I realized we both were going to the City News floor, so I smiled and explained myself, "First day."

She looked me up and down for an uncomfortable few seconds, and then pronounced, "I thought you looked like fresh meat." The door opened and she charged into the office ahead of me.

The man who ran the place had been equally chilly during my job interview. Jim Peneff, the general manager, who was almost fifty years my senior, questioned why anyone would leave the good money I was making in house painting and construction for the miserable pay of a reporter. The hours were bad, too, he said.

Are you sure you want to do this? he asked.

No, I wasn't sure, but I felt like I had to convince him. This was a job interview, and it was my challenge to win him over.

I smiled, leaned forward in my chair, looked him in the eyes. We weren't connecting, though, and I was beginning to doubt I would get the job.

After a few strained minutes, he put his palms on his desk, stood up, and asked when I could start.

So, wait, am I getting the job? I still wasn't sure what was happening. I said I was finishing up a few construction projects, but I was eager and could start next month.

He shook his head no. We'll see you Monday.

I didn't realize until later that the meeting wasn't an interview at all. I got the job Chicago-style: somebody had made a call. Chicagoans were open about how things worked. The saying was, "We don't want nobody nobody sent." The man who sent me to City News was about as powerful as could be in the news business, and for some reason, he took a chance on me.

After graduating in 1979 from Lawrence University in Appleton, Wisconsin, and traveling around Europe, I was living alone at our family cottage in northern Michigan. I painted a few nearby houses, built a shed, and installed a split-rail fence across a neighbor's wooded property. I had done that kind of work through high school and college, having learned from my grandfather on my father's side, who was a carpenter and general contractor. I liked the satisfaction of a job completed on time with a tangible result.

On my mother's side, my grandmother and grandfather had worked at newspapers, so that was a respectable profession, too. My grandmother gave up her career after my mother was born, but my grandfather went on to become a newspaper editor in Illinois and then the Washington bureau chief for *Business Week* magazine.

I first tried journalism in 1975 when a fellow student convinced me to volunteer for the weekly paper at our small liberal arts college. My first story was about bike racks; not very exciting. I was an average freshman student from a good high school in the Chicago suburbs. I played on the hockey team and went to parties on the weekend.

My happy-enough, B-student life changed when I fell in with student activists who were fighting racism, sexism, and injustice on campus and in society. They ranged from progressives to socialists and radical Marxists, and I was drawn to their passion and commitment, their vision of a better world. They were smart and cool and arguing about things I had never considered. We sat on the floor of our dorm, drank coffee, and debated whether revolution would be necessary to bring about the changes we demanded.

Professors and the other students, probably the majority, regarded us as weird, dangerously misguided, or dreamily nostalgic for the radical 1960s. We thought we were on a mission.

Seeing the campus newspaper as a means to advance the cause, I became the editor in chief during my second year. No journalism classes were offered at Lawrence, but an English professor, Peter Fritzell, gave me a one-on-one tutorial in newspaper writing. He tore up my editorials and stories, not just because he disagreed with them, but because they were sloppy, fuzzy, and poorly written.

I learned about editing, photography, and page design from the other students working on the paper. With no one to teach us, we laid out each edition as if it were the first time, and we learned newspapering by doing it. On the long nights before publication, we ordered pizzas and worked happily until morning.

I hadn't even read a newspaper regularly before I was editing one, but I liked the rush and focus of deadlines. Seeing my name in print was a thrill. I liked asking questions and trying to figure out things. Crafting a story and laying it out in the paper felt like building something from scratch, and it made me feel proud. The camaraderie among the newspaper staff was as tight as on any sports team, and on a few occasions we had the chance to right a wrong, or at least expose it.

I only worked on the school paper for a couple of terms, though, because I was more interested in politics than journalism. I never really considered a career in journalism for two reasons: it didn't seem impactful enough merely to report about what other people were doing, and my friends and I considered the media to be part of the repressive political system we opposed. After graduating with a degree in Government, I agonized over what to do with my life. I wanted to do something good and important that would make a difference.

When I looked at America and the world, I saw only the problems, especially racism, sexism, and economic inequality. My ideals had become more radical, far to the left of the established political parties, but I didn't know how to make them real. I considered community organizing or even factory work to be on the front lines of political change, but an older person who had been an activist during the '60s convinced me that wasn't the best use of my skills. You can write, she said. Use that.

At age twenty-one, my plan was to divide the day into thirds: work, sleep, and write. I could make a living with carpentry and painting houses eight hours a day. I would sleep eight hours, leaving eight hours to write about the problems of the world. When I tried to execute my plan, I did manage to build and paint houses eight hours a day. Working outdoors in northern Michigan was physically demanding. I might have a beer after work. Then dinner. Pretty soon I was asleep in my chair. After a few months working and living alone in the Northwoods, I felt less passion about politics, and I didn't write at all except for a journal. My plan wasn't working, but I liked living up north. I had friends and was making enough money.

Then one of those things happened that didn't seem like much at the time, but changed everything.

I had signed on to paint a vacation home owned by a family from Chicago. The father, Karl Hoenecke, was a businessman, the mother an artist, and they had three smart, cute daughters around my age. I spent long days there, and while I was the help, they treated me more like family.

At the end of the day, Mr. Hoenecke and I talked politics, even though we agreed on little. I liked him, but he was a right-winger who spouted all kinds of craziness about free markets, individual rights, and the pursuit of happiness without excessive government control. Where did they get that stuff?

I rose to the challenge of setting him straight. How can you support a capitalist system you can't even understand? I asked. Nobody can comprehend how markets operate. They are irrational and unfair and allow the few to profit from the many. Wouldn't it be better to sit down and plan how we are going to work and share the fruits of our labor?

Since I was so worldly, I also explained there were people in other countries who were different than we were but not inferior. Did you know, I asked, that there were people who not only brushed their teeth but also cleaned their *tongues,* as if that should end the argument about diversity.

He smiled and said, "I brush my tongue."

One day after I finished work, he was standing on his dock talking to another man with the same bearing and yacht-club style of dress. I pegged him for another titan of industry.

Mr. Hoenecke called me over. I want you to meet someone, he said. This is Stan Cook. He's at the *Chicago Tribune.*

I wiped my hands on my paint-splattered pants and shook his hand.

We started right in on politics, but now it was a tag team of them against me. I could handle them.

This country's greatest export is oppression, I patiently explained. Look at Latin America: we benefit from their misfortune, and if they get out of line, we change their governments. And at home the deck is stacked in favor of the privileged and their children. It's almost a hereditary system where the rich pass on their money and opportunities to their own kind, freezing out everyone else . . .

When I stopped for air, Mr. Cook said, "I see you're interested in politics. Have you ever thought about journalism?"

I have thought about journalism, I said, and told him I had been the editor of my college paper and had quite a bit of experience. I did not mention that I would die before working for the bourgeois media, especially the conservative *Chicago Tribune.*

Still, it was flattering to be thought of as a potential journalist, and I knew in my heart that my current plan wasn't changing the world. Maybe I could take a job inside the system and fix it from within. I imagined working inside, literally, in an office with doors and windows instead of scrambling around job sites. I was confident I could cover government, since I had a degree in political science and considered myself very knowledgeable. Maybe journalism could be my way to make the world better. I kept all this to myself. It was pleasing enough that successful men were talking about my career, my future.

Would you be willing to move back to Chicago? Mr. Cook asked. I was excited if a little unsure. I knew enough not to close an open door, even if I wasn't positive I wanted to walk through. He told me to call the next time I was in town visiting my family. The two of them beamed. I wasn't sure what had just happened.

Later, I thanked Mr. Hoenecke for the introduction. So what does Mr. Cook do at the *Trib?*

"Stan? He's the publisher."

I drove down to the Chicago suburbs, where my mother lived with her new husband. My father, whom I was very close to, had died when I was 16, while we were living in northern Wisconsin. The next year, my mother married a good man, a widower with four sons, and she and I moved into their house in Winnetka, Illinois. My stepfather adored my mom, and my mother and I were fortunate to join a big and loving family.

I made an appointment with a senior editor at the *Tribune.* Next, I went to the local men's store to buy my first suit—gray, with a vest—a blue shirt, red and gray tie, and a pair of heavy dress shoes. I visited the barber for the first time in years, and then displayed a clipped ponytail in my room like a beloved stuffed animal from childhood.

The *Tribune* editor was close to three times my age and burrowed into a comfortable office. I looked around and could imagine myself working on stories, talking on the phone, feet on the desk, sorting out the messy and corrupt politics of Chicago and Illinois, and then the world.

He asked a few questions and quickly picked up that I was more interested in changing the world than writing about it. If you want to do politics, he said dismissively, as if politics were something vile and beneath him, you should go to the governor's office, not a newspaper.

No, I said, I think I can make a difference as a reporter.

He shook his head but seemed resigned. He told me to head over to the City News Bureau of Chicago and gave me the address in the Loop.

I was a little confused—I had never heard of this City News Bureau—but I smiled and nodded. I didn't realize the fix was in, and I was about to start my first paid job in journalism.

In military terms, *Tribune* publisher Stan Cook was the general leading a storied infantry division. The *Tribune* editor he ordered to meet me was a brigade commander. City News was boot camp. The drill sergeant at City News was Paul Zimbrakos, a compact man with a dark mustache who sat at a large desk in the middle of the room. Other editors had desks that touched his, and the rest of the writers and reporters occupied cluttered desks around a large open area lined with yellowed windows that faced the tall buildings of the downtown area known as the Loop. City News, they explained, was a news agency—called a wire service because the stories once moved over a telegraph wire—started in the late nineteenth century. It covered local news for all the radio and TV stations and newspapers in Chicago.

At the entrance to the office was an old-fashioned switchboard: a console with cords that plugged into holes to make the connections. There were bulky industrial-looking contraptions, which I learned were the Teletypes used to transmit stories to the TV and radio stations as well as newspapers in the city. On the walls were the remains of pneumatic tubes that once had sent hard copies of stories whooshing under the streets to the newspapers.

The noise in the newsroom was raspy and percussive. Police and fire scanners crackled over the steady hum of all-news radio. The writers had to type through multiple-sheet carbon paper, which required a sharp snap of every key on stiff manual typewriters. The place felt as old-timey as a black-and-white movie from the 1940s.

I was assigned to shadow a more senior reporter for a week before working a shift from 5 p.m. to 2 a.m., every day except Tuesdays and Wednesdays, which would be my days off. City News never closed. Ever. The more senior people worked the day shift, and enjoyed regular weekends and holidays off. I was starting at the bottom, so I would work nights, weekends, and every holiday.

An editor introduced my trainer. Theo, she said, firmly taking my moist, limp hand in hers, Theo Stamos. I tried not to stare, but my young male brain registered only big eyes and high cheekbones. She ignored my awkwardness and was polite, if not all that enthusiastic, about training a new guy. Theo set me up with notebooks and pens, and introduced me around the office.

The reporting staff at City News was young, mostly right out of school. A few adults supervised the operation, but the place was powered by what cops and politicians called "City News kids." Theo was senior to me but only by a matter of months.

The office desks were occupied during three shifts, but I was going to be working out of a police station. There was some discussion about where to send me because I did not have a car, so the editors decided I should stick to the relative safety of the North Side, where I had rented a threadbare studio apartment in an old building that smelled of pot roast. My mom was a little concerned about the late hours in the big city, but she was pleased I was working as a reporter like her parents, and mostly that I had a "real job."

Soon I was a familiar face at the police area headquarters at the corner of West Belmont Avenue and North Western Avenue. The headquarters building included a police station, a holding cell, and offices for detectives. Nearby was a cozy tavern, painted with faux jail bars, called The Slammer. I didn't drink much, and never while working, but the bar was a place to meet cops when they were more relaxed.

My job was to sit at a desk or on a bench in the lobby and wait for crimes. I monitored the scanners, grabbed the officers when they came in at the end of their shifts, and stood by hungrily for the reports they had to file whenever something happened. I took it for granted that the bigger the crime or the worse the tragedy, the better the story. Over time I was allowed to walk behind the counter and poke through the paperwork. I wasn't one of the boys, more of a friendly pet, but they looked out for me and threw me the occasional bone.

Because I worked nights, I usually was the only reporter in the building, probably the only civilian who wasn't locked up. The detectives were divided into offices for property crimes, gang crimes, and homicide. I spent my shift schmoozing them and calling other police stations and firehouses looking for a story, which was called a beat check. Sometimes editors in the office, collectively known as "the desk," would call with a random and mostly unhelpful tip from the police scanner, such as "man being chased by woman with hammer" or "sirens in the Loop."

My growing familiarity with cop ways kept me out of serious trouble one night when I was off duty. It was on the morning side of midnight when my childhood friend Matt and I left a new club called Neo and headed toward another bar.

"I gotta pee," Matt said, and led us into an alley. When he had finished, we walked back down the darkened alley toward the lights of North Clark Street. A patrol car was waiting, the windows down.

One of the cops spoke to us from the car. "What were you guys doing in the alley?"

Matt, who was pretty wise to the city, was suddenly and uncharacteristically quiet. I, normally the silent partner on our late-night excursions, was talkative, if not especially courageous.

"Taking a shortcut?" I offered.

"First you peed in the alley, and then you lied about it," the cop said. "Get in."

Matt and I piled in the backseat behind the two cops.

You got any ID?

We handed over our driver's licenses. The car was running, and I could hear the familiar police radio. I recognized the voices of different dispatchers, the codes and the jargon. We stayed parked by the curb. The cop at the wheel looked slowly at our licenses, until he turned to stare directly at our faces. Then he spoke. "You'll spend the night in jail and see a judge in the morning." Matt was frozen next to me.

"I wasn't even peeing," I whined. "He was peeing."

The cop put the car into gear and started to pull out, heading north on Clark.

"Where are we going?" I asked. "The Belmont lockup?"

The officer stopped the car. He looked at me in the rearview mirror. "What do you do for a living?"

"I work for City News," I said.

That got a dashboard-pounding laugh from both cops. Matt remained silent, probably thinking not about jail, which was scary enough, but about what his father, a strict disciplinarian who had been a prisoner of war during World War II, was going to do to us.

"I can see the headline now," one of the cops said. "Promising Young Reporter Arrested for Peeing in an Alley." They both laughed. The cop behind the wheel looked up at us again in the mirror. He tossed the licenses back onto the seat between Matt and me. "Get outta here, City News. And take your friend with you."

The cops drove off. Freed from the patrol car and back on the street, we laughed hysterically, high from the relief of our narrow escape. Matt didn't say anything about being betrayed, but I knew what I had done. And I was the one who had lied to the cops, not him. He was such a good friend that he didn't blame me.

I had been raised to be respectful of police officers. Then in college, I began to see them, in theory anyway, as the armed force of a repressive state. This point of view, or bias, seemed absurd after a few months spending every day with real police officers. My opinions about law enforcement were still narrow, however, because I rarely talked to victims of crimes or the suspects. Most of what I learned about crime and justice came from the police. The cops were loyal to each other and didn't let in strangers, except for the occasional City News kid like me.

Part of my regular beat check was to call the morgue. I was looking for any death out of the ordinary, something that might be a story. An eighty-five-year-old who died in the hospital of natural causes was probably not a story. At City News that was a "cheap" death and would be ignored, or "cheaped out." Most deaths did not merit a story.

A gunshot victim, a young person, or any death classified as "unknown causes" was worth examining. I also was taught—not in a spoken way but still unmistakable—to think address. A death in an upscale neighborhood was unusual and therefore more newsworthy than a death in a poor neighborhood. A young black man shooting another young black man might be a story, but usually not a big one. An older white newspaper reporter made me cringe when he called those stories "Tyrone shot Willy."

The older reporter and I were competitors, but one night we both were writing about the same gang of kids sent out to rob jewelry stores. The police told us that adult criminals had trained the children to steal because they could fit into tight spaces and would not get in much trouble if caught. I overheard the white-haired reporter ask a cop on the phone, "So, they are kind of like latter-day Fagins?" Then he chuckled and nodded and took more notes.

When the reporter hung up, I asked him about the reference to Fagin, whom I vaguely remembered as a Dickens character who trained child pickpockets. The reporter laughed and said, "The cop probably thought I said 'faggots.'"

The older reporter's story the next morning was filled with colorfully literary cops spinning clever bits from *Oliver Twist*. The desk yelled at me because my story had not a word of Dickens.

I called the morgue every two hours. The man who answered the phone at the coroner's office had a slurred way of speaking as though he were blowing air out the side of his mouth. He would recite the names of the deceased, ages, addresses, the apparent causes of death, and the police stations and hospitals involved. His favorite joke was to challenge us with a good Chicago name. I could see him smiling over the phone when he would say: "Wojciechowski." Pause. "Common spelling." Laughter.

After a final call to the morgue, my shift ended at 2 a.m., a time when the bus ran only twice an hour. If I could leave the police station ten minutes early, I could catch the 1:50 a.m. bus and be home in thirty minutes. If not, I had to wait until 2:20 a.m. and not get home until almost 3 a.m. The editor on the desk, who wasn't much older than I was, never let me leave my post ten minutes early. There was no discussion. He was the editor, and I was a reporter, the ranks and status as clear and rigid as in the army, a hospital, or the police stations I covered.

Standing alone at the bus stop after 2 a.m. one night, I tried to stare straight ahead to avoid eye contact with passing drivers. At that hour, the ratio of weirdos and predators to normal people was high. I felt a car approach and slow down. I looked up and saw it was an unmarked police car, dark and riding heavy on worn shocks.

The detective at the wheel rolled down the window and yelled, "Hey, City News! You can't be standing out here in the middle of the night. Get in."

I jumped in the back and told them where I lived. I was thrilled when the detective put a flashing light on the dashboard and raced me home through the dark streets, slowing barely but never stopping at the red lights.

When I reported to the office at the start of my evening shift, I was given an envelope stuffed with clippings from that day's Chicago newspapers. Each story was a version of something I had covered the day before, cut and pasted into a long single-column strip topped with a label that read "Scoop Recovery." The facts or sentences or entire paragraphs that had not been in my story were marked with a pen. That was where I had been scooped by the papers.

Shame and dread greeted the envelopes, depending on the thickness of the packet. I often reported on four or five stories a night, so there were going to be things I missed. We were being compared word-for-word to experienced reporters from the newspapers, and my envelope was never empty.

It wasn't enough to be criticized for the missing information. We had to dig it out the next day, or "recover" it. So each shift began by revisiting the incomplete stories from the previous night. The challenge was to find a way to restart the same story, using "police continued to investigate," or some other phrase to initiate the process again.

The good thing was that it made us thorough. The bad thing was, we tended to include everything and didn't know what to omit. That was fine for a wire service that had unlimited space but a problem when we went to newspapers governed by the laws of finite space for stories—called news hole—among the ads.

The rookie reporters were free to ramble because we didn't write complete stories but called in the facts to a rewrite, who shaped the story and typed it. Then more senior editors made corrections and improvements, marking the pages with a precise set of lines, arrows, notations, loops, and swirls, which I soon could read like a second language. The editors quickly passed the marked-up copy to the Teletype operators for transmission to the papers and TV and radio stations.

I filed so often that I became very fast. As I got better, I roughed out the stories in my notebook and dictated the finished product to the rewrite. After my first year, I could compose an entire story in my head without writing it down. When I walked out of a news conference, I would have the lede, or first sentence, in my mind. While I was dialing the office, I would mentally compose the second paragraph. By the time I got a rewrite, I had the third paragraph in my head. The rest of the story came easily. Soon I was dictating stories all the time, which eventually would prepare me for a job as rewrite.

I don't remember how I learned to identify "the story" in the whirl of events, but I soon picked up the unique way of seeing things like a reporter, structuring the world into tight sentences, neat paragraphs, and complete stories. It came naturally to me, like learning a sport by playing it. Some cub reporters had trouble recognizing the lede of a story. An editor told us, "If you call your mom after something happens, that first thing you tell her about it, that's the lede." It was unclear why we spelled the word "lede" instead of "lead," but that, too, was part of being in the club.

I moved up to the day shift and through a series of beats including transportation, the courts, and local government. Each time, I followed the person I was replacing on the beat for a few days until he or she moved to another beat and I took over. We learned by watching other reporters, imitating them, and then doing it on our own.

I was expected to become an expert on the fare structure of the Chicago Transit Authority or a trial procedure or a hearing on water taxes. There were no books or lectures or even teachers like those in school, and all my study of political theory explained little about the nitty-gritty of urban life. I was starting fresh in a new world, learning by seeing with my own eyes and then trying to write about it.

The one thing we were taught was to ask questions. If you didn't ask you wouldn't know, and if you didn't know, you would be scooped, which was a powerful motivator. There was nothing worse than the sour look on Paul's face when he handed over a particularly heavy envelope of scoop recoveries. "Pete," he would say, exasperated at some failure of mine, "you're one of my best guys..."

The more experienced editors and reporters in town regarded us as a farm team for the big leagues, or tipsters who might point the way to good stories. We regarded the older reporters as imposing, a little scary, and the true professionals we hoped to become. They were the competition and our teachers.

For example, when I was assigned to cover the county courthouse, City News had a desk in the pressroom. Within a few feet from me were the desks of the *Chicago Tribune, Chicago Sun-Times,* and a couple of suburban papers, all publications I admired. I worried most when the desks were empty. What were the other reporters up to?

The *Sun-Times* reporter was Lynn Sweet, who stopped to chat with everybody in the courthouse, worked all the time, and beat me on stories every single day. At some point she took pity on the City News kid and offered to show me how to be better, but only after she had filed her own story.

Lynn didn't care about competing with me, as long as she broke stories before the *Tribune* and her bosses knew she was first. On days when she got beat
by the *Tribune,* she would be almost sick with anger and would immediately
seek revenge and reassurance with a scoop of her own.

Sometimes Lynn would nod discreetly for me to follow her into the hall
outside the pressroom. Then I was allowed to run along behind her while she
chased down a judge or a clerk for information. I took notes during the interviews, but I was not permitted to file my story until one second after Lynn's
story was in print. The arrangement worked for me.

After Lynn filed an exclusive story, we would wait anxiously until the next
edition of the *Sun-Times.* Then I was free to file my version of the story. Minutes after Lynn's story hit the streets, the *Tribune* guy at the courthouse, an
experienced, hard-working reporter with deep sources, would get a call from
his editors saying he had been scooped by Lynn. We watched him bang down
the phone. Then he would glare at Lynn with dark eyes, and begin to plot his
revenge.

Lynn would just wink at me, but she barely could contain her delight.

The back-and-forth, the keeping score, pulled me into the game. I got a
scoop or two of my own, but my exclusive stories lasted only a short time
because they went on the wire and were shared instantly in all the competing newsrooms around the city. The best moment came when, shortly after
I quietly filed a good story, the phones in the pressroom would start to ring,
and the more seasoned reporters at the papers and the radio and TV stations
would acknowledge a scoop by me, which they had been ordered to chase.

Most of the time, however, I was chasing them.

# 2

# CITY HALL

—— ON GETTING IT RIGHT ——

Chicago's top beat was City Hall. Formidable pros, including radio reporter Fran Spielman and the *Tribune*'s young political ace, David Axelrod, were regulars. When I walked into the City Hall pressroom for the first time, it was like walking into the friendly confines of Wrigley Field. But not as a major league player. More like a fan who had tumbled out of the stands. I sat down at the City News desk, and kept my mouth shut and my eyes open.

One of the aldermen we covered—a powerful, elected member of the City Council—came by the pressroom to complain about that morning's commute to City Hall. He told us he had just about run over a bicyclist because the kid had some kind of headset covering his ears and couldn't hear the car honking. Can you believe that? Listening to music or something crazy on a bike!

This was unusual at a time when music was played inside cars and living rooms, but not on bikes.

You should make that illegal, one of the reporters suggested, mostly joking.

It's dangerous, the alderman agreed, getting more upset. People are going around listening to music instead of watching where they are going!

There oughta be a law, someone chimed in.

You're right, the alderman declared.

Pretty soon a reporter put a piece of paper into the typewriter and hit the keys: "Whereas . . ."

In a few minutes, the alderman had a proposal to ban listening to music while operating a bike. We filed our stories about the headphone ban and had a good laugh in the pressroom—on some days it felt like the best clubhouse ever—and then we returned to trying to scoop each other with an exclusive story nobody else had.

The mayor was Jane Byrne, elected in 1979 as an efficient alternative to the previous mayor, who had unforgivably failed to get the city running after a snowstorm. She was tough, as she had to be as the first woman to run the city. She was married to a reporter on leave from the *Chicago Sun-Times,* Jay McMullen, who bragged about being able to scoop the *Tribune* by rolling over in the morning. Not very classy, but it reflected the spirit of competition between the *Tribune* and *Sun-Times,* then the last-standing giants among the dozens of great Chicago newspapers that had battled to their deaths.

The *Sun-Times* reporter assigned to City Hall was Harry Golden Jr. Harry's desk touched mine, and I learned a lot just being near him. Harry was small and tough as a welterweight, with a tan, lined face like a hawk and perfectly done hair. He always dressed smartly Chicago-style, which meant a suit with wide lapels, a tightly knotted necktie, and shined shoes. His sharp, raspy voice cut through any other conversation in the room.

Harry's phone rang, and he picked up right away. I always monitored Harry's calls. He had covered City Hall for years, had sources in every city department, and was considered the dean of the press corps. People called with tips, and Harry would hunch over to cover the phone to protect his sources from people like me. This time he was listening instead of talking, nodding his head as if in agreement, then shaking it in silent protest.

Someone on the other end was yelling nonstop. Then Harry spoke: "No I'm not trying to ruin the city. No, I love the city, too." I pretended to be looking out the window, wondering who was powerful enough to chew him out and keep him on the line. "Yes, I do love the city, just like you do," Harry repeated, exasperated. "Yes, I do, Madame Mayor."

The mayor and her press-secretary husband followed news stories closely, and they objected to many of them. They also were very good at Chicago politics, something I was about to learn the hard way.

I was working in the office one night when the phone rang. The mayor's husband was calling. I recognized his voice; everybody in the city knew him.

I tucked the phone between my shoulder and my ear and rolled a fresh piece of paper into the typewriter. By then I could type faster than I could write longhand, and my notes were easier to read. How are you tonight, Jay?

He was mad, frothing. I could hear the mayor in the background, equally outraged and egging him on. They often were angry, and this night the target of their wrath was the *Tribune,* for yet another story criticizing the mayor's administration.

They were sick of the paper's unfair attacks on the mayor, and they had decided the *Tribune* should no longer be allowed to use a desk in the City Hall pressroom, which was property of the city. Nor were they going to allow city officials to talk to the *Trib* or provide city records. No more cooperation with the *Tribune,* McMullen told me several times. None.

I typed as fast as I could and tried to ask questions, but they kept complaining about the *Tribune* and making threats. We had a little back-and-forth, but mostly it was them ranting. Then they hung up.

I wrote the story and handed the pages to the night editor. He made a few changes and gave a copy to the guy operating the Teletype. In minutes, the story was fed to all the newspapers, TV stations, and radio stations in the city. It was late but still in time for the final deadlines of the morning papers. I had a nice little scoop, all to myself.

I had no idea what a mess the story would cause.

On Monday morning every news outlet in town sent someone to City Hall to see if the *Tribune*'s reporter would defy the mayor and be at his desk. Bob Davis did show up, wearing a tie for the cameras, and declared he would not be moved. The *Tribune* ran the eviction story above the fold on page one—self-righteously treating their reporter like the Rosa Parks of the pressroom—and ran an angry editorial denouncing the mayor for restricting the paper's virtuous and constitutionally protected coverage of City Hall.

At a press conference, the mayor's husband pulled back a little. "We ordered the *Tribune* to vacate rent-free space in the pressroom," he admitted, but nobody was told not to cooperate with the *Tribune.* "I don't know where you got that idea."

From me, I thought, with a knot in my stomach.

The following day the *Tribune* headline—over a photo of a defiant Bob Davis at his desk surrounded by reporters—read, "Byrne backs down, *Tribune* stays."

I was called into the office early because the *Trib* had questions about my original story, which the mayor now was disputing. The paper wanted the complete transcript of the call. I had not recorded the conversation, but I had my notes. We sent the transcript to our clients, and it ran in the paper the next day. The *Trib* didn't dispute my version of what had happened, but now the mayor had decided to let the *Tribune* reporter stay. She claimed she never tried to limit the paper's access to official information, and that part of the story was typical media exaggeration and lies.

I went over my notes again and again. I was sure I had reported accurately what the mayor and her husband told me. I could still hear their angry voices in my head. But now the mayor had a whole new, more reasonable version of our conversation. She delivered her threat to the *Tribune,* and then dodged the criticism by blaming me for an inaccurate story. After a few days, the mayor moved on triumphantly, as if the whole thing had never happened.

I felt confused and humiliated. No one had ever lied to me like that or challenged my integrity, least of all a respected public official. Nor did I feel comfortable being part of the story instead of the one writing the story. The tussle with the mayor cost me a little of my rookie self-confidence, and it would not be the last I would hear about the incident. At the time, all I could do was sit there in stinging pain, hit for the first time by a major league fastball.

Working in the office usually was not as exciting as being on the street, but I enjoyed the company of other reporters. For most of our shifts we were on the phone or banging out stories, but just underneath the workflow, there was a steady chorus of banter and teasing, a contact sport for word lovers.

I was friendly with the support staff, and on slow days I tried to learn their jobs, too. I loved the antique switchboard, and Leo the operator was delighted to show me how it worked. I sat there happily plugging in the lines and connecting calls, while Leo, his feet up, read a thick novel.

The guys who operated the Teletype machines—all of them were men—included African Americans and Latinos, while the reporting and editing staff was mostly white. The operators were surprised but tolerant of my interest in learning to work the industrial-sized machines.

The Teletype keyboard was unexpectedly quick because it was electric. Each keystroke punched holes into a ribbon of paper, similar to ticker tape. Then the tape was run through the teleprinter to transmit the pattern of holes across town to machines receiving our stories, where the holes were translated back into words, IN ALL CAPITAL LETTERS. Pretty soon I could "read" the holes on the tape that spelled out words and entire stories. It was a little like reading braille.

Operating the switchboard and Teletype were great skills to have, until somebody got sick. If Leo didn't come in, I had to run the switchboard. I wasn't fast enough to do a full shift on the Teletype machine, but I could operate it in an emergency. I even remember going "live" on a breaking story, which meant typing a message directly to the receiving newsrooms without first cutting a tape. That was risky because there was no way to call back the words once they were typed.

I also took a turn on the broadcast desk, where we rewrote the newspaper stories for TV and radio. The trick was to boil down the essence of the story and write it for the ear rather than the eye. For example, a standard newspaper story had all the facts loaded into the top and included less important things as it continued. That way the story could be trimmed from the bottom if it didn't fit the allotted space in the paper. Writing for radio, you had to catch the listener's ear before delivering the big news. So instead of writing "John Smith was killed Thursday," you wrote, "A South Side man was killed Thursday." Gets their attention. Then, "John Smith was shot twice by a robber."

Our most important reporting tool was the telephone. We didn't have time, or the means, to cover every story in person, so we worked the phones fast and hard. Sometimes this had awful results.

I was told to look into the death of a male child, cause unknown. The death could have been from an accident, an illness, or a homicide. Maybe the family was newsworthy. I called the police station near the family home, but they hadn't heard about a boy who had died. I called the hospital where the child had been pronounced dead. I asked for the nursing supervisor, identified myself as City News, and sweet-talked her for details. The nurse working that shift had left for the day, I was told, and nobody else knew anything.

The last resort was dreaded by all of us, but I knew what I had to do: call the family. I looked up the number and dialed. A man answered and I identified myself. Yes, the man said, he knew about the dead boy. The man was the father. I started to ask questions, and the father broke down crying. The boy had been sick and died suddenly. He was so young.

I apologized and felt my throat tighten while the man told me about his little son. Big tears plopped onto the desk in front of me, and I tried to hide my face from the newsroom.

I'm sorry, I said. I'm so sorry.

I hung up and told the desk there was no story.

The editor pushed back for details.

No story, I said. Cheap it out.

Those family calls were made on every shift, and the editors forced us to dig for telling details, no matter how painful. One such story I was told about a call, which I absolutely believed was true, concerned a child who died one Christmas morning. The parents told the reporter their toddler was playing under the tree, surrounded by presents, when he accidentally swallowed an ornament. Before help could arrive, the child choked and died in their arms.

The reporter clearly was upset by the call with the family, but he turned in his story to the desk.

The editor, hunched over the copy with a pen, yelled out, "What color was the ornament?"

The reporter didn't know.

"Call them back!"

Along with the telephone, reporters relied on the big, heavy Chicago telephone book. We were required to look up the name of every person mentioned in a story to confirm the spelling and middle initial. Most people didn't use middle initials, so you had to remember to ask. We also had to include their ages. Neither detail mattered that much, but this was how we were taught to get the facts and confirm them. If we couldn't get the little things right, we were going to miss the big things.

The valuable companion to the telephone book was a directory called the Criss Cross, which was organized by address and phone number instead of by name. So if you heard over the scanner about a fire on West 63rd Street, you could look up the nearby residents. Even at 2 a.m., the call usually was, "Hello, can you tell me if there is a fire across the street?" Perfectly normal at City News.

The emphasis always was on getting the story quickly and getting it right. Storytelling or fancy writing didn't matter as much as getting the basic facts correct. We were taught to ask and then to confirm. Never assume, guess, surmise or ever, ever predict the future. It was hard enough to describe something that had happened, let alone speculate on what might or could happen next. Even things you were certain about had to be verified. "If your mother says she loves you," went the unofficial City News motto, "check it out."

After nearly two years of reporting and editing, I felt I had learned everything I could from City News, and I was ready to move up. Most people left City News for small papers in the provinces, maybe Flint, Michigan, or if they were exceptionally good, Milwaukee.

A *Trib* reporter who had worked at a paper in New Mexico told us that editors out west would appreciate a reporter trained by City News. He made a call, and two of my City News friends went to Albuquerque for newspaper jobs. Once they had proved themselves, they called back to City News—they might as well have been on the dark side of the moon—to say the paper was scrappy and the region was fascinating. I was happy for them, but I was staying in Chicago and headed to the *Trib* as part of my original plan. I didn't need to go to a small paper; City News was training enough for me.

I called the editor who had first interviewed me at the *Tribune*. He was not available. After several tries, I managed to get him on the phone. Another thing I had learned at City News was to keep calling. Just because somebody didn't call you back on the first try, or the fifth, didn't mean they wouldn't talk to you. The editor finally picked up and was kind if not encouraging, the way you might be with a kid hanging around the fire station who dreamed of becoming a firefighter. Go to a small paper first, he advised, and then call me. I was disappointed he didn't understand the plan, but I was stuck.

I started writing to some of the 1,700 daily newspapers around the country. I made copies of my better stories and sent them off with letters asking for a reporting position. The help-wanted ads in a weekly magazine called *Editor & Publisher* were the main source of job information, although reading the magazine in the office was best done discreetly, so no editor would think you were trying to leave.

Fortunately, my former City News friends working out west had put in a good word for me. This I learned when my phone rang with an unexpected call: some guy named Tim Gallagher from a paper called the *El Paso Herald-Post*. Tim said he had hired my City News friends for the Albuquerque paper. Now Tim was staffing up a sister paper in El Paso, and would I be interested?

Interested, yes, but not very informed. While we talked, I pulled out the atlas, one of the many reference books on my desk. I opened the tall book and listened while Tim told me about his plans for the paper. I found Texas and searched the map of the big state, up and down. There was Dallas. There was Fort Worth. I couldn't find El Paso. I was pretty sure it was in Texas. Tim mentioned something about the border. I dragged my finger along the line between Mexico and the United States, and there, way out at the end of the page, I found it: El Paso.

Two years at City News had raised my level of skepticism from near zero to maybe 20 percent. Less when it came to my own situation. Of course this guy wanted to hire me. I hustled and I could write. He had talked with people who had worked with me, so I was "sent" by somebody. On the other hand, I had been applying to papers I wouldn't even read, and they were rejecting me. Many of them never responded to my letters and calls. Here was a paper I had never heard of, in a town I couldn't find on a map. And they were offering a job without ever meeting me. How desperate could they be?

I hung up and announced the job offer to everybody in the City Hall press-room. Somebody sang the Marty Robbins country classic about falling in love with a Mexican girl out in El Paso. They started calling me "Pedro" and won-dered why I wasn't packing up my stuff and heading to the border. I wasn't sure. It seemed so far away. And I had never heard of this paper. Go check it out, the other reporters said. Make them have you in for an interview. Not one of them said it was a bad offer.

I had done one other job interview, in Seattle. I sent the paper my resume, barely a page long, even in a large font, and a packet of clips. I flew there on my own and stayed with my college roommate to save money. The editor was serious, unsmiling, and much older than I was. Everybody at the paper was older than I was. He invited me to sit, and I noticed my resume and clips on his desk. (Every reporter learns to read material on a desk, even when the words are upside down.) We chatted for a few minutes, and then he floored me: "What is the worst mistake you've ever made?"

Wait a second. Mistake? I didn't think we were supposed to talk about mis-takes. Weren't they to be buried, pushed down so they never would surface or repeat themselves? Did he mean in my personal life? A lot of mistakes there. Is that what he meant? No, I thought, he must mean a professional mistake.

But my career was limited to two years at City News, and we weren't allowed to make mistakes. The whole thing was about not making mistakes.

"Well," I said, trying to buy time. My mind was racing. What was an error that was bad enough to mention but not so bad as to be disqualifying? I needed something between journalistic jaywalking and a felony. What's a mistake I learned from, that made me better? Come on, think. "Well," I said again.

Then I thought of something. "I got a call one night from the mayor and her husband. She wanted to kick the *Tribune* out of the pressroom at City Hall." That got his attention. He looked up from the papers on his desk.

"I should have assumed they were drinking; it was late," I said, encouraged to see he was listening intently. "I could hear them egging each other on. The whole thing was strange."

So what was your mistake? he asked.

"I guess I should have been more careful writing it," I said, not sure exactly what my mistake had been, but still burning from the mayor's denial of my story and my shame at having to reproduce my notes. I explained that the mayor cleverly got to have it both ways: she used me to put the *Trib* on notice, and the next day she was able to appear magnanimous in her denial of the story.

He picked up a sheet of paper on his desk and waved it at me. "If that story was a mistake, why did you include it in the clips you sent me?"

Bad. Floored again, just when I thought I had pulled myself up off the rug. "Well. I, uh, learned from that experience that you have to be careful with the writing even when you have all the facts. . . ." I went on for a few agonizing minutes. He just looked at me. There was no way I was going to work in Seattle.

I called Tim at the *Herald-Post* and asked if I could visit. He was enthusiastic. There's somebody here I want you to meet, he said, a photographer we just hired. I think you guys will get along. I tried to get a couple of weekdays off, but I was denied. I called Tim back, apologized, and asked if I could come on a weekend. No problem, he said, they worked all the time.

I flew for hours to get to El Paso. From the air, I saw flat, dry ground. There were mountains, which was a surprise. A few earth-toned buildings were clustered together, about the size of a shopping mall at home. Downtown El Paso, I guessed. The only water was a muddy canal encased in concrete. Later they told me that was the mighty Rio Grande. It was late Saturday afternoon before I arrived at the newspaper.

Tim, the city editor, was eager and smiling, pulling me into the newsroom. He was about my age, twenty-four, but he seemed old, like forty, meaning mature and competent. He joked with everybody on the staff, but he clearly was the boss. People followed him because they wanted to, not only because they had to.

Tim walked me around the newsroom and stopped at a cubicle piled with camera gear. A silent young man with a cool mustache looked up at us, making his eyes wide, the only sign he had noticed me.

This is the guy I told you about, Tim said, introducing John Hopper. Tim left us alone for a minute.

I told John I had heard all about him and looked forward to knowing him better. Apparently I was a little too eager, or people didn't talk that way out west (even if John was from Indiana), because he looked at me like I had proposed a kiss on the mouth.

The instinctual rejection of a newsroom outsider was familiar because it was the same reception I had received on my first day at City News.

Awkward conversation over, I was led into the office of Tim's boss, editor Harry Moskos. Both Tim and Harry had worked at the paper in Albuquerque and had been transferred to El Paso by the parent company of both papers, Scripps Howard. The company was one of the largest American newspaper groups, the owner of United Press International, a large news bureau in Washington, DC, local television and radio stations around the country, and many nationally known columns and cartoons, including *Peanuts* and *Garfield*.

Harry had big ambitions for the paper, even though his resources were small. He bounced up and down in his chair, laughed out loud at his own jokes, and gushed about all the great people he was recruiting, hinting that maybe I would be one of them. Let's go to dinner, he said, and he jumped up from his desk and headed out the door. I stumbled to keep up.

As we got into the car, Harry extolled the virtues of the town, the people, and especially his staff. I nodded and smiled. He drove us through the streets of downtown El Paso, where traffic was light, and pointed out the landmarks, such as they were. A few people were shopping in little stores that had signs in English and Spanish. The only thing big was the sky.

I was on my best behavior. I liked Harry's enthusiasm, and I already had fallen in love with Tim. The town seemed kind of slow, however, and the paper wasn't much. I had never seen a copy before arriving that day, and it felt thin in my hands, an unfamiliar typeface on newsprint so cheap it appeared gray.

Then Harry announced: "Well, you're in Mexico now."

I looked around, startled. I had been focused on Harry's chatter and wasn't paying attention to where we were going. I looked out the window and saw the streets suddenly were busy with people shopping, strolling, and eating at food carts, including one serving corncobs slathered with cream and powdered chili. Kids were hawking full-color newspapers in Spanish and selling Chiclets in tiny packs. I turned in my seat and locked eyes with an exotic woman wearing a tight blouse stretched over a push-up bra, high heels and leopard pants painted onto long, curvy legs.

I don't remember talking during dinner about pay or what my job would be, or any of the details of getting from Chicago to El Paso. I knew I was going to work there, however, and if I could have started that night, I would have. Most of the papers I had applied to were not interested in me. I sure wasn't going to be hired in Seattle. Driving back across the international bridge between Ciudad Juárez and El Paso, I took in everything. Harry made me feel I would be part of something exciting and meaningful, but the border is what closed the deal. This was a place where you could eat dinner in another country.

Back home in Chicago, just before Christmas, I had second thoughts. El Paso was so far away. What if I never made it back home? There were people who lived in El Paso their entire lives. If my goal was to work at the *Tribune*, maybe I shouldn't take such an extreme detour. What if the *Trib* forgot about me? I knew Chicago and the issues. I had covered all the beats at City News and even had supervised a few reporters when I was on the desk. The transition to the *Trib* would be seamless. I was ready for the *Trib*, and I was sure the *Trib* needed me.

I snuck out of the pressroom to a pay phone in City Hall. This wasn't a conversation I wanted to have in a roomful of professional busybodies. I called the *Tribune* editor who had interviewed me.

The editor was surprised to hear from me again so soon. You still need to go to a small paper, he said, and then we'll talk.

I did have an offer, I said, raising the ante. I told him about El Paso and how much they wanted me. If he didn't pick me up now, I subtly warned, he might lose me forever.

The editor laughed gently at my persistence, and he sounded genuinely happy I had a good job offer. Saying good-bye, he said encouragingly, "It sounds like Santa came early."

# 3

# THE BORDER

—— ON HONESTY ABOVE ALL ——

I bought a used Datsun station wagon and packed my few belongings for the drive to El Paso in early 1982. I said good-bye to my mom, her husband, and my four brothers. My family was proud of me, although disappointed I would be so far away. I promised that within two years I would be moving back to Chicago to work at the *Tribune*. The editors at City News were happy for me. A new crop of cub reporters had been hired, and I didn't even know their names.

For the first day of work in El Paso, I got up early in my new apartment and used a city map to plot the route to the office. I remembered little from my earlier visit; I had been so tense I hadn't paid attention to directions. I wrote the street names on a piece of paper, put it on the passenger seat, and headed for downtown. My hands were sweaty on the wheel, even though the desert morning was cool. Had I made the right decision? What was I doing here? I turned on the radio and skipped through the many Spanish stations to find rock. I looked down again at the directions.

Damn, I missed the turn. I glanced in the rearview mirror, signaled, and cut across two lanes onto the next street. A siren whooped, and in the mirror I saw flashing red lights close on my tail. Great. I pulled over, took a breath, and rolled down the window.

The police officer came to my side of the car and bent down to look inside. "Do you know why I pulled you over?"

"Yes, sir," I said. "I changed lanes in the middle of an intersection."

He nodded, looking at my license.

He was just a cop. Even though I was in a strange land, he had a familiar uniform, a gun, and a car with flashing lights. I knew all about cops. "I'm kind of nervous," I said. "It's my first day at work. I'm a reporter at the *Herald-Post*."

He looked at me again and handed back my license. "Be more careful next time."

"Hey, officer," I called out as he walked to his car. "Got any news tips?" He just laughed. I should have gotten his name.

For the first time in my career, I had a desk all to myself. When I worked rewrite at City News, I had a desk for one-third of the day, but other people sat there during the next two shifts. I also got my first computer, which actually was a clunky terminal connected to a room-sized mainframe computer somewhere in the building.

The work tools I supplied were a notebook, a pen, and a tape recorder. In the old days, you had to turn in a worn copy pencil to get a new one. The *El Paso Herald-Post* wasn't known for spoiling its employees, but on my first day I was feeling pretty flush.

I rode into El Paso on a big reputation, most of it unearned. First, I was from Chicago, a tough city with a no-nonsense reputation. In fact, I had grown up in northern Wisconsin and the gentle suburbs of Chicago's North Shore, but that distinction grew weaker the farther you got from Illinois. Second, City News had a fearsome image as a boot camp where real journalists were made. I had success at City News, but two years of chasing stories did not make me a seasoned professional.

I was fast and I was accurate, but most of what I had covered were things that had happened: fires, crimes, press conferences, government meetings. "Cover" was the right verb. At City News we tried to record what happened because that was what the clients wanted. There was less emphasis on, and little time for, breaking a story or investigating something.

The *Herald-Post* was different. The paper appeared in the afternoons, following the morning paper, the *El Paso Times*. As editor, Harry explained he had the challenge of making our paper different from the morning paper to attract new readers. The *Times* was the bigger paper of record; the *Herald-Post* had to be feistier and more creative. The veteran reporters at the paper were solid and knew the community. Harry was bringing in fresh blood like me to shake things up.

My job was to be an investigative reporter, an exotic species found mostly at bigger papers. Even Bob Woodward and Carl Bernstein were local news reporters for the *Washington Post* before the Watergate story made them famous, when I was still in high school. Like most young reporters, I liked the sound of the job title. Investigative reporters were an elite force who weren't going to wait for something to happen, they were going to make things happen. They didn't cover news, they made news. What nobody told me was that the job required a killer instinct, tenacity, a passion for conflict, the judgment that came from experience, and a constitution that could stomach fear, hatred, threats, reprisals, self-doubt, and resentment. Of all those traits, I probably had tenacity, or at least thoroughness.

I worked with Harry and Tim to come up with story ideas, which really were targets. My editors were far more experienced journalists, but they also were newcomers to El Paso. The advantage of being recent arrivals was that we saw things through fresh eyes. The downside was that our understanding of the community was incomplete, and what we saw as novel or even shocking was regarded by regular readers as just another day along the border.

One of my first targets was the local art museum, where the editors had heard grumbling about the management. My initial guide was the paper's veteran culture reporter, Betty Ligon, who introduced me around town as if I were her own son. Betty covered the art museum, and while other reporters might have resented a newcomer poaching on their beat, Betty launched me at the museum like a guided missile. The one advantage I gave Betty was that she wouldn't burn her own sources there.

I met secretly with people who knew about museum operations. They complained about the artistic focus of the museum and how money was spent. Part of it was personal, and some of the staff simply didn't like the director. They didn't allege any criminal activity, just mismanagement. More accurately, the museum wasn't being run the way they would run it. For example, the critics would have focused on Mexican or Chicano art rather than on European classics. Fair enough, but that was a question of taste and artistic direction, not of being incompetent or squandering money. I spent weeks trying to define a story that might be interesting to readers—not just museum patrons—from the mishmash of allegations and complaints.

With the museum project, I began to develop a technique for working investigative stories. I started with a tip or a hunch, just a hypothesis, and tested it with reporting. The information I collected from investigating helped refine the theory until it became a theme for a story supported by the facts.

This was a journalistic version of the scientific method, where a hypothesis was tested with experiments. Like in a lab, it was easier to disprove a theory than to prove one. In other words, it was easier to knock down a story idea as false than to develop one as true. Unfortunately for me, my juiciest tips were better than the final, verified stories. That's why reporters joked that some tips were "too good to check out."

I taught myself about museum management by talking to people in the art world, including at similar museums in other cities. I had a short time to become an expert on a new topic, just as when I had learned about cops and city government in Chicago. The stakes seemed higher now because the paper carried a lot of weight in a small town. The other reporters and I would regularly bump into the people we covered, which helped keep us honest and careful with the facts.

I tried to focus the story on spending rather than artistic merit because money was more quantifiable than taste. I had been taught at City News to write from the point of view of people receiving a service, rather than those providing a service, especially when tax money was involved.

The first installment of my series ran on the front page. I was happy to see my byline, but mostly I was relieved the project was finished. I hadn't found a smoking gun, or even a stolen painting, but I managed to stir up the little community that supported the art museum. Most people in El Paso had never visited the museum and probably didn't care. I did send my parents a copy of the story, which they saved with my other clips.

Just before the story ran, somebody doing layout asked me what name to use for my byline in the paper. I always had gone by Pete as a kid, and that's what my family called me, but "Peter" seemed more appropriate for a real newspaper. And in one snap decision, I became Peter to most people for the rest of my life.

My editors seemed happy enough with my stories, but I wanted something with an edge. I worried I merely was explaining things rather than exposing them. I couldn't sit around any longer and wait for assignments. I needed to be bold and find my own stories. I wanted to kill something and drag its bloody carcass back to the office. I asked everybody I knew for tips and ideas, but it was hard to find something when I didn't know what I was looking for.

One of my regular sources was a prominent Mexican American judge. I met him covering a trial, and he trusted me, so some evenings after work I would visit him in his chambers. A lot of what he told me had nothing to do with his cases or even the courthouse, but he knew how the town was run. I learned to just let him talk, and to listen deeply. A good interviewer is alert but still. I never quoted the judge by name. Nor did I publish anything I didn't verify, but he never had steered me wrong.

Something was bothering the judge. He had noticed that many of the adoptions going through the court were arranged by one woman. The number of these cases was suspicious, he said, and he was angry. It looked like this despicable woman was setting up adoptions for a fee, or "selling" Mexican babies, often to non-Mexican families, known locally as "Anglos." I pulled out my notebook to get the details.

The next morning I searched the "morgue," which is what we called a room with metal cabinets packed with decades of newspaper clips filed by name and topic, but I couldn't find anything on the mystery woman. She had a common Mexican last name; it probably filled a page in the phone book. I started at the top and worked my way down, calling every number. I needed to find the person with the right name, but also a person who was involved with adoptions. Finally, I got a hit.

A lady who answered the phone said she had a daughter with that name. Could I speak to her?

No, she's not here, the lady said. You can try her at the health clinic.

Gotcha.

I didn't know what to do next. I couldn't come right out and ask the woman if she was selling babies. She would deny it and try to cover her tracks. I thought about finding some of the adopting parents or birth mothers, but they were not going to admit to something unsavory or illegal. These adoptions appeared legal—they were in the court record—but any kind of cash payments on the side would have been suspect.

I needed a way to check out the adoption lady without tipping her off. Walking around the office or driving in the car, I practiced what I would say and rehearsed my story. When I had it down, I called the clinic and asked to speak to the woman. Her name was Rebeca.

"My wife and I are thinking of adopting a baby," I told her, "and we heard you might be able to help."

"I'm not sure how I can help," Rebeca said, "but I'm happy to talk with you." She told me she also worked at a hospital in El Paso, and we could meet there.

This is going to be good, I thought.

I paced around on the day of our appointment, unable to concentrate on anything but this woman. The story was huge. I had it from a good source that she was selling babies. Court documents proved she was in the business. In my mind, she was a heavyset, rumpled, middle-aged woman. She had a slight accent, so I guessed she was born in Mexico but raised on this side. The story would make a splash in El Paso because it exposed corruption and played on the worst fears of Mexicans and Mexican Americans about how people took advantage of them. And you couldn't go wrong with a story about babies.

I was uneasy about one thing: I never before had misrepresented myself for a story. I had lied to this woman about being married, wanting to adopt a baby, and why I wanted to meet her. In my entire life I had never told such a big lie, for a story or for any reason. I justified it to myself by rationalizing that I couldn't get the story any other way, and that the good of protecting babies outweighed the bad of lying. I took a deep breath. I made myself relax. She was the one doing wrong, not me.

The hospital setting threw me off. I walked through the whooshing electric doors into the cool air of the lobby. Everything was spotless, efficient. I had expected to confront this woman in some shabby clinic. The hospital felt professional, legitimate. I followed the signs to her office. I knocked on the open door and started to enter.

Sitting on a tall stool was a woman in stockings and heels, a tight skirt and a white lab coat. She had thick black hair, fashionably oversized glasses, and the clearest, whitest skin I had ever seen. She was not much older than I was and looked like the kind of glamorous, skilled doctor you would see on a TV medical drama. I froze in the doorway.

She stood up, walked toward me, and shook my hand. She offered me a seat and let me talk.

"I'm not really here to adopt a baby," I blurted out, embarrassed but already relieved. "I'm not even married."

She laughed. "I didn't think so," she said.

"Am I that bad a liar?" I asked.

"We'll see," she said, raising a perfect eyebrow.

"I'm a reporter for the *Herald-Post*," I confessed. "Someone told me you were selling babies."

"Ask me what you want to know," she said.

"Are you?"

"Am I selling babies?"

"Yes."

"No," she said.

Oddly, I was relieved. My big story had just evaporated, but I felt better. I promised myself I never again would lie to get a story.

Her clinic did help women offer babies for adoption, she explained, but there was no money involved. Come with me, and I'll show you, she said. We got in her car and drove across the bridge to Juárez.

When we reached the other side of the bridge, a Mexican official flagged her down. Mexican customs agents never stopped me, so I wasn't sure what was happening. I assumed the agent stopped her car because of the Mexican plates, or more likely, because she was so attractive.

"What are you bringing?" the officer asked.

"Nothing," she said, smiling up at him. "Just some things for the clinic."

This was the first time I heard her speak Spanish, and she was even more graceful and refined. I watched, fascinated to witness how a Mexican in her own country was treated so differently than I was.

"What's in that box?" he asked, pointing to the backseat and a large container that I noticed for the first time.

"*Preservativos,*" she said, a word I didn't know. She reached back and pulled up a handful of individually wrapped condoms. "Here," she said, "take some. For your wife." She pushed a bunch of condoms into his hand.

The officer looked around shyly and shoved the condoms deep into his pocket. Thank you, he said. Have a good day. He waved us into Mexico.

The clinic turned out to be a clean and pleasant place staffed by friendly people. Rebeca had a calm manner and made time to visit with everyone. She had several degrees, and was well traveled and highly regarded in her field. I wrote a story about her and the clinic and adoptions, but it was not the story I had hoped to ride to fame and glory. A different story I would write about her later would change my life, but that was still months away.

When at last I did break a major investigative story, it was by accident. I was looking into how the local court appointed defense attorneys for people who couldn't afford them. I wondered if lawyers were getting rich off this pool of captive clients. The records were kept by hand, but they were public documents, and I was able to tally up the lawyers taking the most court-appointed fees and the judges doling out the assignments.

Making two columns on a large sheet of paper, one column for lawyers and one for judges, I quickly found a pattern: one of the top-paid defense lawyers was getting his assignments from a single judge, a well-known figure in town. This looked suspicious to me. Maybe the judge and the lawyer had a deal to split the money. I made a few calls about the pair—everybody in the legal community knew them—and I learned that the lawyer was actually the uncle of the judge, a fact I noted in passing in my story.

What I didn't know when I wrote the story was that a judge appointing a relative, even a nephew appointing an uncle, to a role like public defender could be illegal. The judge's political enemies quickly figured it out, however, and pounced. Now I had my big scoop, but it wasn't the story I had intended. Everybody was patting me on the back for exposing a scandal, but I felt sick.

The reason I felt bad was because of what I had learned during my reporting. The judge had political rivals, but nobody had accused him of corruption, until now. The lawyer, the uncle of the judge, was one of the best criminal defense lawyers on the border. He didn't need the small hourly rate he was paid by the court. In fact, every time he took a court-appointed case he lost money. So the indigent defendants were getting a great lawyer, and the lawyer was eating the costs. The judge was guaranteeing a high-quality defense for the accused, and he was saving taxpayer money.

But that's not how my story was seen in the community. I had exposed nepotism, corruption, and venality. I got high-fives at the paper, and people started to take notice of the hired gun from Chicago. El Paso was a small town, and I ran into the judge at a reception. We noticed each other across the room but did not speak. A woman at the reception told me later, "You both looked like you had been kicked in the stomach."

I never felt good about that piece because while the facts were accurate, it was not the whole story. The judge had indeed given public funds to his uncle, but he also had secured an excellent defense for the accused. I realized then how facts without context could be misused as a political weapon. It wasn't enough to mention both sides of a story and pretend I was being fair. There were many more than two ways to look at any issue, and being accurate or even "balanced" wasn't the same as being honest and true.

The story about the judge earned a notch on my gun, but not because I was a good shot. I felt as though we had mounted the head of a trophy buck on the newspaper's wall, but I had hit the deer with my car. I wasn't interested in getting more trophies that way. I had not printed a single word that wasn't true, but I could not just fall back on being factually accurate; I also wanted to be fair.

What I really wanted to investigate was El Paso's defining feature: the border. I was starting to see this place was not divided by the line between two countries; it was created by the line. The resulting community was an overlapping area that included both El Paso and Juárez, a unique hybrid of two cities, two countries, and two cultures. The border I was experiencing didn't conform at all to my college theories about underdevelopment and the US exploitation of Latin America. In fact, El Paso and Juárez were deeply dependent on each other.

The main barrier to understanding the border was my high school Spanish, so I paid for night classes. The great thing about studying Spanish in El Paso was that you could go all day without speaking English, and many people did. A few older women at the paper got a kick out of my efforts to learn. One of them, Cuca, sweetly called me *corazón de melón*. I had no idea why she called me "cantaloupe heart," but it felt nice, and I grinned back at her, happy as a puppy.

My first reporting trip using my beginner's Spanish was to the coast of Mexico in search of an American professor who had disappeared mysteriously. He had driven to Mexico for a teaching assignment but never arrived. Two experienced staffers at the paper, reporter Joe Olvera and photographer Ruben Ramirez, were covering the story, and they let me ride along.

Ruben was a jovial former Marine, born in Juárez but raised in El Paso. He was solidly built and formidable, despite the boyish curly hair and wide smile. Joe was a big, dark, good-looking guy who dressed like he was from East Los Angeles in the 1940s. He had a peculiar way of wearing a wide necktie without a knot, which he alone could pull off. We packed our bags, jumped in the car, and started down Mexico's Highway 15, a road regarded as lawless and dangerous.

After a big lunch on the first day, we stopped at the home of someone Joe or Ruben knew. I was never quite sure what was going on and just tried to keep my ears open. The man we visited was a gracious host and asked if we wanted any refreshments. A cool drink sounded good because the day was thickly hot. Then he asked, "How about a *tuna?*"

I looked at Joe and Ruben, and was surprised when they quickly said yes. A tuna? We just ate lunch. No, I said in Spanish, I'm full.

Come on. Go ahead. It's just a *tuna,* the man said, bordering on offended.

Okay, I relented, bring on the tuna.

He served us small plates with light green fruit speckled with black seeds. The fruit was tasty, cool and fresh, but difficult to eat with all the seeds. He showed me one of the fruits before it was peeled; it was the size of a grenade, with thorns. I had seen them sitting on top of cactus plants along the road. *Tuna,* it dawned on me, was not a fish but the Spanish word for prickly pear. And they weren't bad.

We arrived at a luxurious resort in Mazatlán to spend the night. The wide lobby was open to the breeze off the ocean, and women paraded around in bikinis and wispy skirts. I couldn't believe the paper was paying for us to stay here.

Ruben and Joe suggested a swim before dinner. They pointed to a young lady behind the front desk and instructed me, Go ask her for the pool. The word in Spanish is *"alverga."*

I was beginning to know them well enough to be cautious. I sensed them testing me, or sending me into trouble, or both. They smiled and raised their eyebrows a little, pointing the way with their chins. Go on, they said.

I walked up to the desk, offered my most charming smile, and asked smartly for the *"alverga."*

The woman looked at me for a second and then noticed the two guys behind me, now bent over laughing hysterically. She got the joke, proudly ignored it, and pointed me to the pool, carefully pronouncing it *"alberca,"* not *alverga,* which the boys confessed, with more laughter, referred to a part of my anatomy.

Nearby was a hot dusty town called San Ignacio, where we learned that some local men had been arrested for robbing and murdering the professor. The sun was blindingly hot, and the streets were empty. The few people who would speak to us were suspicious or hostile. This was nothing like the resort in Mazatlán. I was glad I was with Ruben and Joe. They asked around until we found a man in jail who had been accused in the death of the professor. I tried to follow what the man was saying, but I missed a lot. Joe grew impatient and then annoyed with all my interruptions.

One thing I didn't get was *"tehuacanazo."* I sort of recognized the word because of the brand of sparkling water called Tehuacán. Ruben and Joe explained that the police had questioned the man for days, encouraging him to talk by shooting carbonated water up his nose. That was a *tehuacanazo.* To be even more encouraging, they spiced the bubbly water with chili peppers. When he still didn't talk, they soaked rags in a dead cow baking along the road. Then they shoved the slimy rags down the man's throat. He did confess to killing the professor, and probably to every other crime committed in San Ignacio.

I had imagined various versions of the professor's disappearance. Maybe he had decided to go off the grid in Mexico. Maybe he had met someone and wanted to stay. Maybe he was kidnapped for ransom. In the end, it seemed he was just the victim of a random, dirty crime, a robbery that ended in murder, a life taken for a few hundred bucks and a used car. He had embarked on a great adventure—probably careful not to drink the water—and never returned home.

This was a Mexico I had never seen. It was mysterious, arbitrary, and scary. There were no rules for the bad guys, or the good guys. The only rule was power, and people accepted it as a fact of life. We drove back home and published our stories and photos over several days.

I was hooked on Mexico. Joe, with a snarl of resentment, called me on it. "Are you going to be one of those white guys who wants to be Chicano?" I didn't argue, because I understood what he meant. Joe thought I was becoming an instant expert on Mexico and the border, even though I had just arrived and barely spoke Spanish. He had grown up on the border and had studied at the University of Texas at El Paso and Columbia University, so his expertise was earned.

I was drawn to the culture, and I enjoyed speaking Spanish. I almost felt like a different person in Spanish. Not a different person entirely, but a more relaxed and fun version of myself, more of the person I wanted to be. I loved the music and the food and found the people attractive. I wanted to know more about the culture and be part of it, to belong to a club of insiders. I had fun surprising people, showing off really, with my Spanish. Mostly, I liked how I felt about myself—lighter and more confident—when speaking Spanish. A second language allowed me to feel like a bird singing a new tune.

My great accomplice exploring Mexico was John Hopper, the photographer I had met during my job interview. John saw the border with fresh eyes and photographed daily life as if he were exploring a foreign land. Renting an apartment in South El Paso, where Anglos rarely lived, he won the confidence of store owners, young mothers, and even criminals, who posed flashing gang signs and tattoos. John never really blended in, but his photos often made the paper because our editors shared this outsider love of the community.

After work, John and I got into his car and drove across the bridge to Juárez. Like many photographers, John had a car that served as a mobile photo studio filled with camera gear, extra clothes, and bags of half-eaten fast food. When he hit the brakes, bottles and cans clanked and rolled from under the passenger seat and bumped my feet.

We had a restaurant in Juárez we liked for beef tacos with a side of grilled scallions. Another regular place had a tiled trough that ran along the floor below the bar. The trough apparently allowed male patrons to urinate without leaving their bar stools, something I never tried. Still, it added to the bar's mystique, or something.

On Friday nights we visited upscale discos to meet women and dance, or at least move around stiffly while the women danced. Our Spanish improved greatly with beer, but the clubs were so loud that conversation was limited to a few shouted words and hand gestures, hopefully leading to flirting and close contact on the dance floor. Every time I started a conversation in Spanish, the Mexican women answered in English. I thought they sneered ever so slightly at my Spanish. I kept trying, though, and it became a contest to see whose second language would dominate. The women always won.

As John and I headed home one night with the windows open, the Juárez dawn felt cool after the hot day. We drove up the bridge from the Mexican side, past the flags from both countries, and down to the US side and the vast expanse of checkpoints that looked like tollbooths. Everybody had a theory about what kind of US inspector to choose: male, female, Chicano, Anglo, fat, old. You had only a second to decide because hesitation or the appearance of choosing made you look suspicious. At least that's what we feared. We never had drugs, or a person hidden in the trunk, so we had nothing to be nervous about, but I still felt on guard, more apprehensive about reentering our own country than about the one we had just left.

"Citizenship?" the agent asked, looking down at us through John's window.

"American," John said.

The agent watched my face when I spoke the words. "US," I said.

"What are you bringing from Mexico?" the agent asked.

"*Nada,*" John said.

I added the usual joke, "Just a hangover."

He waved us through.

The more time I spent in Mexico, working or having fun, the better stories I discovered. When I wrote good stories, people noticed and were more willing to talk, which led to deeper stories. I was hitting the sweet spot for a reporter when I was fresh enough on the beat to be surprised and excited to witness new things, but not so new as to be naïve or to make a stupid error.

The big story at the time was an economic crisis in Mexico. There also were important and dramatic political changes happening, and in 1983 Juárez elected the first mayor from the conservative opposition, a stunning defeat for the ruling party that began an electoral revolution in Mexican politics. I got to know the young mayor, Francisco Barrio Terrazas, and many local party leaders, who would go on to hold important national positions.

I felt comfortable on the border but didn't pretend I knew everything. There was a cliché about Americans in Mexico: the ones there six months were experts, while the ones there thirty years understood how little they knew. I learned something every day, and I got some of it into the paper.

After early afternoon when our stories were filed, the paper didn't publish again until the following day. We didn't regard TV or radio as competition, and the other paper didn't appear until dawn, so we could relax for a few hours. This wasn't like City News, where we updated the news around the clock. The newspaper's rigid news cycle gave us time to digest the stories of the day and consider what we should publish, which made us less likely to make an error of fact, or worse, of judgment.

We were expected in the office before sunrise to get something fresh into the first edition. I always started my day reading the competing paper. Harry hated us reading the *El Paso Times,* however, and I knew not to be seen with a copy in the office. He couldn't bear to speak its name, referring to it as "the other paper." My City News training was to note the stories I had missed and recover them. Harry didn't want us to do that; he wanted us to break stories for the other paper to follow.

The problem for me was named Matt Prichard, who covered Juárez for the other paper. His Spanish was elegant, he was a serious and thoughtful person, and he had sources at the highest levels of the city. I imagined him discussing Cervantes with Mexican intellectuals in smoky Juárez cafes. He wrote with such knowledge and sophistication that I read his stories holding my head in my hands so it wouldn't fall off. He even was taller than I was.

Nobody liked to get beat, but to get beat every day was humiliating. The good news was that my editors didn't care as long as I scooped the other paper just as often. That's what they told me, anyway, but I could not hide my shame when Prichard had an exclusive story on page one, and I learned about something for the first time, like a tourist in my own town.

My secret weapon was Ken Flynn, our Juárez reporter, who wanted me to do well. Ken had served in the army at El Paso's Fort Bliss, married a Mexican woman, Margarita, and raised a family on the border. He knew from his own life about the mixing of two cultures, and he had a passion for all things Mexican that was contagious.

Ken was enthusiastic and open and fit in easily with people on both sides of the border, but he seemed even more outgoing in Juárez, speaking Spanish, hugging and kissing everybody, and always enjoying himself. In addition to being a well-known reporter, he was a deacon in the Catholic Church, and baptized, blessed, and married people in both languages. Every day I hoped he would take me on an adventure across the border, which usually included a long lunch in Juárez, where he introduced me to his large network of contacts, informants, and friends.

I didn't realize how good Ken was until Mexico's president, José López Portillo, was to deliver his big annual address. On the day of the speech, September 1, 1982, nobody had any idea what was coming. We stood in the newsroom watching Mexican TV when the president announced something that would rattle financial markets around the world: in response to the growing financial crisis and weakening of the peso, the government was nationalizing the banks. I understood what he was saying in Spanish, most of the words anyway, but not the significance or what it meant for us in El Paso. Ken got it right away and managed to listen to the TV, answer questions from the editors, and write the story on deadline.

Minutes after he finished banging the keyboard, the building rumbled when the big drums on the presses started to spin. Then the first batch of papers came up, warm as baked bread and smelling richly of sour paper and flinty black ink. Ken's story, below a giant headline, was flawless. Even better, the other paper couldn't publish the news until the following morning.

The weakening Mexican economy was devastating to El Paso, and Harry was increasingly aware of how decisions in Mexico City affected life on the border, and even the future of the paper itself. If Mexicans could not afford to shop in El Paso, local businesses would decline, and the first thing they would cut was advertising. Without advertising, we couldn't cover the news, and without news and advertising, nobody would buy the paper.

I knew vaguely that the paper had an advertising department, but I don't remember any salespeople or what they did. The business operations were completely separate from the newsroom. I had heard about newspapers with bright yellow lines painted on the newsroom floor to prevent ad salesmen from influencing the reporters, but no paint was needed in El Paso. Everybody knew where Harry stood, and no ad salesperson would have dared to pitch a puff piece about a car dealer or big advertiser to curry favor. The opinion of the advertising people, if they had one, wasn't something I heard discussed, ever.

Harry wasn't oblivious to the business side, however, and part of his financial survival plan was that the *Herald-Post* would make its name as the best little paper covering Mexico and the border. To do that, he had a bold idea: Harry wanted to open the paper's first bureau in Mexico City, and he wanted me to be the correspondent. I was thrilled, a little nervous, but brimming with a youthful confidence I could do the job.

Harry needed corporate approval for a new position, especially a rare and prestigious foreign posting, so the head of Scripps Howard's newspaper division, Bill Burleigh, was coming to El Paso in the fall of 1983 to talk about the proposed bureau and to meet me. We had to convince the corporate guy that the paper needed a Mexico City bureau and that I was ready for the job, so I was told to write a story with an audience of one. Harry and Tim said they had just the thing. And then I got a lucky break.

I didn't know anything about the corporate office, but Harry said Burleigh was a conservative Catholic who appreciated serious journalism. Tim, also Catholic, decided we should pitch a curve and write something about family planning in Mexico.

I had stayed in touch with Rebeca, whom I had falsely accused of baby selling. By staying in touch, I mean trying to date her, without much success. I had resigned myself to being "friends." I talked with her about the family planning story, interviewed experts and mothers, and arranged for photos and graphics, which newspaper people called "art." We wanted the story to be displayed well, so I had it finished days before deadline. The plan was for the Scripps Howard boss to see the first edition and then take me to lunch, where I would dazzle him with my knowledge of Mexico and my readiness for the new job.

Just before the boss's arrival, the world provided an unexpected gift. Reporters had a saying that we hoped nothing bad happened, but if it did, "let it be on our time." Meaning, if a good story was going to break, let it occur before our deadline and after the deadline of the competition. Then we could own the story for a few hours.

On the big day, I read the *El Paso Times* (discreetly to prevent Harry getting upset) and didn't see anything about Juárez or the border. I was safe if the corporate guy tried to do a head-to-head comparison. There was a little item in a Spanish-language paper from Juárez, something about a Hollywood film crew getting in trouble.

Harry figured if I had the family planning story in the can, there was plenty of time to find another story. No editor ever was satisfied with what already was written; they always wanted more, different, better. Photographer Ruben

Ramirez grabbed a handheld radio and his camera bag, and we headed out to his red pickup. Let's go to Juárez, *ese*, he said, using border slang for dude. My chest puffed up when he talked to me the way he would to a friend. Ruben was confident and fun; I was in good hands.

I had torn out a clipping from the Juárez paper about the Hollywood dustup. Now they were ranting about the story on Mexican radio. Every station seemed to be talking about it. Ruben drove us across the bridge to the hotel hosting the cast and crew filming *Conan the Destroyer,* starring body builder Arnold Schwarzenegger in the second big role of his movie career. There we met with a reporter from a Juárez newspaper at the center of the "incident" that was lighting up the media in Juárez.

She was shaken, upset about what had happened to her, but she agreed to tell me the story. I took notes and nodded my head sympathetically. She was well educated and had a good vocabulary, including some words I didn't understand completely. She was bright and articulate, so I got the general idea. Ruben worked around us without speaking, unobtrusively taking pictures of her.

We said good-bye, and Ruben and I jumped back into the truck to return to El Paso. If we got stuck in traffic on the bridge, and risked missing our deadline, I would dictate the story over the radio to a rewrite in the newsroom. It wasn't much of a story, though. To be honest, I couldn't understand the big deal. The Juárez press association was furious and wanted Schwarzenegger expelled from the country. The other media in Juárez were calling for strong government action against the film crew. It all seemed blown out of proportion to me.

The reporter told me she was just doing her job and taking pictures of the film crew relaxing by the pool. One of them complained it was an invasion of privacy, roughly grabbed her camera, and removed the film. He returned the camera but kept the film. Schwarzenegger told us the woman should have stopped taking pictures when asked. He said the crew gave her $4 to cover the cost of the film.

Taking her film was totally wrong, and something reporters should protest, but it didn't appear to me to be grounds to declare an entire film crew personae non gratae and expel them from Mexico. I went through my notes, putting together the story in my head.

We were almost to the bridge when Ruben shook his head and said, "Damn. I can't believe that dude mooned that chick."

"What?"

"That dude who dropped his trunks and mooned that reporter chick."

My face must have given it away. Ruben looked over at me and said, "You missed that?"

Completely, entirely, 100 percent missed that. Suddenly all the other stuff, which I had shoved aside as extraneous to the main story, started to fit. All that talk of honor, sanctity, womanhood, the moral fiber of the nation. I got it now. I understood why the reporter was flustered talking about what had happened to her and why everybody was so angry. The Hollywood actor (not Schwarzenegger but another cast member) had exposed himself and insulted her in the most vulgar way. She had told me about it, but using modest euphemisms.

Ruben went over the entire interview, helping me flesh out my notes, which now made more sense. I filed the story, and it ran on page one. I should have insisted that Ruben share a byline, but that would have called attention to my poor Spanish on the day I was supposed to shine. Ruben never spoke of it.

After the main edition with my two page-one stories—birth control in Mexico and the much-more-talked-about indecent exposure—Harry and I walked to lunch with our visiting dignitary. Mr. Burleigh was deeply serious and thoughtful, showing little emotion during the meeting. He was a foot taller than I was and had a commanding presence, and a much better suit. He made a favorable comment about the birth control story—"I read every word"—and I thought things went well.

Harry told me later that the boss liked the idea of a Mexico City correspondent, but he thought the concern—at Scripps Howard one did not use the crass word "company" or even less the word "chain"—could use a man (it was not going to be a woman) covering the region for all the papers, not just El Paso. Our man would roam from the pampas of Argentina through the jungles of Central America and the beaches of the Caribbean, with cosmopolitan Mexico City as home base. His stories would run in all the Scripps Howard papers, plus papers around the world through Scripps Howard News Service, a news agency based at the company's Washington, DC, bureau.

The newspapers had maintained a few overseas bureaus in Asia and Europe, especially during the war in Vietnam, but mostly reporters were sent from Washington on temporary foreign assignments. The company had just sold its major international news organization, United Press International (UPI), in 1982.

The new, expanded plan for the Mexico City bureau sounded good to me, but Harry seemed a little anxious.

I was sent to Denver to meet the editor of our paper there, along with the chief of the Washington bureau, a feared and powerful newsman known as the "lean gray wolf of Washington."

At this point in my career, I was supposed to be a professional reporter, skilled at gathering information and making sense of complicated issues. Like many reporters, though, I was terrible at applying those skills to my own situation.

I got my first clue when I arrived at the *Rocky Mountain News* in Denver. Outside of the *Chicago Tribune,* I had never been in a newsroom where I looked up to so many reporters. I had a similar queasy feeling in a good bookstore: a mixture of awe and insecurity, a realization that I would never write that well or even read all that work.

The Washington bureau chief, Dan Thomasson, was a confident, firm-handshake kind of guy who looked good in a fedora—someone my dad would have called a "man's man." He had broken major stories during Watergate and was an influential voice inside the company. He could be charming or gruff, patting reporters on the back for a good story, or pounding his desk in rage when they missed one.

After the introductions, Dan excused himself to use the restroom. I said I would join him. I was so self-conscious trying to keep up that I had trouble walking. I focused on my stride—too casual? macho enough?—and I almost tripped. Older editors waved hello to Dan, and younger reporters jumped up to kiss his ring. The ambitious ones wanted to work in the Washington bureau some day, and Dan was the one who could take them in, or not.

Inside the men's room, one of those ambitious types grabbed Dan's hand, held on so he wouldn't get away, and said, "I heard we're opening a Mexico City bureau."

I stopped dead, trying but failing to look as though I weren't listening. Dan said, "You bet, kid. I've wanted to do it for a long time."

The eager interloper said, "I'd like to be considered for the job." Dan promised to keep him in mind.

What job? My job? Slowly the other signals I had not seen or just ignored started to make sense. Now I understood why Harry had been anxious about the company's plan. They were going to open a Mexico City bureau, but it wasn't going to be run by Harry from a little paper in El Paso. And if Harry wasn't going to run the bureau, he wasn't going to send his own reporter. And if Harry wasn't sending the reporter, it wasn't going to be me.

When I had overheard people talking about "green," they weren't referring to the grass. I had just turned twenty-six and had less than four years of reporting experience. Slowly I understood: the corporate bosses wanted the first Mexico City bureau to have a veteran reporter who answered to Washington.

We finished our meetings, and I went back to El Paso, mad and dejected. I was resigned to the fact that I wasn't going to Mexico. Maybe it was for the better, I thought. I had been considering a bigger Texas paper, perhaps the *Corpus Christi Caller-Times,* which was known for good writing. Then I could try for Dallas and then the *Chicago Tribune,* the final destination. After two years in El Paso, I had learned a lot. I had friends at the paper and felt at home in the community, but I had bigger ambitions for my career.

The next day Harry was bubbly, goofy even. Come in, come in, he said, pulling me into his office. He never closed the door, but he sat me in a chair in front of his desk.

You're going to Mexico, he said.

Really?

Yes, he said, telling me I must have done a good job at the meeting in Denver.

More likely, Harry had thrown a fit, threatened to break something or quit.

There was a slight change in the job description, he said, but it would be fine.

I nodded.

You'll report to me in El Paso, Harry said, and focus on border issues.

Good, I said, smiling; that was our plan all along.

And you'll report to the paper in Denver, he added, because they want general coverage of Mexico and the deepening financial crisis.

That's fine, I said. I can do that.

He paused.

And you'll report to Dan in Washington because he wants coverage of Central America, especially El Salvador.

El Salvador? That was not in my plan.

El Salvador in 1983 was in a terrifying civil war, after centuries of poverty and oppression. The Salvadoran army, supported by the US government, was indiscriminately hunting anyone who called for change. Leftist guerillas ruthlessly controlled parts of the countryside. At night, cars with tinted windows and armed men prowled the dark city streets: death squads. Even an archbishop, who had criticized the misery and injustice in his country, had been shot to death—in a chapel. Then, at his funeral, dozens of mourners were slaughtered.

President Ronald Reagan feared the rebels would install an oppressive, communist government allied with the Soviet Union in "our backyard." He vowed to stop them. The Soviet Union and Cuba gave the rebels weapons and training. Reagan and the Soviet leaders had opened a new front in the Cold War, and unfortunately for the people of El Salvador, their country became a bloody battleground.

Great, I told Harry. El Salvador. Good story. I decided not to think about it.

# 4

# MEXICO CITY AND POINTS SOUTH

—— ON LEARNING BY DOING ——

In early 1984, I repacked the little car I had driven from Chicago two years earlier and cruised one last time through downtown El Paso. I left the United States when I crossed the bridge to Ciudad Juárez, which used to be called Paso del Norte. For centuries, this place was the gateway—the pass—for travelers heading north. For me, El Paso would be the gateway south to Mexico City and beyond. I had no idea then, but I was headed toward a serendipitous encounter on a busy street in one of the world's largest cities, a chance meeting that would change me in ways I could not imagine.

A few miles inside Mexico's border, I pulled over at a checkpoint to register my car with Mexican customs. To protect the local auto industry, American cars could not be sold in Mexico, so the government kept close tabs on imported cars like mine to prevent them from being sold illegally.

Several days later, I arrived at my new apartment near the capital's touristy Zona Rosa. I parked in the underground garage and carried my few belongings through a pleasant, walled courtyard filled with plants. The building was concrete—the walls, floors, and stairs. The entire complex could have been poured into a single mold. There would come a day when that solid construction would be a blessing. I unpacked and went in search of groceries and supplies.

The neighborhood market was as big as a hangar, with long rows of stalls organized by product. There were sections for beef or chicken, for example, and a section for vegetables. I didn't recognize half of the fruits, with their knobby shapes and husky covers. The noise was an overwhelming mix of voices, fans, and blowers, cleavers chopping, and blenders whirring. "Hey shoppers," the vendors cried out, "try these strawberries. Very fresh! What can I do for you today?" People spoke Spanish with a different accent than I was used to, with a singsong lilt, and very fast.

I was self-conscious, sensing—accurately as it turned out—that I was the only gringo in the entire market. I felt people looking at me and wondering what I was doing, whether I was lost or confused or a little slow in the head. I walked stiffly, hoping no one would see me or that I would not somehow offend with an imperious stride.

After forty-five minutes and a half-dozen stalls, I had filled two woven plastic shopping bags with groceries. Some of the transactions were difficult because I wasn't sure of the quantities—how big was a liter or a kilo? I also needed to convert the prices into dollars, which was cumbersome for a non-math major. The prices in pesos were meaningless, but when I calculated the dollars, I knew the hours I needed to work to make the purchase.

The final item on my list was eggs. Many vendors carried eggs, but I didn't see a simple carton with a dozen. Instead, the loose eggs were stacked in pyramids or arrayed in neat rows. Some eggs were snow white, others were brown. I was less concerned with the color than with finding ones that were not covered with the pain of birth: flecks of blood and bits of feather. I observed other people order, and the vendor carefully placed the eggs into a clear plastic bag, tying the top into a knot. I bought a bag and nestled the eggs among the other groceries.

Passing the final fruit vendor, I noticed bright yellow bananas. Now the confident market shopper, I asked the lady how much. I pointed to the bunch I wanted, and she reached down from her perch to place the bananas into the shopping bag.

"Not in there," I told her, politely but firmly. "I've got my eggs—*mis huevos*—in there."

She looked at me and burst out laughing. In a loud voice, she announced to everyone within twenty-five stalls, "This young man's got his 'eggs' in the basket!" She was guffawing now, and sending ripples of laughter across the market. "Oh yeah! Got his eggs in the basket!"

Right away I realized my mistake—I should have said *the* eggs instead of *my* eggs—but it was too late, and I was too slow in Spanish to come up with a clever retort. The laughter continued, so loudly that startled birds flew off the rafters, and I tried to shrink myself enough to sneak away with the eggs—or as I had said, "my balls"—in a bright orange shopping basket.

Safely back in my apartment, I got to work. The company had offered me an office downtown or $100 toward my monthly rent if I worked from my apartment. The decision was easy, and I set up the headquarters of the Latin America bureau on the dining room table. I had a Radio Shack computer, a rotary-dial phone, and a television with a handful of Mexican channels. I filed stories from my computer using a cable that connected to the telephone with two black rubber cups attached to the mouthpiece and earpiece of the handset. Then my computer connected over the phone line with a computer in Washington to transmit my stories.

My daily routine began with a visit to the corner vendor for at least five newspapers: one liberal, one conservative, one representing the ruling party, and others for variety. Once a week I bought the news magazine *Proceso*. The trick to reading the papers was getting to know who was writing what, and why. Some of the stories were deliberate leaks by one faction against another or by the ruling party against a dissident wing. Other stories were part of ongoing feuds. A few stories were simply dictated by the people who paid for them, just like taking out an advertisement but more expensive.

I watched TV news every day, especially the *24 Horas* program at 2 p.m., mostly to avoid missing something big. The television news was well presented by smart, good-looking people, but the underlying and unquestioned assumptions were that the ruling party was synonymous with the government, the government existed to protect the citizens, the police were interested only in catching criminals, and the army, well, the army was not mentioned at all except when soldiers marched in parades. Mexico's foreign policy was noble and respectful of others, resistant to the charms and pressures of the United States. The business sector produced the highest quality goods, the national soccer team was unbeatable, Mexican women were both sexy and chaste, and the Virgin of Guadalupe watched over everything with a subtle but pleased Mona Lisa smile.

My efforts to understand Mexico better were interrupted by a call from Washington. Things are heating up in El Salvador, my new editor said, so you should go.

El Salvador, I repeated, staring down at my computer and the Mexican newspapers spread across the table. I was just getting used to my comfy new apartment. El Salvador was the scary place. Every day, students, farmers, even journalists, were "disappeared," as they said of people who vanished, horribly, without a trace. I had never been to a war zone or witnessed mass violence. Mexico felt warm and fuzzy in comparison.

"I guess I could go next week," I offered. "I'm still unpacking my stuff."

"We need you to go today," the editor said.

I didn't argue. I knew El Salvador was part of the territory, although I wasn't expecting to go so soon. Maybe it was better to get it over with. I went to the airline office and bought a ticket. I packed a small bag of clothes and a briefcase with my computer and fresh notebooks. I asked the porter who lived in the building to keep an eye on the apartment and my car. I hadn't made any friends yet, so I didn't have anybody else to tell.

I deliberately did not tell the person who cared most where I was: my mom. She worried enough that I was living so far away in Mexico City, so when I called Chicago to check in, I did not mention I was going to Central America.

My stomach was tight during the taxi ride to the airport, and I stretched my shoulders to relax the burning knot in my neck. I was anxious about the trip not only because of the danger but also because it was my first assignment for Washington. I had learned the basics of reporting during two years at City News and had done some good stories during two years in El Paso, but Washington was in another league. Dan and the editors there didn't know my work, and I felt I had to prove myself from the start.

Even though I originally was supposed to report to editors in Denver, El Paso, and Washington, Dan had used his considerable clout in the company to make himself my main boss, and he let me know it. El Salvador was getting a lot of attention in Washington, so Dan would be reading my stories closely.

No one ever told me what to write, or which side I should take, the angle, or the spin. Just write good stories. My bosses all seemed to take seriously the Scripps Howard motto: "Give light and the people will find their own way." I was starting to believe it, too.

After I checked in for my flight, I joined a long line that ended at a single desk where a man in uniform reviewed the documents of departing travelers. I glanced at my watch every few minutes, starting to get concerned. I had left my apartment immediately, but the line, everything in Mexico City, was moving underwater. I switched my briefcase from my right hand to my left. I checked again to be sure my passport was in my jacket pocket, along with the ticket and boarding pass. At last it was my turn at the desk, the final hurdle before the gate.

"Ticket," said the man in uniform, not looking up. I handed him my ticket. "Documents." I handed him my blue US passport. "Travel documents," he said. I gave him copies of the forms I had filled out at the border when I drove across from El Paso. He paged through the papers, looked again at my passport and then up at my face. "Where is your car?"

I was confused for a second. I'm taking an airplane, I thought, what do you mean, where's my car? Fearing this was a trick question, I looked at him trying to determine the correct answer. "Uh, at my apartment?"

"You can't leave the country without your car," he said.

Now I really was confused. There was no way I could take my car, even as checked baggage. "But I live here," I said. "I left my car at my apartment, and I will be back in two weeks."

He folded up the papers, stuffed them into my passport and handed it back to me. "You must bring your car to the customs lot here at the airport, where it will be impounded. You can pick it up when you return from your travels. Have a nice day."

My stomach dropped, and I felt a prickling current of anxiety. I looked ahead and saw the gate. I looked behind me and saw the line growing longer. People were pushing forward into me. I was holding up the other departing passengers.

"I'm a journalist," I said. "I'm going to El Salvador to write a story."

The official started to look behind me at the next person in line.

"Surely there's something we can do," I offered.

He looked back at me. This was the moment he would decide whether to press an alarm under the desk and armed men would burst out and arrest me for trying to bribe a federal official. I would spend years in the dark pit of a Mexican prison. I would be disgraced and lose my job.

"It would be very expensive," he said.

"How much?"

"One hundred American."

"How about fifty?"

"Sixty," he said.

I peeled off $60 and handed the money to him with my documents. He made no effort to be discreet or hide the money. He opened my passport and slapped it with a clunky metal stamp. "Have a nice trip." He looked behind me at the line and said, "Next."

I took my seat on a perfectly nice jet operated by the Salvadoran carrier TACA. Whenever I flew, I made a mental note of the make and model of the aircraft and the view outside the window. I glanced at the passengers next to me so that they would be familiar if I had to get their names and ages.

The reason for this preflight ritual was that if we crashed, I wanted to be prepared with a few paragraphs of background color for my story. I noted the exit doors and imagined how quickly I could get out of the wreckage and find a phone to file. In these daydreams, the passengers, me included, always survived. I did this on every flight, not just when flying TACA, which I soon would learn the other reporters called "Take-A-Chance Airlines."

We did not crash, and a few hours later, I stepped off the plane into the heat and noisy disorder of the airport in San Salvador: extended families pressed closely together and jostling to get a better view of the arriving passengers, kids running up to carry my bags, taxi drivers soliciting riders, men pushing carts of stacked luggage.

Unlike Mexico City, where the air was dry even when the sun was hot, this place was moist as a jungle, low and close, thick and humid. The smell was warm bananas, corn, and diesel fuel. The people were shorter and darker than in Mexico City. They spoke Spanish quickly and swallowed the final letters of some words, forcing me to pay close attention. It was like hearing Jamaican English for the first time.

I changed some money and allowed myself to be herded into a taxi. The driver tossed my bag into the rusty trunk and we sped off toward the city. The scenery reminded me of rural Mexico: worn concrete houses with tin roofs and faded paint, small restaurants with wobbly plastic tables, mountains of truck tires piled outside repair shops, and the occasional wandering cow or donkey, untethered and feeding on grass along the highway.

I had reserved a room at the Hotel Camino Real, a gathering place of the international press corps, where permanent residents from the big newspapers, the wires, and television networks had offices. Visitors like me filled the upper floors overlooking the pool and the green countryside.

From my room, I looked out the window at this new country and wondered how I was going to understand it enough to write a decent story. I had followed El Salvador over the years, but writing a story was much harder than reading one. Writing required knowledge, of course, but also the self-confidence to feel mastery of the subject. I feared I didn't really know anything. I wanted to be able to hold the entire country cupped in my hand, turning it this way and that, to learn its secrets.

The next morning I woke up early, not sure what to do. How do I cover an entire country? Who do I talk to? Where do I go? I didn't have much guidance from the office, other than "things were heating up," so I guessed they were interested in the war. I had a vague idea of the issues based on stories I had clipped from the US and Mexican papers. There were guerrillas on one side versus the military and politicians supported by the United States. All I had to do was find the right people on both sides and convince them to talk to me, without getting blown up, shot, or kidnapped.

First, breakfast. I went to the dining room and saw it was packed. The buffet was piled with fresh fruit, bread, and steaming trays of eggs and sausage. Some tables were filled with Salvadorans: men in white *guayaberas* or suits and women in fitted skirts and dresses, stockings, and heels. They were eating, smoking, and laughing.

At other tables were foreigners. There was no international tourism because of the violence, but the war had attracted aid workers, activists, opportunists, spies, and journalists. Most of the foreigners were Americans dressed in casual shirts and jeans. Some of them wore khaki Domke vests with many pockets, bulging with notebooks, film canisters, and camera equipment. The floor was piled with TV cameras and folded tripods. The Americans were eating and talking quietly, huddled together, and no one looked up when I approached.

I grabbed a plate of fruit and took a seat by myself. The waiter brought me coffee, which I sipped slowly, hoping I would come up with a great story idea or some veteran reporter would invite me along. What the heck was I going to write? Even before I started to write, where was I going to go? This wasn't like being in El Paso, where I could run across to Mexico and come back with a story in time for lunch. I was all the way inside now. How would I find people to interview? What would I ask them? How would I get there? Taxi? Rent a car? Walk? I had no idea.

From my seat, I tried to overhear the conversations at other tables. My worst fear was missing something big that everybody else was covering. I figured if they all were eating breakfast and smoking cigarettes, things must be quiet. I recognized a few of the nicer looking reporters from television. The preppy men and women were probably reporters for the East Coast papers. The scruffier, bigger guys must have been cameramen. There were a few Salvadorans with them, most likely local reporters or fixers, the invaluable men and women who arranged interviews, travel, and logistics, and kept us safe.

I couldn't drink any more coffee, so I signed the bill and went to my room. I turned on the television, hoping for inspiration. I was pleasantly distracted by a flexible woman doing aerobics. I flipped through more channels looking for local news. What if something was happening a few blocks away and I didn't even know? Maybe the dining room had emptied and everybody was covering a big story that would be in all the papers tomorrow, except mine. I couldn't find any news on TV. Maybe that was good because nothing was happening. More importantly, I wasn't missing anything.

I looked again through the pile of clippings I had brought, trying to see themes or story ideas. The war was big, but so were the political situation and the economy. I took out three new notebooks and labeled them: war, politics, economy. I would take notes on each topic only in the designated notebook and hope a story emerged. I clipped two pens in my shirt pocket, checked that I had enough cash, and walked out of the hotel and into El Salvador.

The doorman asked if I wanted a taxi, and I settled into the spongy back seat. I knew from Mexico that I could negotiate an hourly rate, but I wasn't sure how much to pay. We came to an agreement—less than I paid in Mexico but probably more than the rate in El Salvador—and I told the driver to show me the city. I asked questions, and he was full of opinions about his country, my country, the war, the future, soccer (which I didn't care about), and the local cuisine, which was more interesting.

Like many rookie correspondents, I got my introduction to a new place through the eyes of a taxi driver, the first source of last resort for reporters without a clue. After a few hours, I had moved up to the passenger seat, and I enjoyed seeing the city like a curious tourist. It was manageable compared with Mexico City, and life seemed normal. It did not feel like a war zone. Soon it was time for lunch, which I agreed to buy if the driver would pick an authentic local place.

First he returned me to the hotel because I had to check in with the office. Every day at 12:30 p.m., the Scripps Howard editors in Washington transmitted a budget of coming stories—the "sked"—to our papers and the hundreds of client papers around the world that paid to print our stories. I needed to tell the desk by noon if I was going to file that day, with a two-sentence description of the story, the length in words (usually five hundred to eight hundred), and the "slug," or the story's one-word identifier. After I filed the skedline, I had up to five hours to finish the story.

By the time I called at noon, the editors already had seen the *Washington Post* and the *New York Times,* the wires, and news radio, which were not available to me. There was little news on daytime television at home, except for a startup called CNN, which the big networks dismissed as the Chicken Noodle Network. The imbalance of information—the editors knew everything and I knew nothing—made me feel more anxious and unprepared.

I asked the hotel operator to dial the number in Washington. I turned on the TV, thinking I might need more aerobics. In a few minutes the operator rang to say my call was ready. I said hello, someone in Washington answered after a few clicks, and the operator left the line. I explained to the desk that I had a couple of things going but was vague about the story.

The editor who took my call was patient and encouraging. Give it a day, he said, and then file. What a relief. I gave my cab driver a high-five, and we jumped back into the taxi to resume the search for news. The driver chose an expensive place for lunch, where the menus were covered in hairy cowhide, which put me off ordering steak.

Fortunately for me, the country was small, and the players were few. They were accustomed to talking with American reporters because their country's future depended in part on the US government, which was in part influenced by US public opinion, which was at least in part influenced by us in the media. The conservative Salvadorans recognized this explicitly and complained that we were biased toward the left-center politicians or even the rebels. Their bumper stickers declared: "Journalist: Betray Your Country, Not Ours. Tell the Truth!"

This might have been funny if reporters were not being threatened, beaten, and killed. Everyone, even the print reporters, taped the shorthand "TV" on their vehicles or attached white towels borrowed from the hotel to the antennas. Somebody had made t-shirts that read in Spanish: "Journalist—Don't Shoot!" It was hard to know whether the shirt was a shield or a bull's-eye.

At the American outpost in the capital, the fortified US embassy, my first press briefing was so crowded I had to sit on the floor with other reporters. I started to recognize the journalists and learned two things from their questions to the US military officer briefing us: how much they knew about the story and whether they were friendly people. I didn't ask any questions, but I took pages of notes.

After a few days, I felt more comfortable. I saw some of the reporters enough that I started to introduce myself. At least now when I went to breakfast, I could eat with someone. To a newcomer, the seating arrangements appeared as deliberate as a state dinner. The "A-team" was the *New York Times,* the *Washington Post,* the *Wall Street Journal, Los Angeles Times,* and maybe a reporter from a TV network, especially if the person had started his or her career at a newspaper. There also were reporters from the Associated Press, UPI, Reuters, and news outlets from Europe, Asia, and Latin America.

The reporters often plotted together where to go, whom to interview, and less directly, what to cover. There were several reasons to do this. First, it was safer to report in small groups than alone. Second, while the news organizations were competitors, the reporters often were friends who trusted each other. Finally, it was better to know what the competition was doing than to be called by the desk at midnight asking why the other paper had something different. Not necessarily better, but different. I had experienced all of this covering City Hall in Chicago, where competitors routinely agreed on "the story" for the day.

Reporters still competed for scoops, however, which had a trickle-down effect on the rest of us. If on Monday a *New York Times* reporter discovered armed conflict in a rural area, the story would be in the paper Tuesday. The network correspondents in El Salvador received early copies of the *New York*

*Times,* so at dawn they would race off to the same rural area in search of combat video called "bang bang" for Tuesday's nightly news. By Wednesday, editors across the United States, including mine, had seen this new "hot zone" in the paper and on television, so they would assign their correspondents to cover the action, furthering the impression that something big was happening. The predictable process was annoying and defeated the whole purpose of having independent eyes and ears on a story.

The reporters who were not on the A-team did not consider themselves to be in the minor leagues, and rightly so. Many were experts on the region, but they worked for the wires, news magazines, radio, television, newspaper groups, or regional papers in Dallas, Baltimore, or Philadelphia. The *Miami Herald* considered itself the paper of record for Latin America, and the *Herald's* excellent reporters owned the story as much as anyone.

As the new kid with little experience, and working for a venerable company that lacked snob appeal, I was not going to start on the A-team. I barely got up the nerve to speak to them. These people were legends and my heroes. The *Washington Post's* Ed Cody had covered wars around the world, spoke a half-dozen languages, and didn't even take notes. He had a tiny notebook he rarely removed from the breast pocket of a golf shirt. He wrote down only the occasional word or phrase. Mostly he just listened, really listened.

I heard that one of the stars, Julia Preston, taped and transcribed every word of every interview and permanently archived all her notebooks. Another guy, Clifford Krauss, had been shot in the head covering a story here, and now he was having breakfast a few tables from me.

Just as impressive were the photographers like Jim Nachtwey, Susan Meiselas, and Cindy Karp. They not only had to understand the story, they had to anticipate what would happen so as to be there to photograph it. Photographers never had the luxury of covering the story by phone, or recovering a scoop they had missed.

I remember standing under a tree to avoid the burning sun and watching *Newsweek's* Bill Gentile shoot photos with the intensity he brought to everything. While I watched, the back of his light-colored, cotton shirt began to darken with sweat. He lowered the camera only to wipe his eyes or adjust the heavy bag of gear on his shoulder. Soon his shirt was completely dark, soaked. All in the time it took me to drink a soda in the shade.

My three notebooks filled up quickly, and I filed a story every day. Much of my work focused on El Salvador's coming presidential elections, and I met all the candidates and memorized their platforms. After two weeks, one of the Washington editors told me to slow down. Take a breath, he said. When you write, let us know you are there. Have a dog step on your shoe or the sun warm your back.

His guidance released me from my fear of getting scooped on something minor. After that, I spent more time writing the stories and really thinking about what I wanted to portray, rather than just shoving out facts and figures. I wasn't working for a cushy monthly magazine, however, and I would be judged not by how much I learned but by how often I filed good stories.

My regular taxi driver, Alejandro, agreed to guide me to a small mountain town that had been tossed back and forth between the guerrillas and the army. We had just met, but I didn't hesitate to go anywhere with Alejandro, even a conflicted area. He took me to dangerous places, at some risk to himself, partly for the US dollars but also because he was interested and cared about his country. He cared enough about me to invite me to backyard barbecues with his extended family, where the little kids held my hands and jumped on me, the exotic American, and I cheerfully swung them by the arms in dizzying circles.

On the road leaving the capital, we were stopped at a military checkpoint. After I presented a press credential issued by the Salvadoran Army, I interviewed the young soldiers, dark-skinned boys from the countryside, about what they had seen.

Later, far from the capital, armed men flagged us down at a guerrilla checkpoint. The "Gs," as some reporters called them, were thin and hard, with scraggly beards, homemade uniforms, and weapons ranging from a farmer's shotgun to automatic rifles. I showed identification issued by the Salvadoran press association, not my army ID, so they wouldn't mistake me for a government agent.

I interviewed the young men, and a few women, about where they were from and why they were fighting the government, looking over my shoulder in case an army patrol was approaching. At least nine foreign correspondents had been killed in El Salvador at the time, often in crossfires.

Alejandro drove us up a winding unpaved track through a pine forest, watching carefully for fresh dirt where a mine could be hidden. I suggested we follow a bunch of cows walking up the road to let them discover the mines first. When darkness fell suddenly in the dense forest, I was briefly but intensely afraid, and I promised God that if we made it out safely, I would not return to this place.

The power had been knocked out by the rebels, and no food had gotten through for several days, so that night we ate leftover tamales by candlelight at a solid wooden table in an empty hotel. The windows were open, and we could hear distant gunfire and occasional yelling. The mountain air was pleasantly cool; I hadn't known this country could be anything but hot and humid. The other guests at the dinner table were a heavyset Salvadoran Army captain in fatigues and a human rights lawyer from the city.

After quite a few beers, the captain vowed to fight the rebels to the last man, saying, "You can't turn the other cheek if you've been shot in the face."

The lawyer just sighed, again. He shook his head in the darkened room and said, "That's a parable, *mi capitán.*"

A reporter friend, Larry Jolidon, silently approached the table in the dark, not wanting to intrude if I was doing an interview. I nodded for him to take a seat.

The lawyer, who had been matching drinks with the captain for a couple of hours, said to me, "You treat us like animals. You want to know how many have been killed, which side is killing more today. No one wants to know, 'How can the United States help El Salvador?'"

The truth was that El Salvador mattered to the US media only because it was part of the struggle for world dominance between the United States and the Soviet Union. Backed by the United States, a small, wealthy elite had long used the army and police to crush protests and kill opponents. In response, rebels took up arms and sought help from Cuba and the Soviet Union. The Salvadorans might have fought a civil war without us, but I was there as a reporter only because President Reagan and the Soviets were focused on Central America as a battleground in the Cold War. Washington and Moscow drove the news coverage here, more than events on the ground.

The next day, I could not help but smile when Larry took the lawyer's advice and asked every person we met, "How can the United States help El Salvador?" Both of us used the responses in our stories.

El Salvador was the place I had feared the most, but soon it was just another story on my beat. Covering elections there was not all that different from covering elections in Chicago or El Paso, except that the stakes were much higher. The war was terrible for the Salvadoran people, but I made Salvadoran friends and developed sources. I found my place among the press corps, and soon I felt comfortable, if not completely relaxed.

I did have a moment of doubt when I filed my expense report. I had paid a $60 bribe at the airport to get through Mexican immigration, but I wasn't sure if the company would reimburse me, or if that was even legal. I called to ask the Washington bureau's office manager, a chain-smoking old-timer, whom I found a little scary.

I explained about the bribe, and surprisingly, she said, "We'll call it a 'gratuity.'" She also noticed on my hotel bill that I had crossed off the charge for one movie in my room, because I considered it a personal expense.

"I'm putting the movie charge back in your expenses to be reimbursed," she said, from that moment adopting me as another of her boys in the bureau. "What do they expect you to do at night when you're all alone?"

# 5

## HOW WE MET

—— ON LUCK ——

When I returned to Mexico City, it felt more like home. I had a daily routine, a growing list of sources, and the story was more clear. I went back to wearing a coat and tie in the big city, instead of jeans and hiking boots in Central America, and relaxed a little. No longer so worried about getting hurt, I remained in fear of missing a story. I felt responsible for everything from the US border to the tip of South America, and I always was anxious something was happening that everyone knew about except me.

I worked all the time because it didn't feel like work. I couldn't believe this was a job: I traveled to exotic places on the company's dime, saw new things, met interesting people, and asked them anything I wanted to know. Then I wrote about my adventures for people back home. And I got paid.

When I wasn't reporting or writing, I didn't have anything to do. I didn't have hobbies or interests outside of work. Some nights I felt restless, too tired to work but too wired to sleep. On one of those nights, I tried writing in my journal, which I had kept since college, but I couldn't focus. I called a friend to see if he wanted to go to a movie, but he wasn't home. I paced some more, stared into the empty refrigerator. Nothing on television. Got to get out. It was a cool night in the fall of 1984, so I grabbed a jacket and walked a few blocks to Paseo de la Reforma, the main avenue near the US embassy.

A movie called *Sebastian* was playing at the Cine Elektra. Waiting for the movie to start, munching my popcorn, I glanced around and noticed a young woman sitting to the right and back a few rows. She was medium height and slender, with hair that was dark brown, almost black, cut short and straight. Her face was the color of creamy caramel, with high cheekbones, full lips, and large eyes that were almost as black as her hair. She was wearing a tan trench coat and very tight, stylish blue jeans. The woman looked familiar, but I couldn't place her. She was bouncing her left leg up and down, like she was nervous. I thought she must have been waiting for someone. No way a woman like that would be alone at the movies, or anywhere. I noticed she was not wearing a ring.

The movie was a silly British import about secret agents and codes. My mind wandered. That woman looked really good. Maybe I'll say something in Spanish on the way out, if she's still alone. I could say something easy: Hello. How did you like the movie? I practiced saying it in Spanish.

The movie ended, and the house lights brightened. I stood up and put on my coat, turning around to look at her. She was still alone. I practiced my opening line, timing my exit so our paths would cross. When I got to her, she was standing in front of her seat, waiting to ease into the crowd leaving the theater. I was just a step away when I lost my nerve, averting my eyes as I walked by her. She's probably got a boyfriend. I stood in the lobby, pretending to look at the posters for coming attractions, and watched her leave the theater.

Outside in the fresh night air, I saw the Angel of Independence monument: a bronze, winged angel perched on a tall stone pillar. At the other end of the street, on a hill, the Chapultepec Castle glowed under bright floodlights. Cars drove by on Reforma, and young couples arm-in-arm waited to cross the street. On nights like this I loved Mexico City, lighted up and buzzing. Here I was, a roving foreign correspondent in Latin America. I felt like James Bond with a notebook. Walking toward home, I dashed between speeding cars to the grassy median of the wide avenue.

Waiting for another break in the traffic, I saw her again. The woman from the movie was standing at the bus stop, and two cars were idling at the curb in front of her. The young men in the cars were calling to her and offering a ride. Mexican men assumed it was better to try, and be rejected, than not to try at all. In the old days men whispered *piropos,* sweet little nothings, such as, "Who opened the gates of heaven and allowed an angel to escape?" These guys were more the type who hissed and smacked wet kisses, trying to entice her into the car.

I crossed the street and kept going, chuckling to myself at the attention the woman was getting. I wasn't the only one who found her unusually beautiful. I didn't think she was in danger, just at risk of being annoyed. I looked at her and smiled, but she was staring straight ahead, her jaw tight, trying to ignore the guys in the cars. Those jerks. I should help her. And it was some kind of sign that I kept seeing her.

I had walked by, so I turned around and came up behind her. "*Oiga,*" I said, tapping her on the shoulder and using the formal voice in Spanish. She flinched and took a step away, stopped, and turned quickly to look at me, her eyes wide with fear. I put my hand on her arm, and she relaxed, even smiled a little.

"Did you like the movie?" I asked.

"Yes," she said, "It's good to see foreign films."

I stumbled with my weak Spanish, made weaker by a sudden and unexpected wave of nervousness. "Do you want if I should wait to the bus?"

She smiled again, this time a real smile. "Please."

Her suitors were still idling there, leaning over to see if I was going to fail. Feeling cocky, I snarled quietly, and they drove off into the night.

We started walking, and she seemed not at all interested in the bus. Her name was Maria Eugenia Montero Salud. People called her Maru (MAH-roo), a nickname for Maria Eugenia. Lucky for me, because in Spanish Maria Eugenia was a mouthful of vowels. She said she was a dancer, and I bowed, impressed.

"How old are you?" I asked.

"Why? Because a dancer has to be young?"

"No, I was just wondering."

"I'm twenty-two," she said. "You're young, too."

"I just turned twenty-seven a few weeks ago."

"A Virgo?"

"Yes. What are you?"

"Pisces," she said.

"What does that mean? What are you like?" I asked.

"Conflictive. Serious. Sad."

"I saw you in the movie," I told her. "You seemed nervous, bouncing your leg. I thought you were waiting for someone."

"No, I pulled a muscle," she said, opening her trench coat and turning out her leg to show me the inside of a lovely muscular thigh packed into a pair of jeans. I was unable to speak, fortunately.

"I saw you too," she said. "You looked so serious eating your popcorn."

We walked down Reforma, once in a while lightly bumping into each other just enough to express interest if not desire. Tall palms rose up in front of the sleek steel and glass buildings that towered over the street. Every few blocks, amid the modern offices and banks, there stood a heavy, stone building from a distant era. The night was clear, and everyone seemed to be out strolling. We talked and laughed and she took my arm. I could not understand everything she said, but I nodded and smiled a lot.

"Do you have any friends in the city?" she asked.

"A few but not many."

"*Amigos* or *amigas?*" she asked, men or women?

I knew we were playing a game here, and I was glad to play. "Mostly *amigos,*" I said. "How about you? Do you have many friends?"

"No, I am very demanding."

I asked, "Will you be my *amiga?*"

"*Encantada,*" she said, "delighted," and my heart fluttered.

Suddenly we were at the corner of Insurgentes Avenue, and it was time to part ways. I was leaving the next day, back to El Salvador, but I promised to call her in a week. My trip turned into two weeks, but I called Maru the day I arrived back in Mexico.

"Hi, this is Peter," I said in Spanish.

"Who?"

"Peter, the guy from the movie." Silence. "You remember, the journalist."

"Oh, yes. How was your *trip?*" The way she pronounced *trip* was like I had not really gone anywhere.

The trip was fine, I told her, but longer than expected. I was disappointed she didn't remember me, but after a little gentle prodding, she agreed to meet me for another movie, this time sitting together. We fell back into easy conversation and started seeing each other. She didn't speak English, but wanted to learn. She helped me with Spanish and taught me about Mexico, about dance and the arts, and about herself.

She had music on all the time, and one day she played a catchy tune called "Corazón de Melón." She said the title didn't refer to cantaloupe, as I had understood, but was a term of endearment like "sweetie." Just then I realized why Cuca in El Paso had called me that, and I smiled at the memory.

After a few months, Maru agreed to take me to visit her family, who lived an hour away on an unpaved street in a rough and struggling part of the city called Iztapalapa. Maru had told me she was one of twelve children of an itinerant father and a mother who had raised them while running a small grocery store in the front room of their cinderblock house.

When Maru was about thirteen, she was discovered by a dance company. She was trained rigorously and soon was traveling the world with the famed Ballet Folklórico de México. Someone had opened a door for her, and she rushed in, exhilarated to find herself and a career she loved.

Coincidentally, I had found my journalism career the same accidental way, and it was one of the few things we had in common. Now that same randomness, or luck, or maybe guardian angels, had led me to her.

I was nervous meeting Maru's mother, but I thought we had a nice conversation. Maru complained I didn't talk with her mother, or anyone for that matter: I interviewed them. I thought talking politics was a good icebreaker.

"*Señora,*" I said, "Do you vote in the elections?"

"I always vote," she said.

"If you don't mind my asking, do you vote for the PRI or the PAN?" I said, mentioning the official party and the largest opposition party.

"They're the same, aren't they?"

Either this was a shrewd political analysis, recognizing how the two parties served as counterweights to support the larger system, or Maru's mom was not too interested in politics. "What do you mean?"

"The PRI, the PAN. Who knows? On the day of the election they come and pick me up in a bus. We go and mark little pieces of paper and put them in a box. Then they give us a sandwich or something and they take us home."

I nodded. The only vote allowed on those government-run outings was for the ruling party. Here I was writing all of these detailed analyses of Mexican politics, and I was missing the story. The politicians and experts I interviewed were participants in the system, both for and against the ruling party, and knew well how Mexico worked at their level. But what about the majority of people? Was this how one party had survived so long, through the powerlessness of citizens and the coercion of the state?

"Why do you bother to vote?" I asked her.

"It's my patriotic duty, isn't it?"

Maru's mother spoke differently than Maru did, and I had trouble understanding her. It was not only her accent, but the way she saw the world. She was from old and rural Oaxaca, wrapped in a dark shawl of centuries of tradition and beliefs. She had cut her braids and given up her long skirts when she moved the family to Mexico City, but she still had country attitudes. Life was hard because it was meant to be hard. If things were too good, she would have worried. I was different from Maru, but I could communicate with her, even when we had to pass a Spanish-English dictionary between us. With Maru's mother, I feared the distance was too great.

Because of Maru, and then her family, my professional interest in Mexico became personal. The more I learned, the more I wanted to know. I started to write about films and books, sports, music, soap operas, and travel destinations. One trick I learned from *New York Times* reporter Larry Rohter was to write for every section of the paper, thereby making myself valuable to the entire news organization and less dependent on the international desk (and less easy to fire). I even wrote for the food section, interviewing the great chefs of Veracruz about preparing their famous red snapper.

My editors, however, were less interested in fish recipes than in hard news. I was drinking up Mexico because I found it fascinating; getting my editors excited would require a US angle, and the big story was the crashing Mexican economy and its potential impact on the United States.

During the early 1980s, Mexico was in a full economic crisis, unable to pay its debts, forced to devalue the currency and cut public services, and facing a devastating decrease in revenue because of the world market's low price for oil, its main export. Unemployment was high, people were protesting in the streets, and some US analysts warned about a revolution on our border.

I walked over to the US embassy for a 4 p.m. appointment to talk about the economy. There was a large fence around the building to keep out the occasional protests, which were loud but not violent. While demonstrators shouted anti-American slogans in front of the embassy, in the back of the building many other Mexicans lined up to apply for visas to visit or live in the United States.

I joked to Maru: "Their slogan should be '*Yanqui* go home, but take me with you.'" She didn't laugh. In fact, she didn't get most of my best jokes. I usually had to point at my knee to signal a joke, or "knee slapper."

A serious man named John Walsh came into the embassy press office and directed me to sit on the couch. He sat in a chair across from me. He looked at his watch theatrically. In response I checked my watch; I was fifteen minutes late. "We may be *in* Mexico," he intoned, chiding me for my tardiness, "but we are not *of* Mexico."

His description summed up my situation precisely. I was living in Mexico, working in Mexico, and I even had a Mexican girlfriend, but I was not part of Mexico. I immersed myself in Mexican affairs, wrote stories, and sent them off to Washington, where they were distributed to hundreds of newspapers around the world. But I might as well have sent my stories into outer space: after I pressed that final key on my computer, I never heard a thing about what I had written.

It was not the same as being a reporter in El Paso, where I wrote a story in the morning, and it appeared that afternoon on the rack at the gas station. In El Paso, people called to complain about or praise my stories, and I felt I played some role in the community. The name recognition also was a welcome form of compensation: a byline was a daily bonus in lieu of cash.

Another difference was that in the United States, getting a story was as easy as picking up the telephone. In Mexico, nobody in government would even take my call, let alone give me information over the phone. The telephone book itself was worthless; it had so many wrong numbers that people referred to it as the "Mexican Book of the Dead." I had been spoiled by the rules back home. There, I needed information, and government officials gave it to me, either because it was required either by law or by custom. In Mexico, my reporting techniques weren't working.

When I set out to write about the economy, for example, I called repeatedly to the spokesman for the Mexican Treasury Department, whose job was to respond to questions from reporters. A secretary answered, and I explained, for the third time, what I wanted. The spokesman's not in right now, she said, but I'm happy to take your message.

The next day I called again. A different secretary cheerfully took a new message. Another day went by without a word. My office was pressing me for a story on the economy, so I met with local businesspeople, Mexican economists, and "Western diplomats"—what we were allowed to call experts who worked at embassies representing many different countries, not just the United States.

It was after 9 p.m. when I tried the Treasury spokesman one last time. Officials often went back to work after a late lunch. On the first ring, the guy himself answered. The conversation in Spanish went something like this:

"Hello, Peter," he said, warmly, pleasantly surprised to hear my voice. He either had not seen my earlier messages or he was a terrific actor. "Where have you been? I haven't seen you. We've got to get together for lunch."

"That would be fantastic," I said. "I was hoping for an interview with someone at Treasury about the economy."

"Sure, of course," he said. "Do you have someone in mind?"

"Not really," I said. "I was hoping you could recommend someone."

"With pleasure," he said. "Let me get your number, I'll check around and I'll call you back with something. Deal? And let's do get lunch. I'll have my secretary call you to set up something. Great to hear from you."

I flushed with pleasure. Okay, I thought, now we're rolling. I had met the spokesman a couple times, and that was paying off now. I might even do a longer story—what we called a "takeout" or a "thumbsucker"—on the Treasury interview, if he got me someone big enough. Finally, I had gone from outside the door to inside the room.

By the end of the week, I ran out of time and filed what I had on the economy. I worked on a few other projects and waited for the promised call from Treasury. I didn't make any lunch plans because the spokesman had said we would get together, although he didn't say when. Nor was I sure if we were going to do American lunch, around noon, or Mexican lunch at 3 p.m. I snacked a little and checked the phone to be sure it was working. By 4 p.m., I was starving and made myself something to eat.

I waited until the magic hour—9 p.m.—and called again. He answered cheerfully: "Peter, how the heck are you? What's going on? What's new?"

"I'm wondering if you had any luck getting me that interview," I said.

He didn't hesitate. "You know what? I did ask around, and listen, I was just going to call you. It's good that you called first. The truth is, and I talked to the minister and various people on his staff, the truth is that for you to really understand the economy, this is probably not the right place for you to start. I think, especially because you asked about the peso and its relative strength vis-à-vis the dollar, well, as you know, that's really not in our purview. So what we are thinking is that the best place for you would be the Bank of Mexico . . ."

I started to stay something, but he kept going.

". . . So the Bank of Mexico . . . let me see . . . I've got a friend over there . . . let me just find his number. I'm going to give you to my secretary and she will give you the number. He's a friend of mine so just use my name. Great talking to you. Ciao."

I never did get the Treasury interview. Even when I was granted an audience with government officials, they rarely told me anything, and the more authority they had, the less likely they were to reveal something valuable. I prepared well for interviews, rehearsed my questions, dressed in my best suit, and stopped for a shoeshine on the way. Many times all I received in return was a cup of coffee and cookies on the good china and a lecture about the five historic principles of Mexico's foreign policy.

I should have realized I needed to develop deeper sources. On one of my early reporting trips into Mexico, while I was working in El Paso, I had seen just how helpful the right person could be.

I had traveled to La Paz, south of California, to cover the 1983 summit between President Ronald Reagan and Mexico's president Miguel de la Madrid. The night before the meeting, I was invited to dinner by Ricardo Chavira, a reporter friend from the paper in San Diego, and the top Mexican journalists covering the summit.

Bottles were lined up on the outdoor table along with heaping plates of fresh seafood. The food was delicious, and it was a breezy warm night, but the conversation was annoyingly dominated by one of the Mexicans. He was young and bearded and talked constantly. He tore into a huge lobster, obviously on an expense account. After dinner he sipped a French cognac and smoked a Cuban cigar he carefully removed from a leather case. The guy lived pretty well for a reporter.

He did say one interesting thing. He predicted that Reagan would greet de la Madrid with a Mexican-style embrace, called an *abrazo*. The Mexicans did not want to appear rude but also did not want such a lovey-dovey image to dominate Mexican television, so de la Madrid was going to counter the bear hug with a vigorous, American-style handshake.

I walked back to the hotel with Ricardo, ready to sleep for a few hours before the presidential meeting the next morning. I asked him, "So who was that Mexican reporter who kept flapping his gums?"

Ricardo laughed. He's not a reporter, he said, he's one of the top analysts in the Mexican government, their expert on the United States. Then I understood the deference everyone had showed him, and it made me reconsider what he had said.

The next day, Reagan stepped off the plane, his usual smiling, ambling self, and put out his big arms to hug the smaller de la Madrid, who deftly parried the attempted *abrazo* with a gracious handshake. Reagan smiled, and everybody was happy. I would not have noticed the momentary awkwardness if I hadn't been looking for it.

I asked Ricardo for the phone number of my new friend from the Mexican government, and he became one of my deep, protected sources. Since there is no statute of limitations on "off the record," I can't name him, but years later he rose to a cabinet-level job and was considered for president of Mexico.

I realized, again, that the best way to learn was to cultivate people who knew things. And the only way to get them to talk was to earn their trust. In that sense, Mexico wasn't different from Chicago or El Paso, where my best tips had come from people who confided in me. Trust and loyalty were especially powerful in Mexico, and even in business transactions people gravitated to friends and relatives, willing to pay a little more to someone familiar rather than to risk being taken by a stranger. This made the country less efficient, but it was a cultural trait I could use.

Working for Scripps Howard, which most Mexicans could not pronounce let alone identify as a newspaper company, just made the personal connections more important. If people in Mexico (or any country) wanted to leak something internationally, they went first to the big US newspapers. No one was going to seek out less powerful news outlets, but they might leak something to me, if they trusted me.

I never promised anyone a bogus story (or money) in exchange for cooperation, and I tried to be frank and honest about my job. Mexicans got a kick out of American directness because their political culture was dizzying with polite platitudes and empty promises, like the runaround I got when asking for the interview at the Treasury Department.

I began a series of courtships, usually over lunch or coffee, to develop new sources. I learned to go slowly and be patient. A good Mexican lunch could last three hours, and sometimes the best information emerged in the final minutes. I tried not to ask questions that would make someone feel like he was breaking a confidence, or worse, betraying his country.

As a reporter from the United States, I often was suspected of having a secret agenda to help my country or damage Mexico. Even Maru wondered if I was a spy, since, according to her, I was too nice to be a real reporter. (This was not meant as a compliment.) On the other hand, Mexican officials regarded US reporters as less likely to harm their careers because the stories would not be published in Mexico.

Pepe was a senior official who was close to power, because of both his job and his family. He knew people in the government, and the people behind them in the shadows, and he felt important talking about them. I was deeply curious about how things worked, and my desire to understand Mexico was passionate and genuine. Perhaps Pepe thought he could influence how Mexico appeared in the US media, but really, I think he just enjoyed my company; I was an appreciative audience for his opinions.

During one memorable lunch at our regular spot, *Los Guajolotes* ("The Turkeys," but it sounded better in Spanish), he was colder than normal. The waiter brought him the first of many rum and Cokes. "I told you I wanted a lot of ice," Pepe snapped at the waiter. "I thought the service here was supposed to be good." After a few more drinks, the normally charming and gracious Pepe was more unpleasant. He was complaining about something—I gathered it was something I had done—but he was talking in circles and beginning to slur his words.

"Have you seen *Proceso*?" he asked, referring to the influential weekly news magazine.

"No," I said, "It just came out today and I haven't read it yet. What's in it?"

"You should see it."

"Why? What's in it?"

"And after all I did for you," he said. He pushed his food around his plate like a child refusing to eat. He hadn't taken a bite.

"What? What does it say?"

I couldn't take it anymore. "Excuse me, Pepe," I said, standing up and putting aside my napkin. I walked to the newsstand outside the door, bought the magazine and quickly realized why he was so mad. There was nothing more disturbing than seeing my own name under an inflammatory headline. Then I saw the word "propagandist" and a few other insults. There were damning quotes from me that I never said. Not good.

"You know I didn't say that stuff," I told Pepe.

The story was about a PBS *Frontline* documentary called "Standoff in Mexico" that exposed election fraud in northern Mexico. The producer, Hector Galán, had filmed me during 1985 while I covered the elections, and then allowed me to help write and edit the film. The documentary did not air on Mexican television, but I knew bootleg copies had circulated because Mexicans stopped me on the street and said, "Hey, you're the kid in that movie!"

The news magazine called the documentary an unfair and biased attack on Mexico by "the US government's official television network."

Pepe was especially mad because he had vouched for me to arrange interviews for the film.

"This is messed up, Pepe. I did work on this film, but I didn't say those things, and I'm not a propagandist for anybody. You know that."

"Well that's what I told the big guys when they called me to find out what the hell was going on," he said in Spanish. His voice was getting louder and his speech more slurred.

"After all I did for you," he growled. Now he was almost shouting, but I heard in his voice more hurt than anger. People at other tables stopped eating to stare at us. You could hear the random clink of a fork on a plate as the crowded restaurant suddenly went quiet. "After all I did for you," he cried plaintively, "and you fuck us in the ass."

To repair the damage, Pepe had invited three senior leaders of the ruling party to join us for coffee after lunch. The party was divided into young technocrats who wanted to "modernize" the country and the old guard, known as dinosaurs, who preferred smoke-filled backrooms and elections with predetermined outcomes. Pepe was a proud dinosaur, and he described the three men coming to meet me as even more conservative. These guys, he said, were not just dinosaurs but "woolly mammoths."

When the mammoths arrived, we stood to greet them. Pepe had sobered up a little, but he was nervous and spent a long time on the ritual handshakes and backslaps, larded with effusive praise for the political brilliance of his three great friends. The men had good suits and haircuts. They were polite and quietly powerful.

When everyone had settled in, Pepe whispered to me out of the side of his mouth, "Let me do the talking." After praising the mammoths some more, he tried to build me up, stressing my experience, my love of Mexico, even my beautiful Mexican girlfriend. Too late, though; they already had seen the magazine story about me.

The mammoths began a philosophical discussion about democracy, while Pepe switched from rum and Coke to brandy. Mexican officials loved to speak about "guided" democracy or "controlled" democracy. My favorite protest sign called for a "democracy without adjectives." The mammoths thought I was naïve to believe the United States was a true democracy while Mexico was not. Each country had a native form of government and citizen participation that suited its historical reality, they argued. One system was not better or worse than the other.

They smirked at the idea that the United States even was a democracy at all; they considered it a plutocracy ruled by an elite divided into two parties. The wealthy prospered no matter which party was in power. Their views weren't all that different from my own views in college, but now I heard myself defending the United States like a love-it-or-leave-it patriot.

The lunch was civil, though; the Mexicans had exquisite manners. I was a guest in their country, even if I wasn't as appreciative as I could be. I didn't convince the mammoths of anything, but they showed me the courtesy of opening up and speaking honestly about their country. Instead of ignoring me, or telling me to go to hell, they engaged me. That's all I ever wanted as a reporter.

I walked home with my thoughts racing because they had given me a peek inside the system, and it was different from how I had imagined. I believed Mexico was more ready for democracy than they did, but they were not evil dictators. They gave me a more nuanced view of Mexico's political future than I had considered. Seeing something in a new way, for the first time, was exhilarating.

Not everyone was so generous. The *Proceso* story kept causing me problems. Most people hadn't seen the documentary itself, which was tough but fair; they only had seen the story about me in the magazine, which was tough and unfair. I needed to correct the record, but it made me uncomfortable, and I wasn't sure how to fight back, or even whether I should.

It was a good lesson to be written about because it made me more sensitive to the value (and difficulty) of responsible journalism. After being burned in print, I would be more careful about how I portrayed people. Another reason for my reluctance to speak up was the unwritten rule against publicly criticizing another reporter's work. I didn't feel comfortable taking on a colleague, but this story had the feel of something contrived to damage me and to discredit the documentary. This was fake news with an agenda. And it hurt my feelings.

Reluctantly, I asked for an appointment with the magazine's founder and editor, Julio Scherer, a pioneering and respected journalist. He was my father's age, calm and soft-spoken. I brought him a transcript of what I had said in the film and compared it to the magazine's version, which was entirely invented. He apologized, genuinely. He probably was surprised and disappointed about the erroneous story in his own magazine, but he did not share his feelings with me. I was too nervous, and it felt like it was none of my business, to ask what he would say to the reporter. He did not offer to correct the story, but he asked me to write a formal letter explaining what had happened, which he published verbatim in the next issue.

I went back and forth about whether I enjoyed the attention from the documentary and the public exposure. I got a thrill from every byline of my own, but I did not enjoy being the target of someone else's story. The difference was feeling the power of writing a story versus the powerlessness of being in one. At a gut level, it was the difference between chasing someone and being chased. Also, while being on TV was a rush, I hadn't fully appreciated the freedom of anonymity, until I lost it.

My new celebrity status came up awkwardly during a routine news conference. Mexican and foreign reporters were summoned to be briefed about the Mexican government's response to a series of violent street protests. A senior official played video of people throwing rocks and bottles at the riot police. The police showed remarkable restraint, at least in the video chosen by the government.

Then the briefer pointed to the group of masked people holding rocks and sticks and said, "These guys here? These are friends of Peter Copeland." Everyone laughed. I felt a hot flush climb up my neck.

I wasn't going to pull back. That same week I was thrown out of the US embassy because of a story the American ambassador didn't like. The desk in Washington said if I had upset the Mexicans and the Americans, I was doing a good job. Nobody considered that maybe I was doing a *bad* job and was unfair to both sides. I didn't think so. I just wanted to show people back home what Mexico was really like, the beautiful and the ugly.

I loved Mexico, although the poverty and injustice could not be ignored, and daily life for everyone was frustrating because of bureaucratic inefficiency and the arbitrariness of power. I definitely was a harsh judge of Mexico's government, but after the violence and criminality I had seen in Central America, Mexico felt like Switzerland. Still, corruption and malfeasance were overwhelming and stifling forces in Mexican life, and therefore inevitable topics for my stories.

One kind of corruption Mexicans experienced every day was from the police, so that was an obvious story. After City News, I considered myself an expert on covering cops, but to write about the Mexican police, I needed a way in or a hook. Riding along in a patrol car was a routine reporting technique at home, but when I suggested it to a Mexican official, he was flummoxed. Ride in a patrol car? Didn't I want to interview the chief of police?

Surprisingly, I got the ride-along with Mexico City's finest. They assigned me to a shift that lasted all night, which was perfect. I was introduced to the two officers who were my hosts, and they led me to a squad car. I got in the back, and they sat in front.

"Where would you like to go?" asked the officer at the wheel, looking at me in the rear-view mirror through a protective screen across the top of the back seat.

"It doesn't really matter," I said. "I just wanted to see things from the police point of view. I've been in Mexico for awhile, and I know the police have a public relations problem. There are always two sides to a story, though, and

I figured I should see what it's like. I suspect the relationship between the police and the public is more complicated than people think."

The driver looked back at me again. "That's right," he said.

"I don't know how you guys do it," I said. "You risk your lives every day and what do you get? Low pay and no respect."

"That's right," the driver said.

There were long silences as we cruised around the city. I watched as drivers noticed the police car and then averted their eyes. You could practically hear them praying, Please don't pull me over.

"How long have you guys been on the force?" I asked, trying to keep the conversation going.

"Twenty-seven years," the driver replied. He nodded to his partner. "The lieutenant here has been a policeman for twenty-three years."

"Do you have a regular beat?"

They both laughed. "I haven't had a beat in ten years," the driver said. "I'm the captain in charge of all the squad cars in this area. It's an administrative position."

Despite my request for a typical patrol car, the brass had given me two veterans with supervisory jobs. I was a little disappointed because they were less likely to be candid. The good thing was they could speak about the bigger issues from more than their own personal experience.

The captain pulled over to the curb, where a young female officer was talking and laughing with a young man on the sidewalk. The officer waved at the patrol car, did a double take when she saw who was driving, and saluted.

"Come here, darlin,'" the captain said, leaning out the window and patting the side of the patrol car like it was his horse. She walked over, her eyes on the ground. The older man asked her, "Are you writing parking tickets or flirting?"

"Writing tickets, captain."

"That's my girl. Sharp eye, darlin.' Sharp eye."

After two hours of the officers responding only "that's right" to my questions, we stopped to stretch our legs. I bought soft drinks, and we stood near the patrol car watching the traffic. I was afraid the ride was going to end without anything for my story, so I changed tactics. My Spanish was good now, but I dropped the exaggerated formality and went for American directness. I loved the Mexican expression for speaking frankly: *sin pelos en la lengua,* literally "without hair on the tongue."

"You know," I said, deploying my favorite expression about being blunt, "I have a problem with the police. They try to get too much money from me because they think I'm a rich gringo."

The captain and the lieutenant were leaning up against the patrol car, sipping their sodas. This could go either way: They could feel insulted and not talk to me, or they could open up. The two officers looked at each other and the lieutenant asked, "So what happens?"

"Usually I've done something wrong, I admit it. Maybe an illegal turn or running a stop sign, double-parking. The officer says it is a serious infraction. I say surely we can arrange something. He says how much. I say five dollars, and he wants ten."

"The first thing is, never tell them a price," the lieutenant said. "They're trying to figure out your bottom limit, and they will always ask for more. And don't offer them money. Just pull out a few pesos, take their hand and say, 'Here's a little something to buy flowers for your wife,' or, 'I'd like to treat you to a nice necktie.' Don't argue about prices; just give it to them."

The captain joined in now, warming to the topic. "People say it's a payoff or corruption. Look. Say a guy goes through a red light. If I give him a ticket, we both are going to lose a lot of time at the station. If I just give him a warning, then the next time something happens, he's going to remember the police. Say there's a robbery and this guy sees it happen. We've got a witness. He's going to cooperate with the police because we've cooperated with him.

"If he offers me a little something," the captain said, "That's not corruption. That's good public relations."

The sun was coming up by the time they dropped me back at the station. I had learned a lot, and we had a few laughs. I was looking forward to writing my story. I already had decided not to use their names. No one had told me not to identify them, but I didn't want to hurt their careers, even if my story would not appear in Mexico. They had been honest with me, so I wanted to protect them. The story was much bigger than those two officers, anyway, and I already had interviewed legal experts and victims of police corruption.

A few days later I stopped short when I saw the headline on the front page of Mexico's English-language paper, *The News*. There was my police story with my byline and a photo. I had wrongly assumed no one in Mexico would ever see my story. Once in awhile, the Mexican press printed a critical story from the US media. That way they could publish something negative about Mexico and blame the foreigners. No one in Mexico would have been shocked by my "revelations" about police corruption, but it didn't look good on the front page of the local paper. I was sure the police would be mad. Just to be safe, I left my car in the garage for a few days and used taxis.

This was one of the times I benefited from being in Mexico but not of Mexico. A Mexican reporter had to be careful writing about the police or government corruption. There could be serious repercussions for his or her career and personal safety. I felt safe. If I wrote tough stories, I was rewarded by my employer, and I did not fear reprisals. It was only later, after I upset the wrong people, that my life would be threatened.

The most dangerous stories I covered were not about government corruption in Mexico or wars in Central America, but international drug trafficking. Covering an armed conflict, I always felt some protection being a journalist and an American. The lines were blurrier when covering the "drug war." Which side were we Americans on, anyway? The United States led the global fight against drug trafficking, but we also led in drug consumption. And since the traffickers got their way using bribery and terror ("silver or lead," in Spanish), it was dangerous to trust anyone.

The danger I faced, though, was nothing compared to what Mexican reporters risked. If their editors allowed them to write about drug trafficking, which was rare, few reporters took the chance because of the peril to their families and themselves. This wasn't a question of personal courage; they had no protection at all. Mexican reporters were knowledgeable about trafficking, however, and they wanted the information to be published. That's where I was valuable to them.

I made friends with journalists around the country. One of them, whom I will call Victor to protect him, was totally wired into the drug trade in his home state of Sinaloa, the crime capital of Mexico. I met him through Maru, and therefore he trusted me completely, meaning with his life.

We usually talked in his pickup truck, which was the safest location for him. He drove me around on a trafficking tour: there's the house of a narco, there's his disco and restaurant. That warehouse was used for storage of guns, drugs, and money. This is the home of a politician who takes money to look the other way.

I asked if Victor had written any of this. "Are you nuts?" he said, laughing and swerving around corners so hard that I slid across the seat.

He introduced me to four friends, who worked for the state and local government, and we sat on folding chairs formed into a circle in a big, abandoned industrial building. It was hot, and there was beer. Someone lit up a joint of the local cash crop, and then another and another. The conversation—as it always did when an American journalist was present—turned to politics.

The guys who worked for the government were supporters of the ruling party, both for ideological reasons and patronage. I told them I understood a one-party system because I had covered Chicago, which got a laugh. "If it weren't for the ruling party, the gringos would have taken over Mexico by now," said one of the men, adding to me: "No offense intended, but all the gringos have ever done is fuck us over." Another said, "We'd be better off with the Russians as bosses."

When we started talking about journalism, Victor asked me, "Do you ever take money from your beat here?"

All eyes turned to me. I laughed. In Mexico, there was a whole vocabulary around paying off reporters, including the Spanish word *sobre* or "envelope," which came stuffed with money. "They know better than to offer us envelopes," I said, "because we'd write about it and cause a scandal." I'm not sure they believed me. I didn't ask the same question of Victor because I didn't want to know the answer.

A baby owl appeared out of nowhere and walked into the circle. The guys applauded and greeted the owl with friendly clucking noises. The chubby bird walked clumsily as a toddler, turning its head this way and that. Since I was the guest of honor, someone picked up the owlet and set it on my lap. I tried to pet it, but it bit my finger. Then it turned its head almost completely around and peed on me. The smoke was thick and skunky, and my hosts were getting more upset about Yanqui imperialism, present company excluded. The owl dug its talons into my thighs, popping the fabric on my pants.

This was one of many times when I experienced "magical realism" not as fiction or art, but as just another day at the office.

"Sorry about that," Victor said later, back behind the wheel. "They got a little carried away."

"No," I told him. "I appreciate their honesty. Americans want everyone to like us. We want to think we only do good in the world, and we forget that not everyone sees us that way."

Victor stopped for a six-pack of beer. The day was still hot. We drove around the edge of town watching the sky turn red and orange as the sun went down. "*Salud,*" I toasted him with a beer. "Driving around like this is what we call a champagne flight."

"I love it," he said, laughing and popping open a beer can between his legs. "A champagne flight!"

When I returned a few years later, Victor had taken a government job as a press spokesman. "On the other side of the envelope," he said with a little laugh that did not hide his disgust. He told me a reporter friend had just published a series of stories on drug trafficking. Shortly after, two men walked into the reporter's living room and shot him dead in front of his wife and children.

The threat level to all of us increased when traffickers kidnapped, tortured, and murdered a DEA agent in 1985. If they would kill a US federal agent, an American reporter no longer was safe. The following year, my paper in El Paso got pulled into the violence while preparing a story about a trafficker named Gilberto Ontiveros, known as the "The Mophead."

The Mophead was building a luxury hotel in Juárez. When our photographer arrived to take pictures of the building for a story, he was jumped, beaten, and tied to a chair. The Mophead's men put a pillowcase over his head, screamed at him for being a DEA agent, and beat him bloody. They boiled a pot of water and threatened to burn off his face. They made him lower his pants and said they would rape him. One man pointed a pistol at his head and pulled the trigger. Click. After hours of abuse, they loaded him into the back of a car and drove out to the desert, where the photographer was sure he would be killed. Instead, they released him, battered and frightened, but strong enough to walk back into town.

My newspaper in El Paso went on a rampage against the Mophead. The Juárez papers—which knew the traffickers but rarely wrote about them—republished our stories in Spanish. The federal government in Mexico City was embarrassed enough to send a team of agents who arrested the Mophead. I was called back from Honduras, where I was covering the civil war in neighboring Nicaragua, and told to make arrangements to interview the Mophead in jail.

Jail was too strong a word. More of a modest hotel where the Mophead was earning honored guest points. The Mophead wasn't living in luxury, but he was not without power behind bars. I didn't feel safe meeting him in prison. I could imagine an accident or a fight, then a riot, and there would be no witnesses.

I drove out to the prison with Stephen Baker, a Spanish-speaking reporter from the paper. I was glad to have an ally for courage and a witness in case things went badly. Even if we survived the interview, it didn't mean we were safe from the Mophead's reach. Living in Mexico City, I was more vulnerable than when I had lived across the border in El Paso. This interview didn't feel like just another story for the paper. One of our people had been attacked, and it could happen again. I felt no hatred for the Mophead, just wariness and fear.

Steve and I were led through heavy gates and holding rooms. It was unusual to be allowed into the prison, but the government wanted everyone to know the Mophead really was behind bars. We were put into a small room and told to sit at a table to wait. After a bit I heard distant doors clanging. Then the door to our room opened, and there was no mistaking the Mophead. He was big, thickset, wearing tight black jeans and a bright yellow sport shirt, and he came toward us like a powerful dog straining on a leash. He really did have a mop of curly dark hair, which poked out from under a black cap emblazoned with a skull and crossbones.

Most people are a little nervous before an interview with reporters. This guy did not look nervous. He looked confident, and angry. "What's your name?" he snapped at me.

I mumbled something.

"What? Do you have a card?"

"Gosh, you know, I just ran out." I patted my pockets.

The Mophead wasn't interested in pleasantries. He started talking fast and picked up speed. He spat out the words in machine-gun bursts, punctuating every sentence with creative obscenities. He was used to owning the room and everyone's attention. He told us his life story, cracked jokes, and bragged that he soon would be out of jail. He tilted back in his plastic chair, happy to have an audience writing down his every word.

I found myself laughing with him, trying to remember he was not a normal person.

"I'm not a saint," he said, "but I'm not like they say, either." He called himself a retired drug dealer and a victim of international politics.

"They busted me because the government wants to look good with the gringos." That business with the photographer, he said, was just a misunderstanding. Yes, his men had worked him over, but they let him go once they realized he wasn't a DEA agent.

Then he got serious, big arms on the table, and stared at me. "You know what really pisses me off about you and your fucking newspaper?"

Oh God. Here it comes. I'm dead.

"That fucking picture of me you keep running on the front page. It makes me look like shit."

We promised to get a more flattering photograph, and left the prison as quickly as we could. I didn't hear from the Mophead again until after he had talked his way out of jail. Soon his business was bigger than ever. The DEA and FBI were searching for him, but he had gone underground. And just as I had feared, he was gunning for me.

Back at home in Mexico City, I noticed strange clicking sounds on my telephone. All the reporters assumed our phones were tapped by the Mexican government, but now it felt more ominous. I also worried about Maru. Someone could get to me by hurting her, and she had none of the protections of being an American or a journalist. Had I put her in danger by loving her? Would I have to be more cautious in my reporting to protect us both?

One night my phone rang and Maru answered. An angry man, obviously calling for me, spat in English: "You're dead. You're really dead." He hung up. I hugged Maru, but we both were trembling. What were we going to do, call the Mexican police? I did report the call to the US embassy, but they could not protect us. We had to look out for ourselves.

I begged Maru to be more alert on the street. I was nervous when she came home late after dance performances. I didn't want to scare her, but acknowledging the risk of my position as a reporter could help protect her. She wasn't at all surprised I had been threatened, maybe just that it had taken so long.

"Don't you dare stop doing your job," she told me, ending the discussion about whether I should ease up on drug stories.

Shortly after, on a quiet Sunday morning, I got another unexpected call, this one from the Mophead's American girlfriend, whom I had gotten to know. We chatted a bit and I asked, not really wanting to know the answer, "Where is he these days? He's on everybody's most-wanted list."

"You mean Gilbert?" she asked innocently. She always called him Gilbert instead of Gilberto. "He's right here sleeping. Do you want me to wake him up?"

"No! No!" I whispered. "Let him sleep, please."

"You know he's mad at you," she said. "You keep writing about him."

"I have to keep writing about him," I said. "He bought his way out of jail, and now they want to lock him up again. He's selling drugs like nothing happened. And he beat up our photographer."

"Well, he's still mad at you," she said.

We talked for a while, and she caught me up on the latest narco-gossip. I wanted to end the call quickly for fear of waking up the Mophead. I really didn't want a cranky trafficker on my case.

Finally she said good-bye. "Keep in touch," I said, silently hoping I never would hear from them again.

# 6

# SHAKEN

—— ON WHEN THE STORY GETS PERSONAL ——

Most of the time on assignment I did not worry about getting hurt. When I was scared, I often learned later that I had been afraid of the wrong thing.

I was in El Salvador with Alejandro, my regular driver, cruising along a quiet stretch of country road just after sunrise. The date was September 19, 1985, my 28th birthday, and I treated myself to a day outside the city. Visiting rural areas, I was on guard for ambushes, crossfire, and landmines, but out here on the open road, I allowed myself to relax. I was pleasantly dozing in the sunny passenger seat, listening to music on the radio, when the announcer burst in with a bulletin: earthquake in Mexico City! Hundreds dead, buildings collapsed, bridges toppled, and roads cut in half.

Maru.

"We've got to get back to the hotel," I told Alejandro. "I need to make a call."

When we pulled in front of the Hotel Camino Real, television crews were throwing equipment into vans. Running past them into the lobby, I picked up enough conversation to understand they were flying to Mexico to cover the earthquake.

I ran up to my room and told the operator to put through a call. I gave her Maru's number. I turned on the television to see the news and paced the floor. The operator rang and said the circuits to Mexico were busy. I should try later. I called the office in Washington, and the desk told me to stay in El Salvador. The daughter of the Salvadoran president had been kidnapped, and it was a big story in the US papers. It was too early, the editor said, to know what was happening with the earthquake.

I didn't argue. I just packed my stuff and checked out of the hotel. I didn't care about the story, either the one in El Salvador or the one developing in Mexico. I needed to see Maru. Commercial flights were canceled, but one of the networks had found an old charter plane with a pilot willing to fly to Mexico. I put a few hundred dollars into the pot and got one of the seats. The aged prop plane was banged up on the outside, and inside the cabin was as cold as if the windows were open.

It was dark by the time we approached the airport, and I could see the golden lights of Mexico City spilled onto the black earth beneath us, just as always. I hadn't expected to see any lights, and certainly not all those cars on the road. I had imagined a city squashed by Godzilla, but things looked normal. I had a shortwave radio pressed to one ear, and I shouted the news bulletins to my colleagues above the noise of the engines.

For many of us covering the region, Mexico City was not just a story, it was home. The newspeople on the plane had spouses and children living there. We willingly shared adventure and risk on the road, but now the danger had surprised us at home. I was glad we were together on the plane. I was part of the group now. People used the term *pack journalism* as though it were a bad thing, but a pack was comforting when we feared for the people we loved.

I shouted the names of neighborhoods where the destruction was greatest and translated the frantic news reports into English. The street where I lived, Versalles, was mentioned again and again.

Maru would have been asleep that morning when the quake hit, wearing her blue pajamas and tucked under a half dozen blankets in her dark, musty apartment. She lived in a stubby, four-story building made of thick stone. I imagined getting there and finding it in a heap. I would scratch and dig with my hands, desperate, but there was so much rubble. In my mind I saw her brothers and sisters discussing how to dress Maru's body for burial. I shook my head and tried to concentrate on the radio news. My imagination was flying faster than the airplane.

When we landed, we were told to wait for Mexican customs, but I slipped through a side door, walked into the first empty office, and dialed a phone on the desk. Maru answered—*"¡Diga!"*—and I felt the tension lift. Some part of me had known she was safe, but I had braced for the voice of her roommate saying Maru was dead. Instead, Maru answered with her usual crisp, *"Diga."* It always sounded like she was telling a dog to "speak," and my American friends jokingly had adopted her brusque manner of answering the phone.

"I'm fine, Pito."

She always called me Pito, which sounded like PEE-toh, and was her Spanglish version of my name. Only later, when she yelled for me across a busy flea market and everyone laughed, did she mention that *pito* also was slang for penis.

"Don't worry about me," Maru said. "I was knocked out of bed, but nothing happened." She had been in touch with her family, and everyone was safe.

When I tried to tell her how worried I had been, she told me to stop being silly.

My shoulders relaxed. I took a breath. It was time to go to work.

I arrived at her apartment by taxi, and Maru embraced me at the door. I looked her up and down and hugged her again. She playfully pushed me away, and we jumped into her car. We got within six blocks of my apartment before soldiers stopped us at a roadblock. I showed them my Mexican press identification, and we started walking, slipping under a rope stretched across the road. The streets were dark because the electricity was out, and the air was pungent with the rotten smell of natural gas from burst tanks and broken pipelines.

Behind a line of soldiers, I could see the remains of the Hotel Versalles, which had left its foundation and slid into the street. Five stories had crashed into a heap of concrete and steel about thirty feet high, spitting out beds, tables, chairs, sheets and towels, pots and pans, and magazines. There was no space between the floors—the piles had been squished into a thick cement sandwich.

I always got my hair cut by a woman named Clementina who worked in the barbershop across the street. From the barber's chair I watched tour buses delivering camera-toting tourists to the hotel. I wondered how many guests had been buried under the rubble.

People were camped in front of their buildings, afraid to go back inside. Before the earthquake, kids played soccer on this street using piles of stones to mark the goals. To drive by, cars had to wait for a break in the action, and the players would reluctantly make room. There were no kids playing soccer now. Parents held their children close.

We found a dozen of my neighbors, some of them wrapped in blankets against the chill night air, sitting on the steps of our darkened apartment complex. The building had been evacuated, they said, and they were guarding against looters. "Thank God you weren't here when it happened," said the older woman who lived below me.

Behind her, the underground garage was filled to the top with dirt and bricks, and the only car visible, a white Ford, was flattened. I couldn't see my car at all. At first I thought our building had fallen straight down, but it was the building next door that had dissolved into brick and dirt and poured into our garage like lava. I was grateful for the solid construction of our building.

"Is everyone all right?" I asked Modesto, the porter.

He shook his head. "They say fourteen people next door were killed."

One of my neighbors cautioned, "Don't light a match or a candle. There's too much gas. Don't even switch on a light. The light won't work, but it might make a spark."

Modesto led the way with a flashlight up the yellow concrete steps. When Maru and I got to the door of my apartment, I paused, half expecting someone or something to be waiting inside. I turned the key and pushed open the door. It looked as if the place had been ransacked. The television had tottered off the table onto the floor. Plants had tipped, spilling dirt across the carpet. Pictures had shaken off their hooks and crashed, spewing broken glass. The building had shaken and swayed so much the bedroom doors had slammed shut.

Modesto said there didn't appear to be any structural damage, but we had to stay out for a few days until engineers could check the foundation. He said my car was not even scratched, but it was blocked in by a pile of rubble. He promised to dig it out soon. I grabbed clothes, a handful of fresh notebooks, and my printer, and we left.

I interviewed a few more people, trying to understand how it felt when the earth moved, before we returned to Maru's apartment so I could write. I had been up since dawn, nearly twenty-four hours before, but I was wired awake. I had to slow down and put the story into perspective. I still didn't know the scale of what had happened in the enormous city, just what I had seen with my own eyes. I was frustrated, feeling that I was looking at the world through a straw.

Much of the city seemed undamaged, but certain areas, including my neighborhood, had been shaken to the ground. How was I going to make it seem real to people in the United States? How was I going to capture so much in five hundred words? I decided to write the story like a letter home, describing what I had seen on my block rather than follow the stiff formality of a straight news story.

A more immediate problem was how to get my copy to the United States. The local phone lines worked fine (like normal anyway), but the international lines were down. I finished two stories before the sun came up, made copies on the printer, and took a taxi to the airport. I checked out the passengers waiting for a flight to Ciudad Juárez and found a young American couple. For thirty dollars they agreed to deliver the story to our paper in El Paso, just across the Rio Grande from Juárez. To be safe, I went to the counter for a Miami flight, and a man in line volunteered to phone in the story to Washington when he landed. Both couriers completed their missions.

Since I didn't have anywhere to stay, I took a room at the Maria Isabel Sheraton, a modern high-rise hotel on Reforma in front of the Angel of Independence monument, not far from where Maru and I had met. The monument had been damaged in the 1957 earthquake. I thought it strange that the last bad earthquake had happened the year I was born, and this one was on my birthday, but not once did I worry there might be another earthquake. I figured the earth moved, and then it had settled. So I was not at all concerned when the bellman showed me to my room way up on the top floor of the Sheraton.

On September 20, the afternoon after the earthquake, I left Maru reading in my room at the Sheraton while I walked over to the Hotel Century in the Zona Rosa. I had to plan our earthquake coverage with other journalists sent by Scripps Howard, including my old friend from El Paso, photographer John Hopper. I took the elevator to the fourth floor, and I found them in their room, which featured a round bed that made the place look like a love nest. We joked around, glad to see each other. The intensity of the earthquake story made us giddy; it was a news buzz.

Sitting on the bed, I picked up the phone to call Maru at the Sheraton to tell her I would be late for dinner. While I was dialing, with my back to the room, the bed started to rock. I laughed, thinking John was "playing earthquake" and shaking the bed, but when I turned around, he was running out the door with his camera bag. A woman in the hall yelled, "¡Está temblando! ¡Dios mío, está temblando!" Oh my God, it's shaking!

The room rumbled and dipped as deeply as a ship at sea. The overhead lamp clanged like a bell. I felt a rush of adrenaline, and at first it was surreal and exciting. I was fairly calm collecting my things, but the shouts from the hallway grew louder and more panicked. The reaction of the people was more frightening than the movement of the building. My colleagues already had run down the hall headed for the stairs.

When I got there the narrow stairwell was packed with guests and hotel employees pouring down at full speed. They were screaming and crying, and someone was yelling, "Don't run! Don't run!" But you had to run or you would be trampled. I took the stairs three at a time, seeing cracks opening and closing in the walls of the stairwell. Chunks of cement and plaster rained on our heads. Around and around, down the stairwell, four flights to the street.

Outside there was a terrible noise of buildings clapping together and rubbing their concrete shoulders, shattering glass, and crashes of concrete falling to the street. Standing on the sidewalk I had to crouch and bend my knees as if I were surfing on the shifting pavement to keep from falling. There was no way to run; even trying to walk was like wearing magnetic shoes on a metal plate. You could feel the pull of gravity. I sensed for the first time the movement of the Earth and the precariousness of my position upon it. People had their arms around thick palm trees. A man was on his knees holding a crucifix to the sky.

I looked at my watch. I would need the exact time for the story. The worst shaking stopped within ninety seconds. Half-dressed guests, some wearing only towels, staggered back inside the hotel and yelled for their bills. People were packing suitcases in the lobby and in the street.

Maru.

I had left her a few blocks away in the Sheraton. I ran so hard my chest ached. I pushed through crowds of people who had emptied out of offices and apartments and filled the sidewalks. They were crying and embracing, looking up at the buildings. Cars, doors left open, were abandoned in traffic. Why had I let them give me a room on the top floor? What if the whole thing had collapsed? Why had I left Maru there?

I ran around the corner and saw the Sheraton still standing. I relaxed a little, but I was afraid to use the elevator, so I raced up 18 flights of stairs. I ran down the hall to my room, and since I hadn't stopped for a key, I knocked hard. No answer. The hall was deserted, quiet. I ran back down the stairs and outside to where people were staring up at the hotel, wondering what was going to happen next. I pushed and shoved my way through them, frantically scanning their faces. Sitting on the curb, crying with her head on her knees, was Maru.

"Where were you?" she wailed, mad and relieved, hugging me hard and kissing my face.

"Oh, baby, I'm sorry," I told her, holding her tightly and kissing the streaks of tears from her cheeks. "How was it? I bet this sucker really moved."

"Don't joke, Pito," she said, punching me in the arm. "It was terrible. It started to shake, and I didn't know what to do. There was an American man in the hall who tried to talk to me in English. I think he was telling me not to be scared, but he was more afraid than I was. Why did you leave me here?"

"Come with me, hurry," I said, taking her hand and running. "We've got to get back to the other hotel."

People were walking around in a daze. I stopped to interview one man, careful to get his name, age, and occupation. We ran into the lobby of the Hotel Century and past all the guests trying to check out. I had to file. I had to get the news to Washington. The receptionist told me the phones were not working, and I knew that with everyone calling at once, the international circuits would be jammed. I had to beat them somehow.

I searched the hallways until I found an unmarked door behind the front desk; it had to be the phone room. I opened the door and looked inside. The room was empty, the switchboard unstaffed. The operators were still on the street, afraid to return to the weakened building. But I smiled when I saw something familiar from when I worked at City News: a Teletype machine.

I grabbed Maru, closed the door behind us and sat at the Teletype. I needed a minute to remember, but then I punched out the code for Scripps Howard in Washington. The keyboard made a clunking sound, and I was on line. I wasn't sure the signal was getting out of Mexico, but I had to try. Normally I would have cut a tape and fed that into the machine, but I was afraid of losing the connection or getting kicked off by the operator, so I went live, making it up as

I typed. I clicked the keys as fast as I could: "A second earthquake hit Mexico City Friday night . . ."

I wrote about three hundred words and stopped, not sure if the story was being transmitted. I sat there for a second, and the keys started to move by themselves: "Great story. Send more."

I did send more, lots more during the next few weeks. I knew this was page one all over the world, and I didn't want to slow down. I tried to convince Maru to come with me when I worked, thinking she could help do interviews and monitor the radio. "Come on," I told her. "Keep me company. It'll be fun."

To me it was a story, something I was expected to cover and wanted to cover. During my career so far, I had written about murders, car wrecks, fires, coups, and wars, and interviewed plenty of grieving relatives. I saw events as "news," not my life, and people as sources; it was a psychological survival mechanism. And this wasn't even my town, not really. I had lived in Mexico City for nearly two years, and I called it home, but I still was an outsider, a visitor. If things got too scary, I always could go back to the United States.

Maru refused to go reporting with me, and, although I had hoped she would, she never asked to read my stories. We didn't talk about it, but she was living something I was only covering. In the weeks after the earthquake, I did not sleep enough because I had so much work. I worried about being able to find a good story every day and file on time. I worried because the *New York Times* had five people there, and I didn't want to get beat on my story. Maru did not sleep because she was afraid to close her eyes: her nightmares were vivid and terrifying. In one dream she saw her entire family standing in the stairwell of a crumbling building. I used her dream in a story I wrote about the psychological scars left by the earthquake.

I was still trying to get a handle on the damage. If people in charge had a true estimate of the casualties, they weren't saying. The government seemed embarrassed by the destruction, knowing it would make them look bad, and the "official" death toll was kept low. Government leaders understood no one believed anything they said, so if they released a low casualty number, people automatically would calculate a higher and more accurate number.

There was no way to survey all the ruined buildings, but I could get an idea of the number of dead. People would be missed, and relatives would demand answers. In search of numbers, I planned to visit the makeshift morgues set up around the city. There were so many bodies, there was nowhere to put them, and many large buildings were used for storage. Modesto had freed my car from the garage, so I went for a drive.

At the first morgue, people were standing outside or sitting on the grass, some of them volunteer rescue workers, others looking for lost relatives. I walked inside to find someone who could tell me how many bodies they had. I was hoping to get a list. I didn't even need the names. If I could just get the number of bodies, I would seek out the biggest morgues until I had a rough count of the dead. The number was in the thousands.

"I'm a reporter from the United States," I explained to a young woman wearing a white smock and a surgical mask. "I would like to speak to the person in charge."

"Upstairs," she said.

There was a crush of people walking up the stairs. I climbed along with the crowd, not sure where I was going, looking for someone carrying a clipboard or sign of authority. At the top of the stairs, at the entrance to a room the size of a basketball court, I found myself being pushed onto a trail of wooden pallets spread on top of the floor. I was already in the doorway and could not go back because of the people shoving me forward. The smell was of an old dusty hospital ward: thickly medicinal but not crisp and clean. The air was dank and heavy, cooler than outside.

The room had no furniture, only the wooden pallets on the floor. The pallets snaked through shallow puddles of bloody water mixed with formaldehyde. I took a few steps into the room on the wobbly pallets before I realized what had caused the floor to be so wet.

The path wound among hundreds of bodies packed side by side, their middles covered with plastic garbage bags full of melting ice. Only their heads and feet were showing. There was a little girl in a flannel nightgown. There was an old man, his head turned to one side and split like a dropped watermelon. Their faces were blue, sort of a frosted blue because of a coating of dust.

The earthquake had struck at 7:18 a.m., so many of these people had been asleep. Some had been crushed by the rubble, others had suffocated under its weight.

I felt guilty, like a vulture, but I was strangely fascinated and wanted to look. I told myself it was my job. I thought of all the gore I had seen in horror movies; this was no worse. Had I become so desensitized after being a reporter for five-and-one-half years? The other people on the wooden trail were looking for parents, children, friends, and lovers. I was looking for a body count, color, a detail, a good quote for my story. I walked faster but the pallets were narrow and unsteady, and groups of people, even young children, had stopped to speak in whispers, holding their noses and pointing down at the bodies. I hurried for the exit.

Outside, finally outside, the sun was shining. Volunteers distributed balls of cotton soaked in alcohol to hold under our noses. It would cut the smell, they said. My shoes were wet with bloody water, and my clothes felt clammy against my skin, as though I had climbed out of a damp grave. I wanted to shower and change. People were throwing up on the grass. Someone was selling tacos. I left in a daze and never did find out how many bodies were on the floor. I gave up on my plan to count the dead.

It was too early to write my daily story, so I got into the car, which was comfortingly warm from being parked in the sun, and drove a few blocks to a medical center that had collapsed. I interviewed some volunteers clearing the rubble, and then I crossed the street to what was known as the French Cemetery. There was a long row of flower vendors outside the walls of the cemetery, and business was brisk. I bought an enormous bunch of yellow and white marigolds, dripping wet and wrapped in newspaper, for one dollar. I drove over to Maru's apartment and knocked on the door, the flowers hidden behind my back.

"What have you got?" she asked with a grin and a giggle.

"Flowers," I said, smiling and handing her the bunch of marigolds.

Her smile vanished. Her eyes narrowed, looking at my face for a clue.

"Oh," she said cautiously. "They're pretty."

"What's the matter?"

"Nothing," she said, reluctantly taking the flowers. "I'm just surprised. We'll put them in water."

Surprised? I may not have been the most attentive boyfriend, but flowers should not have been such a surprise. She looked as though she had seen a ghost.

Later I told a Mexican friend what had happened. He laughed and gently called me an idiot. "You should know by now that *cempasúchil,* what you call marigold, is the Aztec flower of the dead. We use them on graves."

There were more than one hundred aftershocks in the weeks following the two big earthquakes. I suddenly would feel dizzy and wonder if it was the earth moving or me. I watched the overhead lamp in my dining room to see if it was swaying, and then debated whether to run outside or brace myself under a doorframe. By the time I decided, the shaking had stopped. We all were so sensitized that I even began to feel when a heavy truck rolled by, setting the building asway ever so slightly.

I knew if another big one hit, I would be as exposed as anyone else living here: my blue American passport and reporter's notebook wouldn't protect me. Then I began to have nightmares, cold-sweat dreams of being trapped in rubble, suffocating, inhaling dust and choking, clawing at the dirt and stone until my fingers bled. When I closed my eyes, I saw the frosted blue faces from the morgue, especially the toothy frozen smile of the man with his head cracked open.

I had to keep working, moving fast and straight ahead. John Hopper and I drove to a hospital to see a baby who had been born three hours before the earthquake. When the maternity ward collapsed, doctors, nurses, and patients, including the baby's mother, were crushed. Days later, rescue workers found the baby kicking and screaming and strapped into a tiny metal bassinet, which, like a wire birdcage, had sheltered the newborn until rescuers dug her out of the rubble. It was a miracle, and I was desperate to write something positive and upbeat.

We walked up to pediatrics, where nurses and hospital workers were gathered to see the baby, thin but healthy, under a plastic oxygen tent. The doctors speculated that her metabolism had slowed while trapped in a dark, quiet corner of the rubble, sort of a concrete womb. Physically she was fine, but no one knew the psychological effects of losing her mother and being trapped in the rubble. "The experience was recorded in her mind," a doctor told me. "What we don't know is how it will be played back when she is older."

The baby's father, Ursino Valencia, was sitting in a waiting room. He was about my age, slim, dark-skinned, and dressed in blue polyester slacks shiny with wear.

"I'm sorry about your wife," I said, looking up from my notebook. "But you must be happy to have the baby. It's a miracle, don't you think?"

"I would rather have my wife," he said. His eyes filled with tears. John stood behind me taking pictures. "What am I going to do with a baby? My mother says she will take care of it for me. We gave it the name Sara. That's my wife's name."

I had expected him to be happy about the baby. I already had imagined the quote I was going to use: "It was a miracle: God took my wife but gave me a child." He never said it, though. Far from it. He was depressed and despondent, lost and unsure what to do. I looked at him but could not think of anything to say. Finally, I said the baby must be strong to have survived.

"Yes," he agreed.

"You must be proud of her."

"Yes," he said.

"People are coming from all over to see her," I said.

He nodded.

"How did you meet your wife?"

"I was working."

"Where?"

"Selling stuff in front of the subway."

"Was it love at first sight?"

"No, it took awhile."

"Was she pretty?" I didn't know whether to use the present or past tense. It seemed so final.

"To me she was very beautiful."

"Do you have any other children?"

"A boy, Edgar."

"If you don't mind me asking," I said, "how much money do you make?"

"About four dollars a day."

"Did you eat meat at home often, or a lot of beans?"

"Beans, mostly."

"Was your wife a good cook?"

"Yes."

I stood up, folding my notebook and putting my pen in my shirt pocket. Not much of an interview, but I had enough for a story. I shook his hand. "Well, thank you, Mr. Valencia. With your permission, we will be going now." He thanked us and kept staring at the floor.

John and I stepped into an elevator full of nurses and visitors. "Did you get any snaps?" I asked John. I always said "snaps" to tease him.

"Yeah," he said. "A few. Good stuff of the baby."

The elevator door closed. I started thinking about Valencia, no longer just as a character in my story but as a man. As someone like me. He was right about the baby. What would I do with a baby? What was he going to do with her? They did not even have enough to eat. I couldn't bear to be unable to feed my children. I imagined losing Maru and being left with our baby. She would have Maru's big eyes, the left one a little more almond-shaped than the right. A faint mole on her lower lip. And when the baby started learning to speak, and would say things the way her mother did, I would hear Maru's voice and remember . . .

I felt my throat tighten and my eyes fill with tears. Damn, I don't want to cry. But my defenses were worn too thin to protect me. Big heaving waves of pain and sadness rose up my back and shook my shoulders. Tears ran down my cheeks, and I looked down to hide my face. "Sorry, Hopp," I said, sobbing. He put his hand on my shoulder.

We got outside, but I couldn't stop crying. Days of tension and fear were draining out with the tears. I had not let myself really feel anything, keeping my distance, treating it as a story, but like baby Sara, everything had been recorded in my mind. These weren't my people, but Maru was, and I loved her more than anything. Mexico wasn't just a place I lived anymore; it wasn't just a story.

Worrying about Maru and seeing her suffer exposed the feelings I had hidden behind journalism. Now when I thought about Mexico, I thought first of her. I could not just pack and leave, because it would mean leaving Maru; but if I lost her, I could not bear to stay. It took the earthquake to shake my consciousness. It made me realize that Maru had taken me into herself and into this place, deeply and forever.

John patted me on the back, and I managed to chuckle through the tears, "Those people in the elevator must have thought I lost my whole family or something."

The office wondered why I hadn't written about Monchito. He was a little boy still trapped in the rubble. I had seen the story in the Mexican media, but I didn't pay much attention. There were people in the rubble, but I didn't think many of them were still alive. I had just sent the desk a great story about a baby found alive. I didn't want to go chase some story that everyone else was covering. Wrong answer.

Monchito was a big story in the United States, and my editors were watching it all day on television. This was a relatively new problem for foreign correspondents: editing by CNN. Editors back home watched the five-year-old news network and therefore assumed they knew what was happening around the world. To the editors, there was no story bigger than this little buried boy. Monchito met the narrative needs of television and must be covered.

I dragged myself over to where they were searching the rubble for Monchito. I pushed through the crowd to get close. Diggers—dubbed "moles"—gently pulled aside bricks and concrete, and then used a hammer or wrench to tap on a buried pipe or piece of metal. They waited for a tap in response and then dug toward the sound. They were tunneling toward a boy who had been buried since the first big quake. Someone said his nickname was Monchito. There was a vigil with candles, but the most illumination came from the television lights. TV crews from around the world camped out to be ready for the moment when little Monchito, dirty and tired but alive and grateful, would be lifted from the rubble by a weary but heroic rescuer.

Against my better judgment, I filed a story. I tried to capture the drama of the scene. It was exciting, and unlike most of the stories I had done, it was about hope and life and the future, not about loss and death and destruction. The tapping was growing stronger, or maybe it was fainter. I was told that some rescuers had heard the little boy's small cries for help, but I never met anyone with first-hand confirmation that he was alive. We had to get to him quickly or he would die, they said. People prayed.

A few more days passed with no sign of Monchito. The media coverage dwindled and then moved on to other stories. When the rubble eventually was cleared, there were no bodies, no little boys. I'm not convinced there ever was a Monchito, and there were various theories about what really happened. The story felt like a collective fiction, a kind of benevolent fake news, greedily exploited and shared to make us all feel better. It worked for a day or two.

Weeks after the earthquake, my neighborhood was not the same. All day and night, heavy trucks rumbled along, hauling rubble. A block away, workers were tearing down a damaged seven-story building that looked like something gnawed by giant wolves. Since there were plenty of laborers but only one jackhammer, they kept it pounding around the clock.

Even before the earthquake, I was attuned to the city sounds, especially the banging, shouting, and whistling from the body shop below my window—laid over the growl of buses, honking horns, and a traffic cop's whistle—but the jackhammer was too much. Unable to sleep, even with a pillow over my head, I imagined tiny men standing on my teeth, drilling into them with jackhammers. I got up in a fury, pulled the mattress off the spare bed, pushed it up against the window and tied it there with rope to muffle the sound. But then there was no light in my bedroom, and I still heard the thumping jackhammer.

Maru and I fled the city for a vacation in her home state of Oaxaca. We stayed at the beach, and I was comforted by the solid feeling of walking in the sand at sea level. You don't appreciate the stability of the planet until you've felt it move. There were no tall buildings, no traffic jams and no noise above the sound of the waves. We finally relaxed, chasing crabs on the beach and floating in the pool.

I wanted to be with Maru forever, and after months of saying no, she agreed to marry me. A year later, my mom, my stepfather, my four brothers, and thirty members of my family traveled to Mexico City for the wedding. Maru's mother had died before the ceremony, but not before giving us her blessing. Maru's father was there along with her big family and our good friends, an amusingly oil-and-vinegar mix of reporters and dancers. The church service was performed in English and Spanish by my El Paso reporting mentor (and Catholic deacon), Ken Flynn.

Maru and I moved into a beautiful little house, suddenly made affordable when real estate prices collapsed after the earthquake.

# 7

# THE CAPITAL OF THE FREE WORLD

—— ON WHY YOU CAN'T DO IT ALONE ——

I soon was offered an opportunity that was hard to pass up but would strain our young marriage.

I was covering the 1988 vote in Chile about whether Gen. Augusto Pinochet should step down, fifteen years after he had taken power in a bloody coup. Some people doubted Pinochet would leave the presidency even if he lost the vote. There were protests and threats of violence, and I spent the days interviewing political leaders trying to figure out what would happen during the vote, and after.

My El Paso buddy John Hopper was there shooting an anti-Pinochet demonstration for the Associated Press when he was knocked down and then kicked in the head by a police officer. Other photographers gathered around to protect him. Being photographers, they also took pictures of John on the ground, blood smearing his face. They wanted to take him to the hospital, but John started yelling, "Wait, wait!"

He handed his camera to another photographer. "Take my picture!" he demanded. The photographer took a picture of John and returned the camera. John removed the film and made sure it was processed for the AP wire. That way John would not get scooped when the competing photographers transmitted photos of his bloody face. Only then did he agree to medical attention.

When Pinochet lost the vote and announced he would allow civilian rule again, the streets filled with people cheering, crying, and hugging. I felt shivers of pleasure for them, not necessarily for the outcome of the vote—I tried not to take sides—but because their will was being respected without violence or repression. It was one of the few joyous political stories I covered during my years in Latin America.

While I was working in my hotel room in Santiago, the phone rang. "Peter, this is Dale."

I worried I had done something wrong. The desk almost never called me, and most of the time they weren't even sure where I was. Now the boss of all the editors in the Washington bureau, the managing editor Dale McFeatters, was on the line.

"Hey, Dale," I ventured. "What's up?"

"How would you like to cover the Pentagon?"

Silence. "Uh, what do you mean?"

"We need a Pentagon reporter."

"Don't we have one?" I asked, stalling for time. I was flattered to be asked, but unsure. I knew I couldn't cover the Pentagon from Mexico, but did that mean I would live in Washington? Was I ready to go there? What about Maru? Would I get a raise?

"We don't have one anymore," he said. "Do you want to think about it?"

"Yes," I said. "I need to talk to my wife." But after five years in Mexico, I knew I was going to Washington, and I was pretty sure I could convince Maru.

"¿Estás loco?" she shouted. Are you crazy? "What am I going to do there? You haven't even taught me English!"

"It will just be for two years," I said. "If we don't like it, we can come back to Mexico."

We talked for a couple of days and decided to give it a try.

On a scouting trip to Washington, I had a drink with George de Lama and other members of the *Chicago Tribune* Washington bureau. I knew some of them and recognized their bylines from growing up in Chicago. I had looked up to George when we both were reporters in the city. It was his story that had upset Mayor Byrne enough to kick the *Tribune* out of City Hall.

When George was sent to cover Central America, I admired how he carried himself with a bighearted swagger. One particular weekend stuck in my memory. We were catching the sun around the pool of a hotel in Honduras. All of the sudden George went into work mode, and he whispered to ask if I knew about the plot to overthrow the government. What plot? I barely knew the name of the president, let alone the people conspiring against him. The plot failed, and thanks to George, I wasn't scooped on something right under my nose.

Now I was full of questions about living in Washington, covering the Pentagon, and working in the Scripps Washington bureau. George was someone I listened to.

"Fifty," George said. "You've got to make $50,000 to live here."

Fifty grand? I was making about $37,000, and that was double what I made in El Paso and just about double again what I had made in Chicago. There was no way they would give me that big a bump. Still, the cost of living was high in Washington, and I didn't want to take a big hit on how we lived, especially if I was going to convince Maru to stay with me. I knew we weren't likely to have the same standard of living we had in Mexico (where I earned dollars and spent pesos), but I wanted things to be nice for Maru.

When the real estate agent learned my salary, she told me to jump into the car. We drove for about forty-five minutes. This is Rockville, Maryland, she explained, as I frowned at grim strip malls and empty fields. She showed me a couple of townhouses, not even single-family homes, and a few condos.

This was not what I had imagined. On an earlier trip, the managing editor, Dale, and his wife, Ann, the White House reporter in the bureau, had invited me to dinner at their huge, old wooden house painted bright yellow and bordered by a comfy porch. There were tall leafy trees on the quiet street, and it was not far from the office. That was the kind of place I wanted, but apparently it was way out of our price range.

I went to see Dan, the bureau chief. I told him other reporters in town said I couldn't get by on less than $50,000.

Dan laughed and said, "Welcome to the real world, kid." Conversation finished.

Maru and I stayed in a downtown Washington hotel during early January of 1989, while we looked for a house. I had to start work right away, which was consuming for me and frightening for Maru.

In Mexico, I had worked from home, and we often had lunch together or interrupted the workday with a *"beso* break" (*beso* meaning kiss). After Maru left the dance company, she was modeling and dancing every night on a popular TV show. Still, we managed to make time for each other. Now she was going to be alone in a strange city while I went to an office, sometimes from early morning until after dark. She didn't have a job in Washington, or even a plan. She didn't have a high school degree or speak the language. Then it snowed.

Maru had not seen much snow before, so I thought it would be fun for her, despite the cold. The city, however, was not prepared, and the streets were blocked with drifts and stuck cars. I worried about getting to the office on time for my first day, what to wear, where I was going to sit, whether I would like my new colleagues.

Maru was still under the covers. I put on my winter coat and sat on the bed next to her. She was tan and gorgeous against the white sheets, her hair black and shiny, her eyes dark, dark, and moist with tears. She reached up and grabbed me. "Don't go, Pito! Don't leave me!"

"I've got to go to work," I said. "I'll be back tonight."

"What am I going to do? Don't leave me!"

I hugged her, buttoned my coat, took the elevator down, and walked out into the snowy cold.

That night after work I walked back in darkness through the snow to the hotel, worried she was still in bed, depressed and angry with me. Or what if she had just packed up and returned to Mexico? What if this didn't work? What if she couldn't adjust? She wasn't at all prepared, and I had not helped her. Had I just made a terrible mistake? She was more important than any job, but I had been distracted by my ambition. I rode up the elevator trying not to panic.

I opened the door to our room and found her bursting with energy, cheeks red and windblown. "I had a fabulous day!" she said, restlessly pacing the carpet. She moved like a panther and appeared larger than her actual size. "I met the most wonderful cab driver. He's from Ethiopia. He is this giant, huge, guy. I mean huge! We spent the day together, and he took me to lunch at this restaurant, the 'Sun' something, and he knew everybody and he introduced me to all of his friends. We are going out tomorrow, too. He showed me the sights and I got to know the city. It's really quite beautiful, you know . . ."

I think my face registered both shock and fascination, barely hidden by the mask of a smile I strained to hold. "Interesting," I managed to say. "Wow."

She also surprised me on our first day of house hunting, but only because I was dense. That morning we jumped into my trusty Datsun, which had carried me from Chicago to El Paso, and then to Mexico City and now to Washington. I cheerfully drove Maru out to suburban Rockville, enthusing about the extensive shopping and easy access to the train.

I lost her when we crossed the Beltway ringing Washington. She looked horrified at the suburban sprawl and declared, "I'm a *flor de asfalto,*" an asphalt flower. "I'm not living in the sticks."

Maru fell in love with Dupont Circle, a city neighborhood with good restaurants, stately row houses, trendy shops, and bookstores. We bought a small condo we could not afford. There were big trees on the street, but it was urban enough that—as Maru required—it was "walk to sushi."

I decided to cover my new Pentagon beat the way I would a strange country with its own language, beliefs, and local costumes. I had not thought much about the Pentagon before being assigned to cover it. I was too young for Vietnam, and few of my friends chose a career in uniform. I never was opposed to the military, even in college when I protested US foreign interventions, but mostly I was ignorant of what they did. Similar to when I first was assigned to cover transportation in Chicago, I had to become an expert in an arcane field (now tanks and warships instead of buses and trains), and it was a similar challenge.

Part of the reason the Pentagon reminded me of a big transportation bureaucracy was that the country was at peace. The Cold War was winding down, so the military leadership's biggest concern was protecting the Pentagon budget from members of Congress hoping to use the "peace dividend" for social programs. This was to be the era of "small wars" and low-intensity conflicts, the experts said. People ridiculed the brass for trying to maintain the capability to fight massive wars using aircraft carriers, jets, and tanks.

I knew nothing about the policy debates or global threats (outside of Latin America). I didn't know how the secretary of defense worked with the president, the armed forces, or the Congress. I wasn't positive about the difference between the Marines and the army.

This was normal for a beat reporter. Ideally, you covered a topic until you mastered it, and then moved on to another beat before you became too bored. In a way, each story was like that, too. For every story, I had to find sources and write what I learned. Then I moved on to the next shiny thing, often forgetting completely about what I had written just days before. My plan for the new military beat was to read a couple of books, talk to some experts, and give myself a graduate course in military affairs before I even visited the Pentagon.

During my first week in the Washington office, I walked over to Dale's desk to check in. "You're in luck," he said. "You've got a war on your hands. Get over to the Pentagon, now."

I wasn't sure how to get to the Pentagon by myself. And then what? I knew from my reading that the building had seventeen miles of corridors, and I had no idea where I was supposed to go. I just nodded to Dale and grabbed my coat. I studied the Metro map and noticed a "Pentagon" stop, so that looked promising.

Just by luck, I boarded the train with a camera crew, and I guessed they were covering the same story. When we arrived at the Pentagon station, they walked off ahead of me and seemed to know what they were doing. I was too shy to say anything, but I followed, close enough to watch them but not so close as to be stalking.

We rode up a long escalator into a windowless mall where military personnel were shopping in the pharmacy, the bookstore, getting something to eat, just like normal people. I followed the camera crew—a big guy with a bulky camera, a sound guy, a well-dressed guy who must have been the reporter, and a woman carrying more gear. They were slow and obvious, and easy to follow. A young man in uniform greeted them and pointed them down a hallway. I jumped in, said I was from Scripps Howard, and tagged along. So far so good.

I should have left a trail of crumbs, because after the first couple of turns I had no idea where we were. The hallways looked the same, and I was a little disappointed. I had expected something flashier, maybe more martial; this looked like a large hospital or an aging elementary school. There were subtle grooves worn in the stone steps where rivers of people in shiny black shoes had coursed through the halls. The occupants were mostly men, and they looked clean in their pressed uniforms, but preoccupied and harried, carrying file folders and coffee cups, briskly marching into windowless offices.

Then I saw it: a sign above a hallway read "Correspondents Corridor." This was where the pressroom was located, and on the wall was a gallery of headshots of the beat reporters who covered the Pentagon. There was a small room called the Ernie Pyle Alcove. I recognized the name Ernie Pyle because he was a Scripps Howard reporter killed during World War II. I didn't know much about him, but I felt a twinge of pride because we worked for the same outfit. There was a portrait of Pyle, in uniform and with a manual typewriter, but the style of painting was from olden times and not relevant to a modern reporter like me. I followed the camera crew into a briefing room with a lectern adorned with the seal of the Department of Defense.

I took a seat in the back, and almost immediately a flourish of uniforms with shining medals charged into the room and deployed around the lectern. This was a big story, so the briefer was Secretary of Defense Frank Carlucci. He launched into a detailed recounting of how on January 4, 1989, two US jets had fired on two Libyan jets over the Mediterranean Sea.

I took furious notes, afraid to look up and miss something. "Jinked the bogeys." Or was it "bogies?" Fox One. Then, "the sparrows left the rails." Some other military-sounding stuff. Engagement. RIO (which seemed to be an acronym). F-14s. Floggers. Kennedy battle group. CAP?

Then Carlucci asked for questions. I kept taking notes. The secretary thanked us and left. I looked at my notebook. I had a lot of notes. I had no clue what had happened over Libya, or wherever it was.

The wire reporters raced out to file stories. A few reporters who were not on deadline lingered to talk. I moseyed along behind them into the pressroom. This was a new pack of reporters, and I was an outsider. I stood back a little and watched from a respectful distance. Just as at City News, and then El Paso, and then Mexico City and Central America, I was the new guy and knew my place. There was one man, maybe twice my age, who seemed to be the big dog. I noticed how the other reporters gathered around him to listen. I waited until he was alone.

"Excuse me," I said, offering my hand. "I'm Peter Copeland. I'm the new Pentagon guy for Scripps Howard. I don't understand a thing of what just happened."

"I'm George Wilson," he said, shaking my hand. "Sit down."

George Wilson, I found out later, was a *Washington Post* reporter and dean of the Pentagon press corps. He flipped his notebook to a clean sheet and drew little airplanes facing each other. These are the "bogeys," he said, pointing to the Libyan planes. The "Sparrows" are the missiles. "Jink" is a move a pilot makes in a dogfight.

A light went on in my head: dogfight. I didn't remember that phrase from the briefing, but that was something that sped up my heart. A dogfight was dramatic, dangerous, a story with winners and losers. I could write about that.

Once I had the big picture, Wilson walked me through the details, even marking his diagram with the times (by the second) when everything had happened. The way he told the story, I could imagine his little drawings as real jets in the air, jerking back and forth, the US pilots trying to decide whether to shoot or evade. Were they going to be shot down first? Were the Libyans playing or was this for real? Why were they doing this?

"You got it?" Wilson asked.

"Yes, sir," I said. "Thank you."

I followed some reporters back to the Metro station and took the train to the office. I typed up the story on the central computer system we shared and saved it in a folder used by editors on the desk. Then I walked over and told Dale the story was ready for a first read. After Dale edited and christened it with a headline, the story would get a second read by a copy editor, checking the details such as spelling and grammar, before being sent on the wire. I was told to stick around in case they had questions. I stood over Dale's shoulder, watched him edit, and nervously awaited his verdict.

I appreciated a good edit. A good editor kept you from making mistakes and helped put your narrow focus into a bigger context. The good ones knew their history and could see ahead, even around corners. You could edit yourself, but it was like giving yourself a massage: it was not very effective or satisfying. I did prefer certain editors, the ones with a lighter touch, and sometimes waited to file a story until the clumsier editors had gone to lunch.

Dale, one of the good editors, read through my Libya story (courtesy of George Wilson, but I did not mention that), made a few changes, and looked up at me. "Pretty good story," he said. Then he asked the question I heard every day of my career: "What have you got for tomorrow?"

The next day I found a military history book in the bureau library and photocopied a chart of the ranks and insignia. I cut the chart small enough for the inside pocket of my suit jacket. Then when a person in an army uniform would speak to me, I would look at the shoulder—silver bird—and then glance at my cheat sheet. "Hello, colonel."

I realized they took their appearance—a uniform appearance—seriously. I visited the Pentagon barbershop for a haircut (they pretty much had just one style), and more importantly, I had my shoes buffed to a deep black. This was just like in Mexico City where I had stopped wearing shorts (no grown Mexican man wore shorts in the city) and polished my shoes. Better to fit in than stand out.

I read all I could on aerial combat, thoroughly preparing to cover the last battle. If they got into another dogfight, I would be ready. I also started to understand how the military was organized, what they worried about and how they trained to fight. I learned about the rivalries between the army and the Marines, how they both thought the air force had it easy, and how sailors referred to ground troops as knuckle draggers or human sandbags. Special operations guys were elite warriors or dangerous hot dogs, depending on who was describing them. My first sources were people from one service grousing about a rival service.

When the next big story broke, I was caught off guard. The battleground wasn't the skies over Libya, but the halls of Congress. This time the weapons weren't jets and missiles, but leaks and rumors. The combatants weren't even in uniform—they were civilians from the White House and Congress—and I had no idea how to cover them.

The story began when President George H. W. Bush nominated John Tower to be secretary of defense. A former senator from Texas, Tower was a proud and determined man who was small in stature, the way Napoleon was small. One of the rules he lived by was that the US Senate was an exclusive club, and he was a lifetime member. Tower had to be confirmed by his fellow senators, but he considered that a formality.

I was the only person more oblivious than Tower about what was going to happen. I knew where the Capitol was; you couldn't miss the dome on the skyline. I knew vaguely that it was split into a House and a Senate and divided among Democrats and Republicans. I had a degree in political science, but through no fault of my professors, I knew more about nineteenth-century political theory than about how Washington actually worked. I was not at all prepared for what was about to unfold right in front of me.

I looked for a seat in the ornate Senate room on the first day of confirmation hearings. The reporters who covered Congress knew where to sit, and most of the Pentagon reporters also covered military issues on the Hill, so they knew their places, too. Photographers clattered up to the front and sat on the floor to be closer to the action. The senators themselves stood behind their seats, touching each other lightly on the lapels or the arm, trying to appear earnest while the cameras whirred and clicked.

Once again, I found myself walking onto the set of a play I hadn't even read. I didn't know the other actors or the plot, and I definitely did not know the ending. I was going to have to pay attention and improvise my part. I took an empty chair at the end of a table, half expecting to be told to move, but the hearing was called to order and the room went quiet.

I listened to his former colleagues praise Tower's many contributions to the Senate and the nation, his familiarity with the military, and his leadership skills. They pontificated about the heroic armed forces in this historic period, peace through strength, and the global dominance of the greatest military ever fielded in the history of mankind. They really talked like that. I wrote it all down, and mentally composed the first paragraphs of what I would write. After the hearing, I went back to the office and filed my story, which went on the wire for hundreds of papers that would appear the next morning from Florida to California and around the world.

My mornings began when, right out of bed, I went down to the lobby of our condo for my copy of the *Washington Post*. Neighbors subscribed to the *New York Times*, the *Washington Times*, and the *Wall Street Journal*, so I also glanced at those front pages. One morning during the Tower hearings, I looked at the newspapers in the lobby and felt sick. My stomach dropped, and a prickly tingle of shame spread across my skin. John Tower dominated page one of every paper, but it wasn't the story I had written from the hearings. These stories had nothing to do with the hearings. They were way better stories. And for Tower, way worse.

There were reports of Tower grabbing military women on the flight line, getting drunk on official trips, and generally being an obnoxious, pompous jerk. Somebody was out to get Tower, and they were leaking insider details from across his long career. Many of his offenses had been documented on paper at the time, but had been buried by the bureaucracy until now. A routine hearing that began with everyone playing by the rules had turned into a feeding frenzy, and Tower was the main course. This was good news for the reporters covering the story, except for me, because I had no idea how to find the juicy bits.

I went to the office with my tail between my legs. Even as a child, I did not need to be told when I had screwed up, but one of my editors did me the favor anyway. Everybody else on the desk told me what they thought with the looks on their faces. The silence from the reporters was worse. I should have asked my colleagues for help covering Tower, but it had not occurred to me that I needed help. Many reporters and editors in the office had deep sources on the Hill, but nobody had offered to share or even gave me a heads-up. This was a time when I could have used some adult supervision. I felt humiliated, powerless, lost, and alone.

That night I stayed at work until 9 o'clock, making calls to find something new on the story. Then I walked to The Jefferson hotel, not far from the White House. I was not a bold reporter, or even that self-confident, but I did not like to fail. I hesitated walking into the quietly elegant lobby, but I pushed myself into the barroom. Tower was sitting on a stool with another person, their backs to me. He was short and round perched on the high stool, his hair slicked back, and still dressed in a dark suit from the hearing. Otherwise the bar was empty.

"Senator," I said.

He turned to look at me.

I introduced myself, my voice cracking with nerves. "I just think that it's not fair," I stammered, "that all this stuff is coming out and you are not getting to tell your side."

"Thank you," he said in a slow Texas drawl, "but I'm not going to say anything to the press right now." He turned back to his drink.

I didn't get a story, but I felt better. I walked out feeling self-assured, that I could do this. What if he had talked to me? That would have been a giant scoop. I felt we had a connection now, that he knew me as an honest broker who would tell both sides. It really wasn't fair that anonymous sources were leaking defamatory stories without verifying them. In one day, he had gone from being—at least in the media—a respected former senator to a lecherous drunk. You could say anything about Tower and not get called on it. I was willing to tell his side, and maybe he would confide in me. In the meantime, if I could have gotten my hands on some of the bad stuff, I would have poked him with it until he burst.

In the end, the Senate rejected Tower, for the first time in history denying a new president a cabinet nominee. The job of secretary of defense then went to a politically safe choice, a little-known congressman from Wyoming named Dick Cheney.

I didn't do well on the Tower story, but I learned how to get better. One of the good things about covering Washington was the amount of paper produced by the federal bureaucracy, a bountiful garden of reports, studies, analyses, and internal memos. Human sources were important, but a paper trail could be verified. Some reporters insisted on two sources for a story, but two people still could be wrong or deny it later. That's what the mayor of Chicago and her husband did to me after they cut off the *Tribune*'s access to City Hall and then lied about it. Something on paper was irrefutable evidence.

Also, I was appalled by the Washington media's facile reliance on hiding sources with anonymity. Admittedly, getting scooped with unnamed sources was particularly galling because I didn't have any anonymous sources of my own. Now I saw that evidence on paper was indisputable, the source was there for everyone to judge, and no one could deny it later.

I needed better human sources, too, even just to win access to the documents. The armed services, for their own reasons, were happy to help. I didn't work for the *New York Times* or the *Washington Post,* but I did write for hundreds of papers that served most congressional districts and military installations around the country. The leadership of the army, especially, made a point of cultivating me, or as they put it, getting me "greened up."

Army leaders urged me to get out of the Pentagon and into the field, which was excellent advice. I genuinely liked many of the officers I dealt with in Washington, but it wasn't until I got outside the Beltway that I understood how the real army worked. I traveled to posts across the country and went on a patrol between East Germany and West Germany. I spoke about military-media relations at the Army War College and the Naval Academy and visited with soldiers and noncommissioned officers wherever I could.

At an Arkansas training center for guerilla war, I spent the night running around the brush with the "opfor." My guys were supposed to be irregular soldiers—the opposing force—against bigger units that parachuted in to fight the "rebels." Everyone in the exercise, me included, wore special vests that lighted up when hit by lasers mounted on the weapons. We hid among the trees, popped up to shoot, and ran from the enemy.

The invaders were no match for my guys, who knew the terrain and how to fight. None of us got shot, but plenty of enemy soldiers were left "dead" on the battlefield. The young soldiers were in much better shape than I was, and I was exhausted after slogging through the thick woods until the sun came up. My back hurt, and blisters popped out on my toes. By morning I was so tired that my vision was blurry, and I gobbled candy bars and choked down a packet of dry instant coffee to stay awake.

The enemy that night was the 101st Airborne Division, known as the Screaming Eagles. My guys called them the "Screaming Chickens," which everyone thought was hilarious. A long night in the Arkansas woods gave me a taste of what it would be like to cover US troops in combat, and the little feature story I wrote about my adventure would come back to help me in a funny way.

# 8

# INVASION OF PANAMA

—— ON FAIRNESS ——

My experience with troops in the field paid off just before Christmas of 1989. Maru and I were with my family in Chicago for the holidays when the phone rang. My mom answered, and I saw her frown. She handed me the phone, disappointment on her face, saying it was Dale from the office. She knew the office wasn't calling to wish us a Merry Christmas. Dale got right to the point: "Your current beat invaded your previous beat. You better get moving."

Dale explained that my current beat, the US military, had just attacked Panama, a country on my previous beat in Latin America. The military mission was to overthrow dictator Manuel Noriega. The desk reasoned there was nobody better than I to cover the story.

From my mom's house, I called sources at the Pentagon to ask how quickly I could get into Panama. They told me the country would be locked down for a week or so until US forces were firmly in control. The story could be over by then.

What about chartering a plane out of Costa Rica? I asked.

"They will shoot it down," I was told.

The commanding general was Maxwell Thurman. He wasn't called Mad Max for nothing.

Once an American ally, General Noriega had fallen out of favor with US officials and many people in his own country. In person, Noriega was surprisingly shy and insecure for someone who controlled everything in Panama and had manipulated the US government for years. The first time I met him, he was more nervous than I was. He did not seem to be a threat to world peace, but he was dangerous to Panamanians who opposed him.

I had witnessed just how dangerous when, almost two years before the invasion, government thugs armed with clubs and thick rubber hoses had stormed the hotel where I was staying in Panama, hunting down opponents of Noriega. I was working in my room a few floors above ground when I heard crashing glass and angry yelling from outside. I looked down from my window and saw men charging toward the hotel entrance. Hiding behind the curtain and not quite believing what I was seeing, I picked up the phone to call the front desk.

"Don't come down! Stay in your room," the clerk shouted in English. "They are taking periodists," meaning *periodistas,* or reporters.

There were banging thumps in the hallway, shouts of anger, and screams of terror. I opened the door a crack and saw bulky guys in civilian clothes pounding on the doors and dragging people into the hall. I quietly closed my door and made a plan. I didn't want any of my Panamanian sources to get hurt, so I tore up the business cards I had collected, and ripped out pages from my notebook that might identify people. I flushed the bits of paper down the toilet. I typed up a few paragraphs of what I had seen, connected my computer to the phone in my room, and transmitted a brief story.

The editors in Washington fretted about my safety, but I told them just to edit the story and move it. They were sipping coffee and staring at computer screens in a quiet office building in Washington. I was talking in a whisper, while outside my room I could hear glass shattering and people screaming. I peeked through the curtains again and saw the attackers swinging thick sticks like baseball bats and chasing people, including reporters, in circles around the manicured lawn and tropical flowers outside the hotel entrance.

Just as suddenly, the attackers left. I watched them drive away, and then I carefully went down to the front desk. There was glass and blood on the floor. Chairs and tables were tipped over as if a hurricane had blown through the lobby. People were helping the wounded and talking excitedly about what had happened. Eight foreign correspondents and dozens of Panamanians were arrested. Noriega wasn't winning the political argument, so he was going to fight dirty.

I had learned a valuable lesson earlier at an anti-Noriega demonstration: don't get caught between the police and the protest. I was on a narrow street interviewing people who had gathered with banners and signs calling for Noriega to step down and be jailed. They were chanting slogans and shaking fists, but there was no rioting or looting or even pushing or shoving. The atmosphere was almost festive. Until the pro-Noriega forces arrived.

Police and soldiers jumped down from buses and trucks and formed into rows. Armored cars rumbled on the corners. Groups of beefy men in civilian clothes—the same type of guys who had attacked the hotel—milled around the police. Noriega called the men dressed as civilians "Dignity Battalions," but there was nothing dignified about how they behaved. The two sides stared at each other. The standoff ended when someone, somewhere, ordered the police to charge.

The crowd surged back away from the attacking police, and I was caught in the riptide. There was no way to move forward or to the side; I had to run with the crowd and away from the police or be trampled. There were women and children, old people. Some of them were just watching the demonstration, not really taking part. Now we all were part of it, running for our lives as the police and club-wielding thugs bore down on us.

The first hint of tear gas tingled through the air. When the cloud hit my face, it didn't feel like a gas: it felt like battery acid or broken glass. I couldn't breathe and I couldn't see because mucus was pouring from my eyes and nose. Terrified of falling, I grabbed blindly at whoever was near me, hanging onto a shirt or a belt, and kept running like bees were chasing me.

A military truck caught up to us and sprayed water at the crowd. I wasn't too concerned about the water until my skin started to itch and then burn. The water was laced with pepper spray or some irritant that stung like barbed wire.

At last I reached a place where the narrow street widened into a plaza. I slowed to a walk, wiped my watery eyes, and tugged at my wet shirt because it felt like it was on fire. There was screaming in the street behind me, and the roar of police and military vehicles. Ahead of me, it was just an ordinary afternoon. People were shopping, going home from work. Vendors sold ice cream from little carts. I walked until I found a taxi to take me to the hotel.

Even with all the violence, I was surprised President George H. W. Bush had invaded to oust Noriega. It seemed like going after a housefly with a wrecking ball, but I did not share my opinion with anyone at the time. It wasn't my job to write about whether the United States should have invaded. We had other writers and columnists who did that. I never read the editorial opinions written by people back in the office and didn't care about their views. More to the point, I didn't want their views to color my coverage. I read every news story on every topic I could find, but I almost never read opinion pieces in any paper. I felt the same way about advertisements in the newspaper: I knew the ads were necessary, but I skimmed right over without reading them. My job was to show what was happening on the ground, not share what I thought about it.

When the desk sent me to cover the invasion, I knew Noriega wouldn't be much of a military opponent. So if I wanted to cover the fighting, I would have to hurry before it ended. The good news (for me) was that the pool of reporters assigned to cover the invasion had been locked up on a US military base "for their own safety." This rightly infuriated the reporters, and it limited news coverage of the invasion from the ground.

Maru stayed in Chicago to celebrate Christmas with my family and then planned to return to Washington on her own. I expressed the proper amount of remorse to my mom for missing the holiday, but I wanted to go to Panama. I loved being a Washington correspondent, but at thirty-two years old, I was excited to jump on a plane to anywhere, especially into the middle of a big, breaking story.

An older editor once told me that he, too, used to love parachuting into big stories, but "then your legs go." I nodded like I knew what he was talking about, but after being a reporter for ten years, I didn't understand the phrase, and I certainly didn't share the sentiment. When Dale called about Panama, the light turned green, and I raced out the door.

I did worry about leaving Maru alone. At twenty-seven, she was teaching Spanish and working as a waitress in Washington, both new jobs for her after a career dancing. She still did not feel entirely comfortable in the United States, and she missed her home, her friends and family, and Mexican folk dance. Some nights I woke to find her at the dining room table, sad and nostalgic at 2 a.m., with a bottle of tequila and Mexican music playing softly. I begged her to come back to bed, fearful that she was so homesick she would return to Mexico without me. She had moved to Washington for me, but I often left her alone while I chased stories around the world. She was very supportive of me, however, and respected that my work required travel.

"You want to go, Pito," she said. "Go."

I flew to Costa Rica where the Pan-American Highway crossed into Panama. There I found frustrated reporters who were unable to get into the country to cover the fighting. They were standing around a big, busy parking lot debating what to do. Cars, trucks, and buses were backed up, and no one was sure what they might find across the border. The initial invasion had been short and sharp, but were there pockets of resistance? Had the Dignity Battalions gone into the mountains to wage a guerrilla war, as they had threatened? Would they try to stop reporters? What if there was fighting along the road?

A dozen reporters from the United States, Europe, and Latin America found a driver willing to "charter" his bus if we paid cash, a lot of cash, in advance. I didn't want to be on those roads at night, so our goal was to get to Panama City before dark. We loaded up and headed for the capital.

A few miles after the bus crossed the border, we ran into the first checkpoint. We could see military vehicles and US soldiers blocking a high place in the road ahead, their weapons pointed at us. The bus driver stopped and refused to continue. The reporters and photographers argued over what to do. We had come this far; nobody wanted to go back to Costa Rica, and daylight was running short.

Since I was bilingual, speaking both Spanish and US Army lingo, I was elected to negotiate. I told the driver not to move, and I stepped down from the bus onto the road. I hoped the driver wouldn't panic and do something stupid. The US soldiers blocking the road had no idea who we were, or if the bus was a threat. I put my arms out wide and yelled up the hill, "I'm coming up! I'm American! Mom, dad, apple pie."

The soldiers did not laugh or even smile. They were young, even younger than I was, and it probably was their first time in combat. I didn't think they would shoot me on purpose, but a misunderstanding or an accidental discharge could be fatal. The turret gunner in one of the vehicles pointed the weapon at me and cocked it, making an unmistakable metallic sound. With one arm still away from my body to show I was unarmed, I used my other hand to show my Pentagon pass, a pink plastic card with my name and photo.

It was not a press credential, but a building pass used by everybody, military and civilian, cleared for regular access to the Pentagon. It read, "Property of the Department of Defense," and looked very official.

One of the soldiers appeared to be in charge. "Where's your lieutenant?" I asked him.

He looked at me, deciding what to do, and said, "Wait one." He jogged behind the vehicles and returned with a young officer.

I showed the lieutenant my Pentagon pass and said we needed to get to Panama City before dark.

"Sir," he said, "will you be escorting these journalists?"

My mouth moved but I did not speak. I stopped and debated with myself for a quick second. I didn't know who he thought I was, but I did not clarify that I was just a reporter. I had been raised not to lie, and lying by omission was still lying. I also had promised myself, after the baby-selling investigation in El Paso, not to misrepresent myself to get a story, but this seemed like such a harmless exception to my own rule. And I was, technically, going to escort these journalists.

"Yes, lieutenant," I said, "I'll be with them the whole way."

He ordered his men to move their vehicles off the road. "Let the bus through," he said, waving his arm at the driver. I walked down the hill toward the other reporters, trying not to grin too widely.

It was getting dark when we arrived in the capital. I found a hotel, dropped my gear and hired a taxi driver willing to show me around. Most of the city looked fine, untouched. The streets were quiet, and I didn't see any damage, except in the old downtown where a fire had burned the densely populated buildings. Many people had died, the driver said. We drove close to the fire so I could see. I talked to a few people about what they had witnessed and what they thought about the invasion. I got their names, occupations, and ages for my story, and told the driver to hurry back to the hotel.

No matter how good the story in my notebook, it was worthless if I couldn't file. I wasn't sure about the phones and didn't want to take any chances, so I decided to cut short the reporting to get something on the wire. The desk expected me to be in Panama and to file. They didn't worry about how it all came together, just the story. I was surprised when I got through easily to Washington and promised to file shortly. I read through the story on my laptop one more time, making little improvements. On every editing pass, the writing got better, but at some point I had to let it go.

I moved aside the table between the beds, unscrewed the plastic cover from the phone jack, and connected two alligator clips to contacts inside the wall. I plugged the other end of the wire into my computer, clicked on the modem and hit "send." I heard the happy sound of buzzing and whining, always a relief, as the story moved across the phone cables, through the hotel's switchboard and on to Washington. A few minutes later I called to confirm. The desk didn't have any questions, and I promised to file again the next day.

I went down to the pool for a beer. The night was warm and pleasant. A few reporters were sitting around tables under big umbrellas, drinking and smoking. There were no other guests for Christmas in Panama. I ordered a beer, and we compared notes. Everyone had filed already, so we didn't mind sharing.

From what we all had heard, Noriega was on the run. Bizarre stories soon circulated—probably planted by the US government—that he was wearing his special red underwear for luck. Soldiers searched his house and found bags of white powder in a freezer, supposedly proof that he was involved in drug trafficking. Further testing would reveal the powder to be flour, but the demonization of Noriega was unstoppable.

In the daylight, I talked my way into Noriega's abandoned office, which had been torn up in the fighting. He had display cases filled with tiny frogs made from glass, ceramic, and wood. They were cute, even beautiful. Maybe Noriega thought he was a prince who looked like a frog. Or maybe he collected the figurines because the word for toad in Spanish was the same as for snitch, and informers were valuable to Noriega. He used to taunt people by saying, "I've got a file on you."

I stepped over broken furniture and books spilled on the floor. I opened the top drawer of his desk and found small black-and-white photos of young men lying on clinical tables, naked from the waist up, and dead. I drew back from the photos, fearing I had crossed a line and should not touch them. I felt ashamed and uncomfortable seeing them, like violating a taboo. I had no idea who the men were or why the photos were in Noriega's desk, but it seemed like an archive of some kind, an archive of murder. Maybe I should have told someone about the postmortem photos, but I was too inexperienced to know what to do. I closed the drawer and left the photos in the desk.

I took a taxi up to Quarry Heights, the US military headquarters in Panama. At the gate, I was stopped by a tall military police officer who leaned in to ask my business.

I told her I was a reporter and showed my identification. Before she waved me through, I said, "Excuse me, soldier. Did you see any action?" I was just being nice. This was the headquarters, with clipped lawns and long lunches, and I suspected she and her fellow soldiers had spent the invasion standing around waiting for something to happen. Anyway, US law banned women from combat.

She looked down at me in the car, deciding what to reveal, before saying, "a little bit."

"Really?"

I told the driver, "Hold on a second."

I asked the soldier, "What do you mean, 'a little bit'?"

"I can't talk about it."

Now I really was interested. "I'd like to hear about it."

"You'd have to get permission from my commanding officer," the soldier said, pointing to an area above the headquarters. "She's right up the hill."

"Your commanding officer is a woman?" I asked, now bursting to talk to her and her commander.

"Yes, sir. Captain Linda Bray."

"I'll be right back," I told her.

I suspected Captain Bray would require the okay from the army press office before speaking to me, so I found a public affairs officer, introduced myself, and made a little small talk. The army was like a global, small town; we knew people in common and traded gossip.

"So," I ventured, careful not to reveal any details. "There's an MP company commander I want to interview. What do I need to do?"

No problem, the press officer said, and gave me permission for an interview.

I didn't tell any other reporters. I was sure I had a good story, and I wanted it for myself. Women had been integrated slowly into noncombat units, including the military police, but the urban battlefield didn't really have a "front" and a "rear" the way people imagined. Women were legally banned from combat roles, however, and the expectation was that they were safe from danger. If I could find women who had fought during the invasion, it would be a big story.

The military police commander, Capt. Linda Bray, weighed maybe 100 pounds and was tightly controlled in demeanor. She was matter-of-fact in her description of what had happened during the invasion. I tried to get her to relax and be more expansive, but she would not budge. Every strap, every buckle, was in place, and she was not going to loosen them for some reporter, or "media puke," as we sometimes were called.

Talking to her and others in the unit, I slowly got the big picture. On the night of the invasion, Captain Bray's 988th MP Company saw action at three locations, including a Panamanian military barracks with a kennel for police dogs. Bray arrived at the kennel after the shooting started, used her vehicle to break through the gate, and fired her weapon at the Panamanians shooting from the barracks. Some time before dawn, the Panamanian forces slipped out and escaped. Bray and her troops moved in to secure the building, where they found forty abandoned bunks and a large cache of weapons.

"Did any other women see action?" I asked.

"Yes," she said.

I asked for the names, and she gave me a list of twelve female soldiers. I mentioned the soldier I had met at the gate, to include her on the interview list. I didn't want to get her in trouble, but I did want to give her credit for fighting well and honorably.

I spent the rest of the day driving around the city looking for more female combatants. I guessed that Bray and her soldiers were not the only women who had seen action, and I thought it was better to have more examples. Once I knew what to ask, I had no trouble finding female soldiers who had been under fire and shot back. I also learned that another reporter, a freelancer named Wilson Ring, had interviewed Bray, so I had to finish reporting quickly to be first with the story.

When I filed the story on women in combat, the editor on duty in Washington was Bob Jones. Bob always had questions for me, and we worked through the holes in the story. I had answers to his questions; I just hadn't included all the details. Usually, I had too much information for a single newspaper story, and the hard part was deciding what to leave out. Bob was such a diligent editor that he never left his desk when he was alone in the office. He worried that if he went to the bathroom, he might miss a call, so he held it until the end of his shift. Bob was thorough, and while his attention to detail was annoying at times, he never let me make a stupid mistake.

My story about women in combat ran January 2, 1990, across the top of the front page of the *Washington Times,* a smaller but influential paper. In the story, I tried to describe what the soldiers, men and women, told me had happened on the ground during the battle. I had talked to more than two dozen participants, enough to paint a good picture of what the female soldiers had experienced. I didn't get into the Washington policy issues about women being banned from combat and just reported what I was told by people who had fought in Panama.

When I called the Pentagon press office the next day, the army major who picked up the call, a regular source and a friend, said, "You really kicked up a hornet's nest around here." I was surprised, but not unpleased. She was delighted. "Everybody is running around trying to figure out what to say," she told me.

I was feeling good about my story, which now was all over television and the newspapers, and other reporters slapped me on the shoulder and offered congratulations. The account of Capt. Linda Bray attacking the kennel was even mentioned during the White House briefing.

Just then, when I least expected it, I was hit by a burst of friendly fire.

The dilemma for army leaders was that they were proud of the soldiers who fought in Panama, male and female. They did not like to single out individuals for special attention, however. Nor did they want the issue of women in combat to take away from their military victory. In planning the invasion of Panama, the brass did not set out to break any rules by putting women into combat. It just happened. Now Capt. Linda Bray, twenty-nine, was being called the first woman to lead US troops in combat, although I never referred to her that way in my story.

The reaction to the story among soldiers in Panama was, so what? There were soldiers, men and women, who didn't like the females getting special attention, or they considered the coverage typical media hype. No one said the combat didn't happen. The higher up the chain of command, however, the more sensitive they were to public opinion and especially to Congress. People on TV were speaking out for and against women in combat. Female members of Congress called for the law to be changed to recognize the new role of women in the military.

More than anything else, the brass wanted the issue to go away. A few days after my story appeared, a *Los Angeles Times* reporter spoke to an army general at the Pentagon and wrote that the army considered the press accounts of women in combat "grossly exaggerated." The story said the army had determined the heavy gunfire at the kennel lasted only ten minutes, and no enemy dead were confirmed.

I was blindsided by the *L.A. Times* story. I felt betrayed that another reporter would undercut me like that, and I was angry with the army for trying to soften what had happened in Panama. The *L.A. Times* story made the whole incident appear to be something minor and insignificant, certainly not real combat.

Then I started to doubt myself. In my story I had called the confrontation a "fierce firefight." Those were my words, not Capt. Linda Bray's. Did I exaggerate what she said to make a more dramatic story?

I went over my notes again and again. Everybody I interviewed from the kennel talked about exchanging fire, about having to keep their heads down to avoid getting shot. I didn't know how many rounds were fired, but to me any exchange of gunfire was serious. A "fierce firefight" might have been redundant, but it wasn't exaggerated.

Bray and her soldiers had told me about three enemy killed at a checkpoint, and that three other dead were reported found later near the kennel, which is what I wrote, trying to word it cautiously. Now the army was saying the three dead at the kennel were unconfirmed. I wished I had left out the body count, because the discrepancy cast doubt on the whole report.

This wasn't a story I had been leaked by a covert source. There was no secret military communication about women in combat that I had exposed. I found these soldiers on my own and convinced them to talk. They told me something that was common knowledge to them but was unknown to people back home. The story of women in combat really was just a description of something that happened in plain sight that nobody paid much attention to, until everyone did when it hit the front page.

Dale called from Washington to warn me the controversy was growing.

"What are you going to say about the *L.A. Times* story?" I asked.

"We are going to say that we stand by our story," Dale said. Pause. "Don't we?"

"Yes," I said. "We do stand by our story. That was chickenshit of the army to do that, and I'm pissed at the *L.A. Times*."

"Dan is pissed, too," Dale said, referring to our boss, the bureau chief. "He's having it out with the *L.A. Times* bureau chief."

I felt sick to my stomach. Was my story solid? Yes. Were people going to doubt me? Probably. The *L.A. Times* was a big important paper. I worried that no matter what, my reputation would be tarnished. People remembered the controversy, not the facts or who had it right.

Dale told me one of our largest papers had not run my original story but now wanted to use the *L.A. Times* story attacking me. Dale, normally mild-mannered, told them they better-the-hell-not run the *L.A. Times* story because it was bad journalism. Forget loyalty or standing by our man, Dale argued, the *L.A. Times* story misrepresented the very real combat role of women during the invasion.

I sat on the floor of my hotel room, relentlessly chewing over what had happened. I couldn't sleep or even lie down. I rarely felt anger but was quick to feel guilt and anxiety. The more I ruminated, the worse I felt. I held a printout of my story in my hand and went through every line, again and again.

My story was about the many women who participated fully in the fight in Panama, and Linda Bray was just one example. Now all the attention was on my coverage of this one young captain, and what she did or didn't do.

Stewart Powell, a reporter for the Hearst Newspapers, sat with me and listened. He was just enough older and more experienced to calm me down. Stewart had covered big stories and had dealt with public criticism. He knew I was feeling alone. He also didn't think I had done anything wrong.

Maru listened to my worries over the telephone, but she didn't really follow the news and had not heard about the controversy over women in combat. She was fiercely protective of me, however, and didn't need the specifics to know I was upset. I felt stronger hearing her voice.

After all the attention, Capt. Linda Bray was not given a hero's welcome when she returned home. She felt her army colleagues resented her, but she just wanted her career to return to the way it was before all the news coverage. She didn't want to be a celebrity; she simply wanted to do her job. Now her commanding officers were riding her and increasing the pressure. She felt she was being driven out of the army, so she quit.

Months later, I tracked Bray down at home in Georgia for a follow-up story. A civilian now, she was more relaxed than when I had met her in Panama, her hair was longer and frosted, and her once-plain nails were painted a reddish color called Maui Mango. She was trying to decide what to do with her life after her army career was cut short. I knew she had been treated unfairly, but I had been so worried about my own reputation that for a moment I had lost sight of hers. She was kind enough not to blame me for ending the career she loved.

I was reminded, again, of my responsibility to be accurate and fair. There was no wiggle room at this level of journalism. A word written could never be erased. I thought my story was good, but I realized every single phrase and characterization mattered, and what seemed obvious to me might not be obvious to everyone.

My story wasn't wrong, but it could have been better. I should have left out information I had not confirmed, such as the number of dead, and been more careful describing a firefight I did not witness.

Covering breaking news means having limited time to determine the facts, and limited space to tell the story. It often feels like there's neither enough time nor space to do the job. There is not a story written or produced, especially on deadline, that could not be improved. It's healthy to be forthcoming and transparent about our limitations, because acknowledging mistakes is good training for reporters and helps maintain the confidence of our audience.

Even though I was careful reporting in Panama and tried to do everything right, it wasn't enough to keep Linda Bray, a good person trying to do her job and get her soldiers home safely, from being treated unfairly. I tried my best as a reporter—and she should have been in her hour of glory as a warrior—yet she was the first casualty of the crossfire I had started.

Holley Gilbert at the City News Bureau of Chicago in 1980. She was the rewrite on my first story, about a fire at an apartment building. Behind her is Kinsey Wilson, who went on to lead the digital news operations at *USA Today,* NPR, and the *New York Times.* Photo by Michael Haederle.

I had my first computer, and the first desk I didn't share with other reporters, at the *El Paso Herald-Post* in 1982. Working in crowded, open newsrooms taught us to write amid the noise of police radios, ringing phones, and lots of chatter. Photo by John Hopper.

After I interviewed this man about the Mexican economy in Ciudad Juárez, on the border with El Paso, he persuaded me to help push a newly filled gas tank to his home. Photo by John Hopper.

Standing on the Mexican side of the Rio Grande (called the Río Bravo in Mexico), I interviewed this young man, known as a "coyote," who was helping people cross illegally (for a small fee) into the United States. Photo by John Hopper.

*El Paso Herald-Post* photographer Ruben Ramirez (*left*) and reporter Joe Olvera (*right*) were two of my best teachers of journalism on the border. We traveled down Highway 15 into the heart of Mexico's drug country in search of a missing American professor. Photo by Ruben Ramirez.

Newspaper rack cards in El Paso announced the opening of a new bureau in Mexico City. The company took a chance sending a twenty-six-year-old reporter on such a big assignment, even though more experienced journalists hoped for the job. Courtesy of the E. W. Scripps Company.

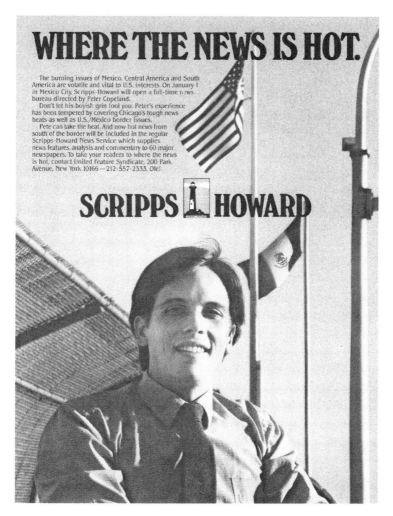

This ad ran on the back cover of *Editor & Publisher* magazine when I was assigned to Mexico City in 1984. My friend John Hopper shot the photo on the bridge between El Paso and Ciudad Juárez, with the US and Mexican flags in the background. Courtesy of the E. W. Scripps Company.

The Mexican Army took foreign reporters on a helicopter tour of a drug-producing region in northern Mexico. Some of the scariest stories I covered were about drug trafficking, including the 1985 torture and murder of an American DEA agent. Photo by John Hopper.

I met Maru Montero in Mexico City during 1984. She had just
left the famed Ballet Folklórico de México after completing
long tours dancing in Europe, the United States, and Asia.
We had little in common, and I was far from home in one of
the world's largest cities, yet somehow we found each other.
Author photo.

My friend from El Paso, photographer John Hopper, covered the 1985 earthquake in Mexico City. We collaborated on many stories across Latin America, looked out for each other in dangerous places, and had some fun. Courtesy of John Hopper.

Journalists from around the world converged on Mexico City after the 1985 earthquake. Reporter Thaddeus Herrick (*center*) came down from our newspaper in El Paso. Photo by John Hopper.

The ghost of Ernie Pyle was with me reporting on wars in Latin America, the Middle East, and Africa. Pyle was a beloved Scripps Howard reporter who covered World War II in conditions far more dangerous than anything I ever witnessed. He was killed in action on April 18, 1945. Photo courtesy the E. W. Scripps Company.

Saudi troops were deployed to the desert in 1990 during the Gulf War against neighboring Iraq. Unfortunately, our military handlers did not allow us to identify the soldiers by name or even our location, except "somewhere in Saudi Arabia." Photo by Frank Aukofer.

NPR's John Ydstie (*front, middle*) indulged my quest to ride a camel during the hot Saudi summer of 1990, just before the Gulf War. He's holding the tape recorder and microphone that got us into trouble in a crowded market. Photo by Frank Aukofer.

My hosts during the ground campaign of the Gulf War were Col. Morris J. Boyd (*center*) and Command Sgt. Maj. John L. Woodley (*right*). They gave me unusual access to the combat operations of the Forty-Second Field Artillery Brigade, including an unexpected drive through a deadly minefield. Photo by David Lawhorn.

# The troops threw them MRE field rations and cigarettes, and one raggedy Iraqi soldier shouted back, "I love you."

One night we watched a line of fleeing Iraqi tanks get chewed up by the Multiple Launch Rocket System, a truck that shoots 12 rockets. Soon the horizon was lined with a string of golden balls that sparkled as the fuel and ammo exploded.

The soldiers watched the battle, eating candy and junk food (known as "pogie bait" and a major Army food group). They cheered the brightest explosions until Sgt. Maj. Woodley reminded them, "Hey, don't forget people are dying out there."

One of the younger officers, staring at the flames through binoculars, replied, "----em." Everyone laughed, but they also understood what was happening. It was hard to get the soldiers to admit the war felt any different than training—that was their emotional protection—but seeing so much destruction was chilling. . . .

. . . The night before the ground war began, I slept in a tent with the brigade doctor, Capt. David Lawhorn, 34, of Chattanooga, Tenn., who told me to start taking little white pills every eight hours for protection against Iraqi nerve agents.

Several soldiers came in that night asking for the pills, even though they were supposed to have them. One mistakenly had swallowed all of his. "Doc" gave me chocolate chip cookies and read his "To Any Service Member" mail, including a poem from a 12-year-old girl named "Rodent" about a man and a woman getting chopped up by knives. . . .

On the first night of the ground war, . . . a junior officer came by and said, "The colonel wants to

Peter Copeland is defense correspondent for Scripps Howard News Service.

know if you want to sit in on the meeting."

I ran to the trailer that served as the brigade TOC, or tactical operations center, and found Col. Morris Boyd reviewing the day's activities with his staff. Behind him was a map with the locations of all the U.S. forces on the move in Iraq.

I had been allowed into the inner sanctum, a place I had only imagined as a reporter. The map alone was rich with highly classified information.

I couldn't write about it, though, because of the military restrictions on the press, but also because I wasn't about to give away our location . . . .

On the down side, seeing the map and being "read in" to the battle plan meant the colonel couldn't let me leave until the war was over. . . .

. . . The last night of the war, the convoy was inching through the Kuwaiti desert in the pitch black.

The tanks kept firing, but by now the Iraqis were fleeing rather than fighting. The troops threw them MRE field rations and cigarettes, and one raggedy Iraqi soldier shouted back, "I love you."

—Excerpts from an account datelined "WITH U.S. FORCES, Iraq" by defense correspondent Peter Copeland.

The story was detailed and memorable because Copeland was right there on the front line. The story was well-edited and ready-to-use because it was from Scripps Howard News Service. Call Irwin Breslauer to subscribe to the most readable wire service available. (212) 580-8559.

SCRIPPS HOWARD
NEWS SERVICE

My company placed this ad on the back cover of *Editor & Publisher* magazine in 1991 to promote our coverage of the Gulf War. After the war, I visited cities where Scripps operated newspapers, and I enjoyed answering questions from readers about what it was "really like" to cover US troops in combat. Readers had seen my newspaper stories but wanted to hear it firsthand. Courtesy of the E. W. Scripps Company.

I rode into Kismayo, Somalia, with these Marines atop a tracked vehicle, swerving and sliding down a sandy road. We had just come ashore during a spectacular amphibious landing from the USS *Juneau*. The Marines stared down the local warlord that day in 1992, but a few months later the fighting would turn ugly. Photo by Kirk Spitzer.

Our children, Isabella and Lucas, dressed in traditional Mexican folk dance costumes for a performance with their mother's dance company, around 1999. Author photo.

# 9

# OPERATION DESERT SHIELD

—— ON COMPETITION ——

One quiet weekend during the summer following Panama, I was relaxing at home with Maru, when the phone rang.

"Mr. Copeland," the caller said, "the National Media Pool has been activated."

This was a call I had hoped for but did not expect. A pool was a small group of reporters who represented the rest of the media when open coverage was not possible. The National Media Pool, called up by the Pentagon from a rotating list of media organizations, traveled with the first wave of troops into combat. I had been told the call could come at any time, and that I would have two hours to get ready, but I would not know where I was going, or whether it was for a training exercise or the real thing.

I wasn't supposed to ask questions on an unsecured line, but I really wanted some details. The most likely destination was Liberia, where crazy rebels wearing bathrobes and pink wigs were fighting the government. The story was all over the news, and I assumed there was going to be an evacuation of US citizens.

"Should I go to Andrews?" I asked, referring to the air base just outside of Washington.

"Negative, sir. You need to come to the Pentagon right away so we can take your measurements," the caller said.

At first I thought, cool, we are going to get uniforms like the ones the World War II correspondents had.

"No sir," he said. "It's for your chemical suit."

Change of plans. We were not going to Liberia, but to the Middle East. A few days earlier, on August 2, 1990, Iraqi leader Saddam Hussein had invaded neighboring Kuwait, and his troops were a short drive from Saudi Arabia's oil fields and control of the world economy. President George H. W. Bush wanted Saddam to leave Kuwait and to stay away from Saudi Arabia. Now it sounded like Bush was sending US troops to fight Saddam if necessary, and I was going along.

Saddam was a brutal dictator, deeply in debt after a long war with Iran. He justified the invasion by accusing Kuwait of pumping oil that really belonged to Iraq, and he further claimed, incorrectly, that all of Kuwait and its oil rightfully belonged to Iraq. The United States was not an enemy of Saddam before his invasion of Kuwait, and for decades the main concern of the US government had been to keep the oil flowing from that little corner of desert, which held most of the world's proven oil reserves. Neighboring Saudi Arabia, a longtime US ally, was key to protecting the oil and would be the base for US troops massing against Saddam.

The Pentagon was quiet over the weekend, even though they were about to go to war. I was measured for my chemical suit and left my passport to get a visa for Saudi Arabia. Then I was told to go home, pack, and report later to Andrews. I was nervous about the chemical suit—getting gassed seemed worse than getting shot—but I was excited to cover the story. I had never been to the Middle East, but I felt confident about reporting on US military operations. Like the soldiers I covered, this is what I had prepared for, this is what I lived to do.

I told Maru I was leaving again, but I didn't have answers to her questions. I didn't know where I was going, for how long, or whether it would be dangerous.

My talk with Maru did not include any details about the chemical suit. I wasn't sure what to make of it myself, so I wasn't going to burden her. Her concern was that I might be gone for months. She did not feel at home in Washington, partly because she was still learning English. Working as a waitress and Spanish teacher helped pay the bills but was not engaging for her. It only made her miss the dance career she left back home. When we lived in Mexico, she was my guide and teacher in a new place and culture. I wanted to do the same for her in Washington, but now I had to leave her.

I was packing my stuff when the phone rang, an urgent call from the Pentagon. Bad news. I was not going with the pool. The military caller said I had been denied a Saudi visa, and I couldn't go on the pool without one. The reason, he explained, was that there wasn't a single blank page in my passport. I had traveled so much that every page had entry and exit stamps from different countries, but the Saudi visa required an entire blank page. I argued without getting him to budge, and then I panicked. This was nuts. How would I explain it to Dan and Dale? How could I ever face the other Pentagon reporters? My passport was too full?

I made a call out of desperation. The head of Pentagon Public Affairs was a former reporter from Wyoming, Pete Williams. Williams was in his office preparing for a major deployment and possibly a war, but he took my call. I explained what had happened and begged him to let me go.

There's nothing I can do, he said, if you don't have a Saudi visa.

I was sunk, disappointed, and embarrassed. I told Maru what had happened, and she tried to console me.

Maybe you can go later, she said.

After a few hours, the phone rang again. It was Pete Williams. Even though it was a weekend, he had personally driven over to the State Department, found somebody with enough authority, and convinced them to graft several blank pages into my passport. Then he took the expanded passport to the Saudis for my visa.

I was good to go, he said. Wheels up.

I owe you, I replied. Forever.

What did you take to a war in the Middle East? I didn't have trouble packing for a war in Panama because I had experience there, but going to Saudi Arabia was a first. I knew it would be hot and sandy, but it wasn't the same as packing for the beach. I needed to be protected from the elements but light enough to move around. I would be wearing boots not flip-flops. Did I even need a jacket? Was it cold at night? Did it ever rain? Would we be in tents or sleeping outside? Was it too hot for a sleeping bag?

"I've got to go," I told Maru.

"I know," she said.

"I'll be back soon."

"How soon?"

"I don't know."

"Be careful, Pito."

I was afraid, but I didn't want her to know. I had left her for a story many times before, starting the day after we met at the movies in Mexico City when I flew to cover the war in El Salvador. I usually knew where I was headed and where I was going to stay. I also was pretty sure I would be safe. This time felt different. Saddam Hussein was in another category of bad guy from a Colombian drug lord or even the death squads in Central America. A firefight in Panama was not the same as tank warfare in the desert. And scarier than anything was the thought of poison gas bubbling my skin and turning my lungs to bloody liquid.

Then, like flipping a switch, my mind locked on the assignment. Everything else that was important to me was left behind. I wasn't afraid, and I had no regrets. The story was everything: the journey and the destination, a jolt of adrenaline, and the magnetic pull of breaking news. If there was such a thing as work-life balance, I broke the scale when I walked out the door.

There were seventeen of us on the National Media Pool, including a television crew, three photographers, a radio reporter, and six writers, known quaintly as "pencils." We would be the only foreign journalists in Saudi Arabia, but our stories and images—whatever we produced—would be available immediately as pool reports to the rest of the media. We had to protect our individual interests (our jobs), but we had a greater responsibility as the eyes and ears of the world's media. A mistake would be worse than normal because there would be no competition to check and correct our work, and the stakes were life and death.

A noisy military aircraft flew us to the headquarters of Central Command in Tampa, where we were hustled into a briefing room. The air was cold, the surfaces clean. It reminded me more of a community college than a wartime command center. We sat and waited for a few minutes. Then a four-star general stormed in, big and strong, filling the room with confidence and an extra-large personality. He shook our hands and welcomed us to CENTCOM. Gen. Norman Schwarzkopf was upbeat, hard-charging and ready for a fight. He also gave a good briefing: clear, colorful, and to the point. The Iraqis had to leave Kuwait immediately, he said, and they would not be allowed to push into Saudi Arabia. Period.

Schwarzkopf went back to work while we huddled over a laptop to write for the first time as a pool. By mutual agreement, the one who sat at the keyboard was John King, a twenty-six-year-old fast-mover from the Associated Press. The rest of us stood behind him and offered a jumble of suggestions, phrases, and quotes, which King managed to turn into a decent story. The pool report was sent back to the Pentagon to be shared with the rest of the media and broadcast to the world.

After a long flight, we landed in Saudi Arabia, tired and stiff but eager to cover a huge story. We were taken to a hotel in Dhahran, not far from the oil fields on the Persian Gulf, and just a few miles from where Saddam's troops were digging in to the Kuwaiti desert.

Saudi King Fahd had tried to keep out the US media, but the Bush administration pushed for some news coverage, so the compromise was to allow the Pentagon pool to represent the media of the world. Our pool reports would be available for all the media to use as their own. While this was an extraordinary opportunity for us in the pool, we were too few to cover a story this big. Also, we represented US media companies, and this was a global conflict. Personally, I was happy to have an exclusive seat for the biggest story in the world.

Reporting was not a team sport, and normally I would have considered the other members of the pool to be competitors. Reporters sometimes worked in packs, and I had shared transportation and sources with other reporters overseas, but I never had written stories with the competition. The exception was at the White House, where most events were covered by a pool. The justification for the pool was that there were far too many reporters in Washington to fit inside the White House. Every day a few reporters, including me, were assigned to cover the president and share the reporting with the rest of the media. Nobody liked the amount of control the pool gave the White House, but nobody stood up to the system, either.

Pools were never the most effective way to cover news because competition and having more eyes on the story were always better. Still, if a pool was the only option, I wanted to be in it.

The handlers who managed the Pentagon pool had restrictive rules for what we could report about what they dubbed Operation Desert Shield. We weren't allowed to name the military people we met, or describe their weapons or their mission. The only permitted dateline was "Somewhere in Saudi

Arabia." Our main escort was Lt. Col. Larry Icenogle, whose day job was in tank warfare, but who somehow ended up in Public Affairs. Icenogle was big and gruff, loud and confident, extremely smart and even a little bit funny. We called him the Iceman.

The Iceman's job was to make sure the pool didn't endanger the troops by revealing too much about their numbers and capabilities. That was exactly the information we wanted, however, because the story was whether Saddam would continue his attack into Saudi Arabia, and if he did, could the US troops hold him back.

When we pressed for details about the size of the deployment, the commanders told us vaguely that the force included "elements" of several divisions. I knew the approximate size of each division and the order of battle, or array of troops and equipment, so it was easy math to estimate the size of the force protecting the oil fields. Except that it wasn't. I didn't realize that "elements" of a division might not be anywhere close to the full 12,000 combat-ready soldiers. The "elements" of a division could have been three guys sharing a room in our hotel.

Without realizing it, I made the US defenses appear more powerful than they were, a mistake that worked to the advantage of the US mission. If Saddam considered taking the Saudi oil fields, he would want to know the size and disposition of the US force. Even at the higher numbers, US forces were thin on the ground. If he had moved quickly, Saddam could have taken eastern Saudi Arabia and controlled a significant portion of the world's oil. He also could have seized the modern Saudi military bases and the military equipment that had been stored there years before by the United States, just in case something like this happened.

The Iceman checked our stories but suggested few changes. We knew the rules and mostly stuck to them. In any case, we didn't know much outside our little bubble. After awhile, the security checks became a formality and then a lark. The Iceman held my little computer in his big paws like a grizzly bear playing with a toy. I stood behind him and read over his shoulder. He scrolled through the text, nodding, and then stopped. He looked up at me and said, "Don't you think 'due to the fact' is a little verbose?"

From the first day, we fought with the handlers over what we could report and how long we could remain in country. We wanted to stay at least until the situation was stabilized, or until Saddam had withdrawn from Kuwait. For the moment, we had deep access to the operation at its most delicate and dangerous stage. Our handlers, both from the military and the Saudi government, regarded us as unruly kids loose in a store filled with fragile objects. They watched and held their breath, waiting for us to break something.

Our Saudi handler was Adel al-Jubeir, a thin, earnest twenty-eight-year-old with glasses and a soft voice. He had gone to school in Texas, earned a master's at Georgetown University, and was working at the Saudi embassy in Washington. He was honest with us and enthusiastic about being our guide, and we grew to trust him. He understood the politics of the Saudi kingdom and the region, and how it all fit with US politics.

He wore nice suits in Washington, but at home in Saudi Arabia, Adel wore a flowing white robe and good shoes and always looked cool and fresh, despite the heat. He seemed able to open any door. He took us to Saudi government officials and members of the royal family, and his presence gave them the confidence to speak openly. We soon had met so many princes that we gave them nicknames.

The Chatty Prince invited us to dine at his palace, which was a desert-brown fort as big as a department store. After a sumptuous meal served from long buffet tables, the prince led us into a large indoor tent, an immense and stylized version of what the Bedouin used in the desert, richly decorated with thick rugs and soft cushions for sitting on the floor. The ambience was desert, but the air conditioner kept the tent as cold as an igloo.

The Chatty Prince had a pretty good sense of humor. Lounging around after the long meal, which we ate Saudi-style (without cutlery and using our right hands only), I asked, "What's the best thing about being a prince?"

He thought for a minute and said, "You get good tables at restaurants. The bad thing is, they expect you to tip a lot."

We spent the days racing around the kingdom in jeeps, buses, planes, and helicopters. Out in the desert, I looked far across the sand to the horizon and saw a silver ribbon shimmering like water; so that was a mirage.

On a trip aboard a Saudi military plane, I tried my first phrase of Arabic on one of our local handlers. "Peace be upon you," I pronounced carefully.

He smiled and returned the greeting in Arabic, adding, "Are you Jewish?"

"No," I said, thinking it was a setup line for a joke. "Why?"

"Because Jews learn fast," he said, not joking and not intending a compliment, either.

The August days were so hot that stepping outside was like being hit in the face with a rolled-up carpet. Even on the stillest afternoons, the heat whipped around like wind. My first reaction was to shed clothes, but soon my head throbbed and my skin tingled from dehydration. Flying in an open helicopter one hundred feet over the desert, I saw the rotors pulling up brown columns of sand, and pockets of hot air rocked the chopper. So much sand slashed across my face that I feared my eyes were bleeding. I felt woozy and nauseous and then shivered with icy chills. The next day I bought a hat, added a long-sleeved shirt, and carried a bottle of water.

General Schwarzkopf followed us from Tampa to Saudi Arabia, and we covered his first visits with the troops. He was a robust man who turned fifty-six that month and appeared grandfatherly compared with the young soldiers.

The general was an inspiring leader, and he loved to be out with the troops. After a few stops at remote camps under the hot sun, I was tired and light-headed from the heat. Schwarzkopf didn't seem to mind the sun and got all fired up with the airmen and women who maintained A-10 attack jets one hundred miles from the Kuwaiti border. "Let's face it," he told the cheering troops, "if he dares come across that border and comes down here, I'm completely confident we're going to kick his butt when he gets here."

I looked at the other members of the pool, raised my eyebrows, and we started shouting mock headlines: "General Cedes 100 Miles of Saudi Territory!" "Iraqi Attack Welcomed!"

Our handlers winced.

The general was energized by the troops, and the more he spoke to them, the bolder he became. By the next stop, he was totally wound up and sounded like a coach getting his team ready for the big game. They cheered, and he yelled back, "Go get 'em!"

Noticing again the TV camera pointed at his face, the general cleared his throat, and backed up a little. "Well, we're in a defensive posture down here, so if he does come down, we'll handle him."

Stop the presses! We shouted, giddy now in the baking sun: "General Orders Attack!" "General Cancels Attack!" "General Indecisive!" Even our handlers laughed, discreetly.

I knew the good times were over when I saw familiar TV network reporters having breakfast in the hotel restaurant. The Saudis had agreed to open the country to more news coverage, and journalists were arriving from all over the world. Our work as a pool was finished, along with our exclusive access. The door of one hotel room now was labeled "Dan's Room," and I saw pressed safari jackets hanging in the closet for CBS anchor Dan Rather.

I sat down for breakfast with an up-and-coming NBC reporter I knew from the Pentagon. She was thirty-three, smart, and very competitive about stories, but in a good way that made me want to help. She was excited to be in Saudi Arabia and eager to hear about the troop buildup. I happily told her what we had seen in the pool, and she shared the news from Washington. Her name was Katie Couric.

Free from pool duty, I was pleased to be invited to the home of a local university administrator. The host greeted me at the door and introduced me to a dozen Saudi men dressed in white robes and headdresses, sitting on the floor or on low couches. We nibbled on snacks and drank hot tea. It was my first adult party without alcohol, which was banned in the kingdom. I had to ask, and the men—amused but not embarrassed or angered—told me that under the comfy robes they wore boxers and t-shirts, regulation white. I could hear the laughing voices of women nearby, but they were behind a wall in another room. The men ignored the sounds of the women.

One of the guests, a worldly university official, said with absolute certainty that Saudi women agreed with the separation of the sexes, which he called an expression of Islam, not of sexism. I was dubious and said, with all due respect, that I would like to hear that from a woman.

"My daughter is coming to pick me up. You can meet her," he said. This was startling because I had been in the country for a month and had not been allowed to speak to a single Saudi woman.

Around midnight, the doorbell rang, and someone announced the daughter had arrived. She did not come into the house, however, and I was led outside to see her. One of the Saudi men, showing me to the door, whispered, "You can meet her, but we can't."

She was a cute seventeen-year-old in slacks and a blouse, with no black robe and no veil. "Oh, daddy," she blushed, whenever her father bragged about her. We chatted in the driveway until they got into the car and drove off. Only later did I realize the girl was driving, even though it was illegal for women to drive. Like a lot of things in Saudi Arabia, the relationship between men and women was more complex than I had thought when I first arrived.

The desk in Washington was less interested in the nuances of Saudi culture than in the preparations for war, so I arranged for a flight to the USS *Independence,* an aircraft carrier patrolling the Gulf of Oman. A minute or two before landing on the ship, I should have been concerned when the navy pilot suggested that we prepare for some "slight discomfort."

The other passengers and I were facing backwards in the heavy metal seats of a Navy C-2 Greyhound, a prop plane used for a COD—Carrier Onboard Delivery. I was in a windowless seat next to an AP reporter, who had asked for an airsickness bag even before we took off. We were groggily enduring another early morning assignment, more of the military's obsession with doing everything at the crack of dawn. What happened to fighting at night? Or at least after brunch.

The pilot explained over my headset that he would fly above the aircraft carrier, then turn sharply ("pull a few Gs") to bleed off some air speed to land on the deck. Watch the crew chief for the signal, he said. When the crew chief waved his hand in the air, grabbed his shoulder harness, and planted his feet firmly in front of him, the meaning was clear. I braced for landing.

The little plane groaned as the pilot pulled it in a tight circle, turning so hard that the force pried open my mouth in a clownish smile. Reassuringly, I touched the arm of the AP reporter, who smiled weakly before bringing the bag to her mouth and filling it with breakfast. I tried to squeeze her arm to comfort her, but the warm, sour smell of vomit punched a fist down my throat. Then BOOM!—we hit the deck, and a metallic chain rang out like from a giant fishing reel, jerking the aircraft to a stop so quickly our heads snapped back into the hard metal seats.

I climbed down slowly on stiff legs, nauseous and squinting like a mole in the fierce sun. On the carrier deck the engine noise was so loud and the heat so intense that I was disoriented, and all I could see were the silver, oily undersides of jet fighters and attack planes. The crew proudly called the deck the "most dangerous three acres on earth." The water of the Gulf was deep blue, darker than the cloudless sky.

I couldn't resist the offer to sit inside the cockpit of an A-6 attack jet. I squeezed into the seat and tried to make sense of the array of switches, dials, and gauges. This plane would be among the first to fly if the shooting started, and the pilot told me he was studying targets in Iraq and Kuwait. I asked if it was hard to drop bombs on targets he knew might include civilians. "You just go where they tell you," he said. "You try not to think about it." The pilot had never flown in combat; none of them had, yet. If this thing kicks off, I thought to myself on the flight back to shore, it's going to be like nothing my generation has ever seen.

By then the buildup to war had started to feel routine. I had exhausted all my ideas for military feature stories, such as, "Logisticians—The Long Poles in the Tent," and I had interviewed my last prince. There was one thing, though, that still got me up in the morning, one thing I wanted to do before I left Saudi Arabia: ride a camel.

We hadn't seen any camels so far, which I complained about frequently. Our local handlers could not understand this unhealthy fascination with all things dromedary. Only one person shared my interest, and NPR's John Ydstie promised we would not leave before we got up close and personal with a camel.

Our chance finally came on a trip to the legendary city of Hofuf, famous for its desert culture. The city's old market was nothing like the modern, air-conditioned malls where we had done most of our shopping. Merchants sold spices, sandals, robes, and trinkets. Pungent sandalwood incense burned in silver charcoal braziers.

"Come, come," said a scruffy, one-eyed vendor. He handed John a battered copper bowl with a design scratched into the side with a nail. "Silver, silver," the man assured John.

I stepped in as John's financial adviser, counseling under my breath, "Silver, my ass."

The merchant understood the tone if not the English. "No, no. Is silver. Forty." Then he went on about something in Arabic.

"What's he saying?" John asked.

I winged it. "He says, 'Today only. I make special price for you. Forty riyals.' About ten bucks. Tell him you'll give him twenty riyals and not a halala more."

The vendor added something in Arabic.

"What's he saying now?" John asked, for some reason accepting the idea that I actually understood. My Arabic was limited to a handful of expressions, but living in Mexico had taught me how to shop in a market in any language.

"Now he says that it cost him thirty-five, and he would take a loss to sell it to you for twenty. Stand firm. He's weakening."

But John, the wimp, pulled out his wallet, making the international gesture of submission. He might as well have bared his neck to a wolf. Forty riyals.

Emboldened by his success, John decided to try his negotiating skills with a Bedouin lady dressed in black and veiled to the eyes. She sat on the ground amid bundles of rugs and bags outside the market, which meant she was too poor to afford a stall. Looked like easy pickings.

John, the son of a Lutheran minister from North Dakota, was the most decent and polite of people. "Hello," he said kindly to the Bedouin lady, looking into her dark eyes, the only part of her showing under yards of black fabric. "What have you got in there?" He leaned forward to peer into a wrinkled plastic shopping bag.

She reached into the bag and pulled out a dozen engraved silver bracelets, worn smooth around the edges. "Forty," she said to John, holding up a small bracelet and a larger one. Forty was either the price of the day or the only number the vendors knew in English. "For baby," she said, holding the smaller one. Offering the larger bracelet, she said, "For madame."

We hadn't seen any Westerners in the market, and we clearly were an oddity. Several armed policemen asked what we were up to. They were most concerned with John's tape recorder and microphone. They wanted to know if we had cameras, which we did not. We had been warned that taking certain photographs was strictly forbidden for religious (and political) reasons, and we had been told to be extra careful not to photograph women.

I was buying a little spice bag of cardamom when I realized John was still talking at the Bedouin lady, who had begun to answer back rather loudly. She folded a stiff paper fan and began to whap John on the leg. She yelled at him in Arabic, pointing at the tape recorder. This could get ugly. I decided to leave the translating to our guide, who was getting flustered and warned us, "She insists that is a camera, and she wants John to stop taking her picture."

"Thank you very much," I told the lady. I pulled John by the arm and hissed at him: "We're outta here." The guide trotted along behind us, moving quickly through the crowded aisles.

I thought we were safe, but suddenly, out of nowhere, the Bedouin lady was on top of John, beating him on the head and shoulders with her fan and shouting at the top of her voice. Ever the rational gentleman, John tried to explain that his tape recorder was not a camera, taking out the cassette to show the lady. This only infuriated her, and now our guide started to panic, pulling John and me by the arms to the safety of our air-conditioned vehicle. He locked the doors and took a deep breath.

"What about the camels?" I reminded him.

"Too late for camels," he said.

"No, no," I protested. "Can't we just try?"

"Why do you want to see camels?" he asked, for the tenth time.

I sighed and tilted my head at him to say, you know why. He relented and directed the driver to the nearby camel market, which we could smell from inside the car.

"Now that we are here, you'll have to ride one," the guide told me, savoring the thought.

"Oh yeah, I'll ride one," I said. "But before that, what I really want to do is talk with some Saudis who work here. Just typical camel herders or Bedouin."

He feared this was some kind of trick. "What do you want to talk to them about?"

"About life," I said, "about what they think about things, about the US troops, the Gulf crisis."

"They aren't very talkative," the guide said, trying to decide what to do. He really didn't want to stop again, but I was a guest. Arab hospitality was a real thing, and he was a good host. He nodded his head and pointed the driver toward a barefoot shepherd standing alongside a dozen long-haired sheep. We pulled up next to the shepherd, and the guide rolled down the window halfway. The guide turned to me and said, "What do you want to ask him?"

It dawned on me that the guide was afraid of the shepherd, embarrassed, or at least extremely uncomfortable asking him questions. I remembered the dates on the local newspaper—one was in 1990, and the other was in the Islamic year 1411. Our guide lived in 1990, but the shepherd was in 1411, and I was not going to bridge the gap between them.

I opened my door and jumped down onto the hard sand. Reluctantly, the guide followed me out of the car. I smiled at the shepherd, who gently shook my hand with his rough hand, which was brown and weathered as a strip of rawhide. In his other hand he carried an orange plastic tube he used for a staff. I made small talk and complimented his sheep. The guide translated my words. Then I asked what the shepherd thought about the American troops in his country. "I think that is a political question," the guide protested, declining to translate.

"Life is political," I snapped. "Just ask."

The guide asked my question in Arabic. The shepherd answered at length, gesturing at the horizon, at his sheep, at me. He waved the yellow plastic staff to make a point. I looked at the translator, thinking I was getting good stuff. I had my notebook and pen ready. The guide told me, "He says it's a good thing."

Wait a second! That's it? What about all that gesturing? Simmering, but accepting my defeat, I started to get back into the car.

"There are your camels," the guide said, pushing John and me back into the sun. "Go over there and see them. But be careful."

The camels were tanking up at a concrete trough, maybe thirty or forty of them. One was sitting in the sand, rubbing himself in the dirt and kicking up clouds of dust. Clumps of long dark hair were bunched on his sides like seaweed. They all needed a bath and a trim. Camels in the cartoons were not nearly so unkempt or stinky. I pushed John forward to tape their bellowing, but when a big toothy mouth tried to eat his microphone he fell over me, running back to the car. The guide was laughing so hard he forgot I was supposed to ride one.

I was happy now: I had met a shepherd from the fifteenth century, and seen a camel from plenty close. The guide, relieved our adventure had concluded, ordered the driver to return to the hotel. We drove back onto the paved road, kicking up a cloud of sand that covered the camels, the sheep, and the shepherd, who was waving good-bye.

When the best story I offered was about camels, the desk decided maybe I should come back to Washington. We never talked about the cost of my stay, but money was a factor. In addition to my meals and hotel for more than a month, the company was paying for a special life insurance policy to cover me in a war zone. The regular insurance would not have paid out if I were killed in combat.

I was ready to go home anyway. The buildup would last a few more months before anything happened. The US military would not attack until all the troops and equipment were in place. My best guess was that there would be no need to attack because Saddam would do the smart thing and start to pull back from Kuwait.

Back to my old routine in Washington, I went to the office, the Pentagon, or Capitol Hill to cover the political debate about the war. I was relieved to be home and to have weekends off, but the story was sterile and remote compared with running around the desert.

Maru was happy to see me, but she also had grown accustomed to being on her own. She was working, taking classes for her high school equivalency, and studying English. While I was away in the desert, she made new friends, was talking about getting back into Mexican dance, and kept busy without me. Maru had been supporting herself since she was a teenager, so she didn't really need me, but she did miss me.

I didn't want to admit it, and I did miss her when I was gone, but I loved covering stories overseas. I liked having one thing to focus on and an opportunity to do something well. I didn't have to worry about anything except the story. I could manage my own time, and the closest editor was 7,000 miles away.

After Christmas with Maru and my family in Chicago, I packed to return to Saudi Arabia in early 1991. I still didn't think there would be a war. How could Saddam be so stupid that he would not declare victory and leave Kuwait? Instead he seemed to be digging in deeper, both in rhetoric and in the desert. Maybe it was all just words, and he was planning to withdraw at the last minute for maximum drama and attention.

I called my mom before I left Washington for Saudi Arabia and told her not to worry. I said I was going back to the frontlines where I wanted to be, but just to cover the peace talks. I kissed Maru good-bye and assured her there would be no war. I'd be home in a few weeks.

# 10

# OPERATION DESERT SWARM

—— ON SOURCES ——

When I arrived in Saudi Arabia the second time, the mood had changed. US forces were leaning far forward and ready to attack. War suddenly felt imminent.

With so many reporters swarming the country, the Pentagon had established an elaborate press pool operation to control access to the troops. Adopting White House rules, the military allowed the media to organize themselves to fill the pool slots, but there were not nearly enough slots for the number of reporters who wanted to go. And as at the White House, the large news organizations thought they were in charge. There were only eighteen slots for media to cover the entire US Army operation. There was no way eighteen people could cover hundreds of thousands of soldiers in combat.

The really bad news was that there was no slot for me.

Frustrated by the lack of access to the troops, I drove to the coastal city of Jubail with Hearst's Stewart Powell, my friend from Panama, to see what we could learn. We ran into soldiers from Great Britain, who were fun and loud and looking for a pub on the road to Kuwait. Their arms were tattooed with snakes and daggers and the words "Death Before Dishonor." What paper are you from, they asked us, the *Baghdad Daily News*? We laughed at the joke, but then they told us their wartime mission.

Media handlers prevented US soldiers from revealing their missions to reporters, but the Brits confidently said they were preparing for two weeks of an air campaign to weaken Saddam's defenses. Then there would be an easy breach of the Iraqi lines and on to Kuwait.

We tried the same trick at a nearby US base—just act like we belonged there—but we were chased away by the military police. We were forced to sneak around because we weren't in a pool and therefore didn't have access to sources among the troops. Stewart and I kept pushing to get on a pool, but we did not have any leverage.

When we heard about a meeting of the reporters running the pools, we decided to just show up. They gathered in an open area of the hotel near the press operations of the US military and the Saudi government. The meeting was for pool members only, and since Stewart and I had arrived in Saudi Arabia "late," we were allowed to observe but not speak.

We were informed we could not possibly be considered for pool membership for weeks, which might be after the fighting had started. There were motions and seconds and votes, but the reporters reminded me of kids playing parliament. If government officials had tried to hold a meeting like this, we would have ridiculed them without pity.

Stewart couldn't control himself, spoke twice out of turn, and was censured. He looked over at me and mouthed, "Aren't you going to say anything?"

Realizing no one was going to call on me, I just started in: "I was here in August before any of you, but the way the system is now, I can't cover the war. I didn't come all this way to read pool reports and cover this through your eyes, as good as they might be. I can't believe I'm pleading with my colleagues to let me cover something. This is a huge pie. There is plenty for everybody." With a dramatic gesture toward the Pentagon's Joint Information Bureau, or JIB, I said, "This is worse than the people over there."

There were murmurs and the shaking of heads, but no one responded. If the war started tonight, I was going to miss it.

Our original Pentagon pool handler, the Iceman, was observing the meeting, too. He leaned over and whispered to me: "Whoa, these guys are cutthroat. I wouldn't want to be in a trench with any of them."

I told him I was embarrassed about how the reporters were behaving. The lack of opportunities to get out with the troops forced us to fight among ourselves. Instead of worrying about stories, we worried about blocking our colleagues from the action. The military could not have planned it any better. "This is right out of Sun Tsu and *The Art of War,*" I whispered to the Iceman.

He laughed and said, "We study that shit. It works."

The mood of the reporters at the hotel during January of 1991 was nervous boredom. The deadline set by the United Nations for Saddam to withdraw from Kuwait was approaching, but the only news was the sound of the clock ticking. We were relatively safe in the hotel, although we knew Saddam could reach us with Scud ballistic missiles, tactical weapons developed by the Soviet Union. The Scuds were not accurate or especially lethal, unless Saddam armed them with chemical warheads.

My biggest worry was how to cover the war. If I stayed in the hotel, I would have access to the briefings and pool reports, plus the computers and phones to file stories. Not to mention a roof over my head, a bed, and hot food. On the other hand, I felt a particular burden to be in the field with the troops.

Fifty years before me, Scripps Howard had a reporter in the Washington bureau named Ernie Pyle, a modest, nice guy from Dana, Indiana. After walking by Pyle's portrait every day at the Pentagon, I wanted to learn more about him. Dan, my bureau chief and a Hoosier like Pyle, told me that Pyle was the bureau's "aviation writer," which was the hot technology beat at the time, and he also did some travel writing. At the start of World War II, the desk sent him to cover the action in North Africa and then to Europe.

Pyle loved covering the grunts, the toughest guys in the toughest conditions, and lived in the field for weeks at a time. He didn't write about the briefings given by the generals, but described how the infantry slept in the mud and how bodies piled up around them like firewood. He was one of the most popular writers in the country, won a Pulitzer Prize, and was known proudly as "the GI's friend."

In our bureau, Dan had decorated the walls with photos of Pyle, a *Peanuts* cartoon remembering him, plus the original of one of his more famous columns, about soldiers recovering the body of their fallen captain. The display I liked was the framed collection of Pyle's expense reports, written on little pieces of notebook paper, requesting reimbursement for "whiskey for courage" and "lipsticks for England." That was a glimpse into a reporter's life that I appreciated. Those little bits of paper represented the hardship he had seen, plus his sense of humor and the warm relationship with his editors back home.

When the Allied victory in Europe was near, the desk sent Pyle to Asia to cover the war with the Japanese. On the little island of Ie Shima, just months before Japan surrendered and the war would end, Pyle was hit by gunfire and killed. He was forty-four. Ernie Pyle did not cover war from a hotel, and neither could I.

The final day of the UN deadline for Saddam to leave Kuwait, I had breakfast with Stewart. He looked different, and it was jarring. Then I realized why: he had shaved his beard to get a better seal for his gas mask. I gave him grief about his new look, and he laughed. We didn't really talk about the deadline passing because it wouldn't be a story until one of the two opponents—Saddam or Bush—made a move. We did feel more urgency to get on a pool.

I jerked awake at 4:30 a.m. on January 17, 1991, and wondered why I couldn't sleep. I was staying in a luxury, high-rise hotel a few blocks from the fully booked hotel where the media operations were located. I turned on the radio and learned the war had begun. Operation Desert Shield, the protection of Saudi Arabia, had become Operation Desert Storm, an attack to drive Saddam out of Kuwait.

I threw on my clothes and went down to the lobby. People were awake, which was unusual at that hour, but otherwise everything seemed normal. Waiters in the restaurant carried gas masks and flashlights in case the power was knocked out, but they were calmly serving early breakfast. I looked around for someone to interview about the start of the war, already roughing out the story in my head. One Saudi man was wearing fully loaded bandoliers crossed like sashes on his robed chest, so of course I had to talk with him. I even found a stray prince staying at the hotel. I ran back to my room and was banging out a quick story when Stewart called from the media hotel with news: we both had landed pool slots. Get over here fast, he said. We're going to war.

I filed what I had, packed a bag, and headed back down to the lobby. My hands were shaking. When I walked past the front desk, the clerk said there was a call for me. I wasn't expecting a call, but I took the phone and said hello. The caller was from a radio station in New Zealand—"We're on the air!"—looking for someone who spoke English. I gave them my most dramatic account of the war so far, based entirely on CNN and the one heavily armed Saudi I had interviewed, and said I had to go.

An American woman grabbed me near the door and asked for a ride. She wanted to interview me, too. My mouth was dry as paste, but I told her what I knew. She said she worked for *Mirabella,* a fashion magazine. I had heard about her. Had she really interviewed female soldiers about masturbating in the field? "It's relevant," she said.

While waiting for news about my pool, I was interviewed by a C-SPAN producer from a live show in Washington. I now had given interviews on three continents and written one story, without hearing a shot fired.

Stewart got a pool slot, and then, finally, someone called my name. A new pool, Number 10, had been formed, and I was on it, along with Tim Collie from the *Tampa Tribune,* Ed Offley of Hearst Newspapers, and a TV crew. We were provided (on loan) flak jackets, helmets, and gas masks, and were driven to the airfield, where we climbed onto a C-130 bound for the Saudi air base in Taif.

Hours later we were standing inside a hangar at Taif when the first F-111 strike aircraft pulled in after attacking Iraqi targets. The American pilot popped open the canopy. He was covered in sweat and trembling, exhausted but pumped with energy. He talked about flying over the targets and dropping the payload. The air force men and women working in the hangar crowded around to listen and cheer.

The TV people in our pool, reporter Judd Rose and a crew from ABC, were happy with the good access to the pilots and their candor. Judd prepared the video to ship to the pool office, which would distribute it to the media of the world. Because we did not have a way to communicate other than through the military, we had to send the tapes on air force flights. I made hard copies of our print stories and gave them to the handlers to be transmitted by military fax to the pool headquarters. Then we waited. And waited. Our stories never moved.

We badgered the press officers to deliver our stories. They told us they were "at the top of the stack" to go out, but then some other priority—ammo, medical supplies, vital wartime communications—knocked them to the bottom of the pile. Our handlers promised they were lobbying on our behalf, but the base commanders did not think news stories were as important as fighting the war. We couldn't argue with that logic, but we assumed that an air force that could drop a bomb on a bunker hidden in the desert ought to be able to deliver a harmless little news story.

We lived in tents on the flight line, just a few feet from a busy runway. The nights were cold, and I slept in my clothes, with a t-shirt wrapped in a turban around my head to keep warm. The roar of the jets kept me from sleeping more than a few minutes at a time, so I stayed up watching the planes being loaded with fuel and bombs. The energy on the base was electric: everybody, from the cooks to the men and women doing maintenance, felt as if they were flying on the bombing runs.

When our pool reports eventually appeared on the TV and radio, it was fifty hours after we had filed. By then they sounded stale and not interesting. Jonathan Wiggs, a *Boston Globe* photographer, told me, "Don't worry. It'll be a long war."

We decided the only way to do our jobs was to get off the base. We weren't exactly prisoners, but we could not just call a taxi into town. A couple of times, we scrambled to catch a military flight out, only to be bumped by someone more important. Finally, we boarded a C-130 and landed in the Saudi capital, Riyadh, in the middle of the night. I was happy to get to a hotel, mostly for the phone. The porcelain toilet was nice, too. I called the office and filed my accumulated pool reports, at least the ones that were not "O.B.E."—overtaken by events.

I was too wired to sleep, so before sunrise I visited the Central Command headquarters. I complained to one of Schwarzkopf's guys about how our pool was not allowed to file, and he predicted all that eagerness to be close to the action would stop when the first journalist was killed.

On the way out of the building, I ran into a source from another story, long ago in another country. When we had met years before, we were just kids starting our new careers. Now we caught up a little, and talked about our wives and families. I told him about my frustrations trying to cover the story. I worried that the ground war would launch while I was still in a hotel far from the action. Relax, he said, the ground attack would not start for a couple of weeks. Until then, they were just going to pound the Iraqis from the air.

I asked how he could be so sure. He just smiled. Then he risked his job, and his high-level security clearance, to tell me exactly where I should position myself to cover the eventual ground attack from up close. He knew me and trusted I never would reveal his name. He wanted me to do well. Normally I liked to have more than one source for a story, and I preferred documents to a hallway conversation, but this was a case where a single human source—one I had not tapped in years—surprised me with a most valuable gift.

Now I knew where to be for the ground war, but I couldn't get there alone. I needed the military to authorize a trip, assign an escort, and find a commander who would take a reporter along for the ground attack. I told Stewart what I had learned, without revealing my source. We were working together, even if we were competitors, and my information jibed with what he had learned from his own reporting.

Stewart and I were in the media hotel plotting how to cover the coming ground war when I heard a deep muffled "whump, whump." The sound was like someone moving a couch on the floor above us. Before I could say anything, Stewart was out the door, a notebook in one hand and a gas mask in the other, rubber straps flapping behind him. Running down the hall after Stewart, I followed other people racing for the stairs. From the yelling and the scattered shouts, I realized the sound I had heard was a US Patriot missile battery trying to shoot down an incoming Scud missile. There was no way for us to know if Saddam's missile, about the size of a telephone pole, had made it through, or if it carried poison gas. We ran down the stairs to the basement and found places to sit on the floor.

The basement filled with hotel guests and staff, most of them wearing gas masks. Sitting on the cool concrete floor, we looked like anteaters. My mind wandered to stories I had read about Israelis in bomb shelters, also hiding from Iraqi Scuds. Some Israelis had panicked inside their masks and suffocated, the stories said, the gas masks actually causing their deaths instead of preventing them. Could that happen to me? My heart started racing and my breathing got harder. I actually was talking myself into a panic attack. Was I going to suffocate? The more I breathed, the more difficult it was to get oxygen. Slow down, be calm. Focus on your breathing. I pretended to be scuba diving.

There was little talking. You couldn't really talk with the masks, and no one wanted to. Everyone was waiting for a sign the danger had passed. A pretty woman was sitting in front of me, pretty even with a rubber snout. I saw her pale hand resting on her leg. I looked at her and she smiled a little with her eyes. I wanted to reach out and touch her, to hold her hand. Breathe, I told myself, just breathe. If gas had started coming down into the basement, I would have taken her hand, one final beautiful thing.

After about forty minutes, the all-clear sounded. We took off our masks and wiped sweaty faces. I scratched my head where the rubber had plastered my hair. People were laughing, still jittery but now relieved. I stretched my legs and back. The woman in front of me was even more attractive without her mask.

She smiled at me.

In the afterglow of our shared danger, I told her my name and said that if this had been a real emergency, I would have taken her hand.

She introduced herself as Della from CNN.

I don't know what I would have done if you had rejected me, I confessed.

I would have taken your hand, Della said, and suddenly we were close.

We talked comfortably, like we had known each other. She seemed to feel what I was thinking, and I wondered what would happen next. The contact, the intimacy, was the other side of fear.

If she had invited me upstairs, I would have gone with her. It would have been a huge mistake.

My happy marriage was momentarily eclipsed. It wasn't that I debated breaking my vows to Maru, or wondered if I could get away with it; right then my marriage did not exist. Nothing existed outside that moment on the floor of the basement when we realized we were still alive.

Fortunately, Della brushed herself off and said good-bye, and I did not see her again. My thinking returned to normal, and the moment was forgotten. Adrenaline, like alcohol, blocked rational thought and loosened inhibitions. Not always in a good way.

I watched military briefings, worked out in the hotel gym, and nibbled nervously on local delicacies: dates and pistachios. US and coalition planes were bombing Kuwait next door, but the war seemed remote. I looked through the pool reports to find a nugget of news. I felt guilty taking stories from other reporters—in normal times this was considered plagiarism and one of the few things absolutely forbidden by our code—but independent reporting on the troops was difficult outside the pool system. I was selective about which pool reports I tapped, however. Reporters were not equally talented, so I used only pool material that sounded accurate or was filed by someone I trusted.

Finally, our pool was called back into action. By action, our handlers meant a behind-the-scenes look at a maintenance company that kept all those trucks running. We went along, happy to get out of the hotel. The lieutenant colonel who greeted us said he wanted to make a few things clear. "Before you roll," he said, trying to use the lingo, "I don't want you to ask anything negative. I want you to accentuate the positive." Simon, the ABC cameraman, was rolling the entire time, but he had taped over the camera's little red light that indicated it was recording. I almost warned the colonel, but kept my mouth shut.

ABC correspondent Judd Rose decided to use the trip to the maintenance company—and our earlier hostage situation at the air base in Taif—for a story on how the military was controlling the press. His timing was good: the day the story aired, CBS reporter Bob Simon and his crew, driving in the desert without a military handler, went missing. No one was saying whether the reporters were lost, captured, or killed.

I called Maru, my mom, and the office to tell them I was going to appear in Judd's piece for *Primetime Live.* No matter how many stories I wrote for newspapers, my family was always more impressed seeing me on television.

The next day, Dale said the consensus in the office was that I should stay off TV, at least if I was going to complain about the military. People back home were rallying behind the troops, Dale said, and if they were going to take sides, they weren't going to line up with the reporters. Judd told me ABC took a lot of calls, all saying the whining reporters should shut the hell up. Maru and my mom said I looked handsome.

I never thought of myself as being on the opposite side of the US military at war. True, our interests were not the same: the military wanted to keep secrets, and my job was to expose them. But if I had to choose, and sometimes I did, I considered myself an American before a reporter. The simple proof was I did not reveal the most sensitive information from the US side, but I would have quickly published classified information from the Iraqis. My duty as a reporter required me to tell the truth about the military, good and bad, but I was careful not to endanger the US troops. So I didn't consider myself an enemy of the US military, even if I refused to be an unquestioning cheerleader.

At thirty-three, I now completely thought of myself as a reporter. It wasn't just what I did; it was my whole identity. My younger, leftist political ideology was gone, replaced by a belief in nonpartisan, fact-driven journalism as a calling and a mission. I had the same level of passion, but I had changed from activist to observer. Having once been steered by my own strong political beliefs, I was suspicious of all ideology in others, whether on the left or the right. My goal was to see and explain things for what they were, not how I wanted them to be.

Journalism also fulfilled my need for a sense of purpose and community and gave me an identity I was proud to share. The same craving for belonging and being part of something important that I had sought in college activism was fully satisfied by journalism. That's also why the infighting over the media pools was so painful. When the pack tightened ranks, I was left outside.

I felt emotionally secure in the pack, but it wasn't always enough to protect me. I was reminded of this one clear dawn when I sat in my hotel room and watched the horizon lighten over the Persian Gulf. The view was vast and calming, shades of deep blue water and sky. The mornings came as a relief, because I knew Saddam would not be dumb enough to fire a missile during the daylight when US aircraft could track and destroy the launchers. Then BOOM BOOM BOOM BOOM—explosions rattled the window.

Now I recognized the sound of a Patriot battery firing at an incoming missile. I grabbed my gas mask and dove to the floor, putting the bed between me and the sliding glass door. Then everything was silent. My face on the carpet, I could hear the air conditioner whirring. There was no other sound. Was it a Scud? Was it armed with chemicals? If it had a conventional warhead, why didn't I hear it explode?

After a few minutes, the curiosity drove me crazy and I crawled to the window. I looked around and didn't see anything unusual. Traffic was light but normal. The water was empty except for fishing boats. I slid open the glass door, stood on the balcony, and sniffed the air like a dog, which was about the stupidest way to check for poison gas. Nothing. Then the air raid sirens went off, which made me tighten up again. I leaned over the balcony, but there were no fires or rescue vehicles. False alarm?

I was shaking a little when I went back into the room and turned the television to CNN. Two reporters I knew, Charles Jaco and Carl Rochelle, were live from the roof of the media hotel down the road. They were reporting on the explosions I had just heard, answering questions from the anchor in Atlanta. Suddenly Jaco grabbed his gas mask and fumbled to put it on. There was real fear in his eyes. I grabbed my own mask and shoved it to my face, holding it on with one hand and staring at the television, my heart pounding.

Then Jaco removed his mask, took a breath and sheepishly apologized. He had smelled something funny and felt dizzy, he said. Wasn't anything.

I laughed and relaxed a little. I had calmed myself looking out the window at the flat blue water of the gulf, at reality, but the reporters on the television screen almost gave me a heart attack. So much for feeling safe in the media pack.

At the end of January, our pool went to the front. The military believed the bombing had weakened the Iraqis, but ground troops would be necessary to drive them out of Kuwait. I needed to be with those ground troops. My strategy, based on what I had pieced together about the still-secret battle plan, was to hook up with the VII Corps, the massive armored force preparing for the ground attack. I was taken to King Khalid Military City, the Saudi base that was an operational hub in the northern desert. I carried a change of clothes, some camping gear, a laptop computer and battery-operated printer, a helmet and flak vest, and a chemical suit, which came sealed in a thick, plastic bag.

I froze the first night in the desert. The weather was totally different from when I had been here in the summer. Now it was gray and rainy, chilly during the day and freezing at night. I had a cot that got me off the ground, but it offered little protection from the cold. By the morning I could see my breath, and I woke with my sleeping bag covered in frost.

The soldiers taught me a few tricks to keep warm, such as putting a bath towel on the cot for insulation, and the plastic poncho on top to trap the heat. I looked forward to the warm breakfast in the mess tent: a scoop of scrambled eggs, a scoop of potatoes, and a scoop of creamed beef ("On top or on the side?"). Lunch was packaged Meals, Ready-to-Eat, or MREs, and dinner was a piece of meat, vegetable mush, and a scoop of potatoes. I looked for tables with bottles of ketchup because the taste reminded me of home.

On the first clear day, I gladly stripped off layers of bulky clothing and curled up on top of a sandbagged bunker with a bunch of soldiers, all of us happy as cats in the sun. Smaller things, even an hour of sunshine, felt more meaningful. I was thrilled when I scavenged a piece of cardboard to put on the sand next to my cot. Then, when I woke up, I had a clean place to pull on my stiff, icy boots. I remembered to shake out the boots first, in case a scorpion had taken up residence during the night. Four days and then a week passed without a shower, and my hair felt like a straw broom. I debated a "high and tight" haircut, and plenty of soldiers offered to provide the shears.

There was nothing to do while we waited for the ground attack. The military handlers tried to keep us busy with feature stories, but our focus was on the actual fighting, which was difficult to cover because it was not safe to drive around the battlefield that was being bombed. Many reporters believed they were neutral in the conflict and should have been allowed to go anywhere. While that was true in theory, it was difficult to cover the bombing without being captured by the Iraqis or hit by a bomb. We learned later that reporter Bob Simon and his CBS crew, driving around the desert, had been taken prisoner by Iraqi forces. A few extraordinarily brave journalists covered the war from Baghdad, under tight restrictions by the Iraqis, but most of the reporters were working out of hotels in Saudi Arabia.

One feature story I enjoyed writing was about scrounging, a venerable tradition in the military. So while the handlers took us to cover "The World's Largest Laundry," I snuck off and talked to soldiers about trading crates of fruit juice for ammo or radios for blankets. The trading wasn't for personal gain (that I saw), but there was no way a distant headquarters could anticipate every soldier's needs, so a freewheeling barter system filled the gaps. There was a cash-free market for everything from clothing to food to weapons.

A military handler tried to prevent me from talking with guys from the 101st Airborne, and he accused me of conducting "unauthorized interviews." I ignored him and kept talking with the soldiers about scrounging.

A different problem emerged when a senior officer from the 101st confronted me. He was big and solid and squared away, and he knew it. I introduced myself, but he already knew who I was.

He snarled: "You're the one who called us the 'Screaming Chickens.'"

Well, I tried to explain, I was just quoting the guys you went up against at the training center, and wow, great memory, that was like two years ago. All in good fun.

He pretended not to get the joke, but in the end, that little story probably helped more than it hurt. At least he knew my name.

One of my poolmates, Tim Collie, declared he was fed up with features and went on strike. He refused to write anything that wasn't directly related to combat. Tim's patience broke when Iraqi ground troops surprised everyone at the end of January and punched down into the Saudi town of Khafji. The attack was a shock because we were assured the Iraqis were dug in on defense, and it played against the US military's preferred narrative of a weakened Iraqi force. This was actual ground combat not far from us, but we were not allowed to cover it.

That night we crowded into a large tent with a television to watch General Schwarzkopf talking about the attack on Khafji. He tried to make light of the Iraqi attack, but the fact that he personally gave the briefing made me worry. When he belittled a news story about the fighting as being "bovine scatology," the soldiers in the TV tent hooted and hollered, stomping their boots on the plywood floor and cheering the boss. After the briefing, nobody but me wanted to watch the news, so we watched a video of "Internal Affairs."

By February 1, I was back in Dhahran, still waiting for the ground war. I was anxious to get it over with, but at the same time I welcomed the delay because I knew US planes were bombing the Iraqis around the clock. The more the Iraqi force was "degraded," the safer it would be for me during the ground invasion. I knew that "degraded" was a euphemism, but I didn't care what they called it, as long as they kept doing it, relentlessly.

I felt a constant, achy fever of low-level fear. I remembered Ernie Pyle writing about the dulled sense of danger, and now I understood why his stories always included each soldier's name and home address, and sometimes the names of their parents and girlfriends. We had to remember that these were people from back home in mortal danger, not characters in our dispatches. The grand strategy seemed important in the hotel and at the briefings, but not in the field. Out there the only things real were the cold and discomfort, the fear, and the person next to you.

I was tired all the time, partly because there was nothing to do and partly because of the uncertainty. My nerves felt scraped. That's how a Marine I had interviewed described his feelings here—"scraped nerves." Now I understood what he meant. I was afraid to stray too far from the hotel because I knew the call to go forward could come at any moment. I hated being dependent on the military and the other reporters for a pool slot. We had allowed ourselves to be penned up in little groups, and then we fought among ourselves.

I called my mom 7,000 miles away to tell her I was fine, still waiting. She wanted to know when I was coming home, but I didn't know. Maru was not taking it well, my mom said, and was going back to Mexico for awhile. I felt terrible about upsetting them, but I never considered leaving the war. My self-respect, the way I saw myself, depended on doing a good job here. This was not about needing a paycheck or feeling obligated to cover the war. The desk would have let me come home any time, no questions asked. This was about pride and doing the right thing and the story of a lifetime.

My mother and wife were under more stress than I was because they got a distorted view of the war from television. If my nerves were scraped, my mom's were rubbed raw. She was a faithful newspaper reader (having grown up as the daughter of two journalists), and now she watched CNN all day and most of the night. She was hardly sleeping. She said the war seemed to be bogging down and not going well at all. I told her to turn off the TV. The coverage was misleading her about the war, and scaring her needlessly about my safety.

The war I was living was not the war she saw on television. Saddam launched Scuds at Israel and Saudi Arabia, where most of the reporters were based, so the missile strikes dominated the TV coverage. Camera crews slept wrapped in blankets on the hotel roofs waiting for Scud attacks to light up the sky. The real story was a few miles to the north, where Iraqi forces were being pounded into the dirt. Their air cover was gone, their tanks were being destroyed, and their supply lines and communications were cut. Nobody was there to report it because of the danger, however, so it was as if it never happened.

Because television coverage was defined by video, the Scud had grown in stature from a wildly inaccurate, flying car bomb to the most feared weapon on the planet. In the TV war, military success was not measured in combat effectiveness but in airtime. No matter what the US military reported in briefings, the images of the Scuds were more powerful. The missile stories were so ubiquitous that NBC reporter Arthur Kent, poor guy, was nicknamed the Scud Stud.

I was discouraged that television was distorting the reality of the war, and furious that my mom was frightened by the coverage. I grabbed a stack of pool reports for quotes and color, checked with military people I trusted, and banged out an explainer about how US pilots were free to fly across Kuwait and Iraq without challenge. They could drop whatever bombs they wanted, wherever and whenever they wanted, and there was nothing Saddam could do. This all seemed obvious to me, but I wrote the story because of the media-induced misperceptions of my mother, my one true barometer of US public opinion.

Tim couldn't stand the waiting and was ready to be strapped to the first tank going into Iraq. Just for something to do, we decided to drive from Dhahran to the capital city, Riyadh, to attend a military briefing. The live performance by both sides was even worse than what we had watched on television. The official information from the military was thin, and the questions from reporters were weak. The military was crowing about having destroyed six hundred tanks. They thought the number was impressive, but I kept thinking about all the remaining tanks. If we were going to roll into Iraq and Kuwait, I wanted the path to be clear of tanks, all of them.

After the briefing, I visited one of Schwarzkopf's advisers. He wanted to know about the pools, and I said they were working well for the military but not so well for journalism. He was upset with reporters ignoring the ground rules and even reporting the exact location of specific units.

"You have obligations," he said. "I want to see what happens when the first journalist is responsible for the death of a soldier. You say, 'Don't worry about our safety; that's our problem,' but when Bob Simon is missing it becomes our problem and we get called every day."

The desk in Washington, as bored with the waiting as I was, suggested a light feature about Desert Storm humor. It sounded like a good idea at first, and I collected a few jokes, although most were too racist (against Arabs) or too vulgar for family newspapers. The bigger problem with the concept was that the closer we got to a ground war, the less funny everything seemed. I kept putting off the story, hoping Dale would forget about it. I wasn't in a humorous mood.

A wall of tears was dammed behind my eyes, and I could feel the pressure of sadness and fear. I finally broke down when I couldn't find my wedding ring. I didn't even remember taking off the ring, until I noticed it was gone. My finger had a white line where the gold band should have been. I panicked. It felt like such a bad omen; I imagined refusing to go forward without the ring. I went through all the drawers in my hotel room, dumped the trash onto the floor, and finally found it under the bed. I suddenly felt all alone and imagined Maru leaving me. That wouldn't happen in real life, I thought, only in my waking nightmares. It was a comfort to know she was waiting for me.

I put the ring on a chain I wore around my neck with a dog tag. Soldiers advised me to wear the ring on a chain because otherwise it could get caught on a hatch or piece of machinery and tear off my finger. When I first was issued dog tags by the military, I tried to make a joke about not being in the army. Why do I need these? I asked. I'm just visiting! The tags were stamped with my name, blood type, and "Christian."

Maj. Barry Bomier, a friend from Washington, advised me to lace one tag on my boot and wear one around my neck. The reason, he explained, was in case I was sent home in pieces.

Then we got the call: the ground attack was on, and I was going. The low-level fear kicked up to full-blown, near-paralyzing dread. Packing my stuff in the hotel, I was half watching the movie *The Great Gatsby* on television, and I wanted to wear one of those sharp suits and to party and have fun at least one more time. Instead I obsessed over an interview with a soldier who had told me about "Bouncing Betty" landmines. You heard the mine "click," it popped up in your face, and it exploded. The mine, he said, turned you into "pink mist."

The tiredness and lethargy, the depression, were gone, replaced by a buzzing fear and anticipation. Even Tim was afraid, which was both scary and comforting. I was glad Maru had gone to Mexico. She would be busy with her family, and I wouldn't be distracted worrying about her worrying about me.

After rushing back to the desert at King Khalid Military City, we waited. It was Day 30 of Operation Desert Storm. This was the regular rhythm of military life and the reporters who covered it: we stood by for a call, hurried to go, then waited some more. I pulled my cot out of the tent to sit in the sunshine and read a book called *How to Make War*. I was interested in the topic, I wanted to write with authority, and what better time than now to learn about warfare?

Engrossed in my book, I heard shouting back and forth, soldiers talking in excited voices. Something was up. I walked over to the TV tent and waited for the *Today Show*. The news came on, and we learned there was a deal to get

Saddam out of Kuwait peacefully. There would be no need for a ground attack. The soldiers cheered and exchanged high-fives, but some voiced skepticism. I felt tremendous relief and excitement that I could return home. Tim sobered me up by saying we should hurry to Kuwait City for the Iraqi withdrawal. He was right, but I just wanted to go home.

# 11

# THE GROUND WAR

— ON LOYALTY —

The peace deal didn't last long. Preparations for a ground attack accelerated. The military handlers divided our pool for broader coverage, and Tim went off with the Seventh Engineers. He, of course, was thrilled to be in the first wave. I was grateful I was not chosen to cover the clearing of landmines, but I missed him.

The military gave me an assignment that was almost the opposite of Tim's spot at the tip of the spear. They chose me to cover the Second Corps Support Command, which supplied the beans and bullets for the troops. I would have electricity, the ability to file stories, and a tent to keep me warm and dry. The bad news was that I would be near the fighting but not in it, and forced to rely on second-hand pool reports.

I had to think about this: How was I going to cover the war from the rear? I ate breakfast and noticed there was no line at the so-called shower, which was an upright, coffin-sized box made of plywood and topped with a bucket of water. Tugging a rope tipped the bucket and dribbled the icy water onto my head and shoulders. Shivering naked in the cold, I soaped up and rinsed, trying to wash away the sand that had found its way into every crevice of my body. The shower felt wonderful. I remembered reading that Ernie Pyle and the soldiers he lived with went weeks without bathing. What would people say about me? "His stories weren't much, but he was always clean."

I didn't want to hurt anyone's feelings, and I really did appreciate the role of the support troops, but I had to go forward. With my hair still wet from the shower, I went to see the military handlers to negotiate a way to cover the fighting. The compromise was that I would write a couple of stories from the rear about beans and bullets, and then I could pick between the artillery and the attack helicopters. Could I fly with the helicopters? Of course not, they said. I chose the artillery.

While the handlers looked for an artillery unit that would let me ride along, I took the advanced course on army life. The soldiers happily taught me important survival techniques, such as how to use the stiff collars on the flak jacket to sleep sitting up while appearing to be awake, and how to warm an MRE field ration in your armpit for thirty minutes. Even better was how to heat the heavy plastic pouch on a tank engine. I learned to prepare a decent peach cobbler from dehydrated fruit, crumbled crackers, sugar, and powdered creamer. Just add water and serve!

The nightly entertainment was passing around a flashlight with the *Sports Illustrated* swimsuit issue. The army was a giant repository of bad jokes and one-liners. Why does that thing have a head on it? So you don't lose your grip. I understood why comedian Bob Hope, a self-deprecating wise guy, had been so popular during World War II.

A big soldier was wheeled into our field hospital on a creaky gurney. He was a black man, but his face was gray, and someone had pulled up his uniform shirt to reveal a thick chest and stomach. He had been in a truck accident. I thought the guy looked bad. Later someone told me that when I saw him, he already was dead. My first casualty of the war.

ABC's Jim Wooten, one of those solid newspapermen who became network correspondents, took me aside after dinner. "It's good that you were upset by seeing that dead body at the hospital," he said. "Don't ever lose your sense of horror. You are going to see more bodies, and don't ever stop being shocked by it."

I felt such heaviness here, and there was so much idle time to wallow in it. I despaired because I was witnessing a tragedy. If Saddam kept up whatever he was doing—it wasn't clear to me exactly what he was doing—there would be a massive war. The two sides were hurtling toward each other, and there was no way to avoid the crash. I felt like a passenger in a fast car slipping on ice; all I could do was hold on.

The deepest, heaviest sadness came from the weight of all this military hardware, all these tanks and trucks and planes, and all these people armed and picking up steam, readying to roll on Iraq. There was little discussion in the US media about the long-term consequences of a war, and I personally never thought about it. Afterwards we would ask whether it was worth it.

Right then, I didn't think about what it meant. I thought only about how bloody and rough it was going to be, and about how long we were going to be there. The right or wrong of it seemed too far away to bother with. I knew that when the fighting started I would hope it went fast and hard so it ended quickly, much the way I appreciated the beautiful sunny days for bombing. I wondered about the Iraqi soldiers in their trenches and couldn't (and didn't) imagine how they were suffering. At night we saw flashes like heat lightning when bombs exploded on Iraqi positions, and the ground rumbled from miles away.

The low feelings were interrupted by pangs of guilt and doubt about Maru. I worried that she couldn't get along without me, and then I worried that she could. I missed celebrating Maru's twenty-ninth birthday and our fourth wedding anniversary. Instead, I visited an artillery brigade.

My escort, a Public Affairs officer, wasn't told exactly where to take me, but the artillery was somewhere to the east, so we put the setting sun at our backs and drove across the desert in a CUCV (or Commercial Utility Cargo Vehicle, and pronounced CUCK-VEE, even though it was a plain old pickup truck). We were hugging the Kuwaiti border, just south of where the Iraqis were dug in for the final stand. We passed a line of US tanks, some Bradley Fighting Vehicles, and then lonely groups of American soldiers in scattered foxholes.

We kept going, and I looked back to see the soldiers staring after us. Soon we were alone in the desert and heading down a dirt road that ended abruptly at a tall sand berm. The bumper was touching the berm before we realized we had been going northeast, not due east, and we were now close enough to pee into Iraq. Resisting the temptation to do just that, the escort slammed the truck into reverse, the wheels spun, and we roared backwards until it was safe to whirl around. I slumped down in my seat, waiting for an Iraqi bullet to crash through the back window. We raced toward the American frontline, and the soldiers stood up in alarm, weapons pointing at our rapidly advancing truck. We waved a friendly greeting, but they angrily shouted at us to slow down.

We found the artillery brigade, and that night the soldiers put me in a Humvee to watch a raid on Iraqi troops. The artillery had been pounding the Iraqis to clear the way for the eventual ground attack, which the soldiers agreed would happen soon. Everyone, me included, wondered what the ground attack would be like, and how we would perform in combat. The first sergeant, Lee Kane, said it best: "It's like having a baby. You don't know until it happens how you will react."

The Humvee smelled of hot coffee, cigarette smoke, and unwashed men—it reminded me of waiting in a duck blind, the same peaceful coziness and quiet anticipation that something big was going to happen involving loud weapons and adrenaline. The difference was, ducks could not shoot back, and people were going to die tonight.

The empty desert was completely dark, and we observed light discipline, meaning no unnecessary lights that would give away our location. I could barely see my hands. Command Sgt. Maj. Harold Shrewsberry was saying that Saddam was in trouble already, but if he really wanted deep shit all he had to do was launch a terrorist attack on army families back home. . . . I was dozing, comfy and warm.

There was a flash of light and a whoosh that rocked the Humvee and shook me awake. Shrewsberry said, "Here we go."

Rocket launchers and howitzers were lined up in a row across the desert, suddenly visible in the dark because of the white flames shooting from the tubes. The darkness went to light so suddenly that the scene looked like a black-and-white photograph. Rockets soared in long arcs toward the Iraqi bunkers a few miles north. Each rocket carried 644 fist-sized bomblets that floated to earth and blew up on top of tanks or in the faces of the dug-in soldiers.

Just as suddenly, the guns stopped like a switch had been thrown, and everything went dark and quiet. The troops, almost invisible again in the night, packed up the guns and rocket launchers to scoot out of range of Iraqi artillery returning fire.

Shrewsberry handed me a pair of night vision goggles that turned the sand a cool, fuzzy green. I noticed an American tank off to our side. The tanker noticed me at the same time, and the turret swung menacingly toward us and locked on our Humvee. The sergeant major saw the tank, too, and he jumped out and waved off the tank, just to be safe.

Still wound up from the raid, I threw down my sleeping bag in the sand and tried to rest. I had been asleep for a few hours when a soldier politely but firmly shook my sleeping bag. "Sir," he said, "it's already 7 o'clock," as if I had missed half the day. I wandered over to a fire pit heating a tub of water to warm little tins of ravioli, which tasted surprisingly good for breakfast.

The soldiers were excited about firing the guns for real. The only time they had fired them before was in training. You should check out inside the gun when it's firing, they said, everybody nodding that was a great idea. We can put you right inside a gun, they promised.

Stupidly, I agreed.

The 155mm howitzers were shaped like tanks with extra-long barrels. Thick as bank vaults, they were set up aiming at Iraq, and we stood around the heavy rear doors waiting for the signal to fire. A sergeant started telling me about the imminent ground attack. He knew I was a reporter, and that this information was highly classified, but I apparently had passed some unwritten test. He dragged his boot across the ground, and pointing with his toes, said, "This is us here, and this is the border." He made more lines in the sand that showed an uppercut punch straight into Kuwait, but the main force, including us, would move up to the west of Kuwait and make a sharp turn to the right to surprise the Iraqis. Looked smart to me, and confirmed what I had heard. I also realized that if I stayed with the artillery, I would be in a good position to cover the action. Then everybody started yelling, "Fire mission! Fire mission!"

A soldier pushed me inside the howitzer's small chamber that held the crew, and I scrunched down to fit onto a bench, bulky in my flak vest and half-blind from the helmet falling in my eyes. I looked up in time to see Spc. Ricardo Moyardo pull the lanyard, just a piece of rope connected to the firing mechanism. The breech slid back in a whumping concussion that boxed my ears. A few inches closer to my head, and I would have become the first journalistic casualty of Operation Desert Storm.

Somebody tossed me into a corner like a duffle bag, and I shoved my fingers into my ears. Wham! Moyardo fired off another round and the blast filled the close metal compartment with noise and pressure and dirt that knocked loose from every joint and crack. Wham! Each time Moyardo grabbed the lanyard, I braced and closed my eyes. Wham! After a few rounds I was covered with dirt and shaking all over. I shut my eyes earlier each time, but my nerve endings were snapping. The crew stopped firing only to swab the steaming barrel, releasing a chemical cloud that smelled of hot ammonia.

After twelve rounds, I sensed a break in the action and bolted out the back, just about falling on my face onto the sand. "Where are you going?" they laughed after me. Very funny. Outside I could see eight guns spitting fire and lobbing one-hundred-pound Joes, as in projos or projectiles, into Iraq. I stopped shaking but was still buzzing. As the soldiers said, it was high speed.

If I had asked, the soldiers probably would have let me pull the lanyard to fire a round, but that would have crossed the line between reporter and combatant. Being that close to the fighting helped me understand the experience of soldiers, but my job was not nearly as committed or dangerous as theirs. If I got hurt, it would be by accident or because I was near soldiers when they were attacked. I didn't have to kill anyone, and I could leave at anytime. If this were baseball, I would not be a player but a spectator, although one standing on the field.

The most challenging part of my job was figuring out what was happening on the battlefield around me, and in the rest of Saudi Arabia, in Iraq, and even at the United Nations and in Washington. I needed to see the big picture, or develop what the military people called "situational awareness." The first time I heard the phrase, it struck me that situational awareness was what I had sought during my entire career as a reporter. How do you figure out—and then describe—what is happening around you? That is the simple, lifelong challenge for a reporter.

I suppose situational awareness also was a good metaphor for understanding my own life and how I fit into the world. I always found it easier, safer, and more interesting, to figure out what other people were doing than to decipher the noise in my own head. I liked reporting because I could observe other people and let their experiences fill my life, instead of doing a lot of introspection or dwelling on my feelings. Maybe I had become addicted to Other People's Drama. Was there an OPD Syndrome? I didn't worry about it.

I briefly went back to the rear to call the office to say I would be out of touch. I asked Dale to call Maru occasionally. I did not tell my editor the ground war was about to start, despite the misleading news stories about peace talks, nor did I tell him the battle plan. I had made a promise of secrecy, I felt loyalty to the soldiers I was with, and I wasn't going to reveal information that could call in an Iraqi counterattack on my own head.

Maru was in Mexico with her family. I managed to get her on the phone and told her I would not be able to call for a few days, but to check with the office if she needed anything. If I only was able to make one call from the desert, it would be to file a story. I knew the desk would get in touch with Maru if something happened to me. Maru said coverage of the war was all over Mexican television, and she was worried I would be hurt. She and her family had lighted candles for me.

I still wasn't convinced there would be a ground attack, so I told her to relax and have fun with her family. Although I didn't realize it, this was a time that my lack of introspection caused a problem for the woman I loved. I ignored my own fear, so I assumed Maru would not be afraid, either. I was wrong.

The guns of the Forty-Second Field Artillery Brigade continued firing steadily on enemy positions, the final preparation for the ground attack. I was told to drop my gear with the brigade surgeon, Capt. David Lawhorn, thirty-four, of Chattanooga. His tent was stacked with junk food—M&Ms, Snickers, and lots of chocolate chip cookies. Most of the food came from well-meaning people back home. The soldiers lived on junk food, which they called "pogey bait" and was a major army food group. I hadn't had a Pop Tart since elementary school, but they were pretty good.

At 10 p.m., Doc Lawhorn ordered everyone, me included, to start taking little white pills to protect us from nerve agents. He passed out foil packets that resembled birth control pills. All through the night, soldiers came by asking for more pills because they had lost theirs or mistakenly had taken all the doses at once.

I mentioned to the Doc that I already had been given an anthrax vaccination. The military worried that Saddam had weaponized the common barnyard bacteria, so I had lined up for a shot with a bunch of soldiers outside a tarp. We were told to roll up one sleeve and walk single file through a gauntlet of medical people standing next to crates of vaccines and needles. I got in the line—I can't say I thought about it one way or another; I just did it—and one of the medical people jabbed me in the arm. Someone else handed me a piece of yellow notebook paper with the date and information about the vaccine, the batch number or something. I threw it into the trash.

Doc Lawhorn said the vaccine probably was a good precaution, but I also needed to take the pyridostigmine bromide pills to protect me from more dangerous nerve agents. I wasn't so sure about that. I didn't think Saddam was going to use chemical weapons, and while I understood the need to protect the troops, I figured I was just observing. The whole chemical thing seemed a little overblown. I had been lugging around a chemical suit and my gas mask, but the longer I carried the gear, the more I took it for granted.

Along with everyone else, I carried a pouch with an injector of atropine, a nerve blocker. The idea was to jab the injector into your thigh if you were gassed. At night I used the stiff little pouch for a pillow, until I heard about a sleeping soldier who accidentally triggered the atropine and injected himself in the head. It was the kind of story that probably was not true, but was much repeated.

The Doc was patient with me. You know the Lincoln Memorial on the back of a penny? You know those little columns? Doc asked. Two of those columns worth of nerve agent are enough to kill you.

I started taking the pills.

After sleeping a few hours, I felt Doc moving around the tent. It was dark, 5 a.m. on February 24, and drizzle tapped on the canvas. I was warm in my sleeping bag and didn't want to get up. Talking on a radio program from Washington, President Bush asked for a prayer for the troops. Then the radio reporter wondered what the war would mean for Bush's political future. Staff Sgt. Jeff Taylor, a twenty-five-year-old medic who was cleaning his M-16 for the final time before going into Iraq, barely looked up and spat out, "Who cares?"

It was time. We were told to go to "MOPP4," or the highest level of Mission Oriented Protective Posture, meaning, put on all the chemical gear. I tore open the bag carrying my chemical suit, which looked like a bulky snowsuit in a forest green camo pattern. The protective boots were weird rubber galoshes that laced up like Roman sandals. I struggled into the suit but left the boots in the bag.

One reason I was willing to wear the suit was to appear the same as the soldiers. I had read somewhere that snipers picked targets who wore unique clothing, thinking maybe they were important or special. I didn't want an Iraqi sniper to think I was special. The boots didn't matter so much because a sniper couldn't see them from far away. I went outside the tent and watched the howitzers fire on the area we were going to cross in a few hours. They called it "prepping the breach."

On either side of us, tanks and armored vehicles rumbled single file into Iraq. The display of force compared to nothing I had ever seen. I kept thinking it was such a waste, all this energy to restore things to the way they were before Saddam invaded Kuwait. What if we marshaled that power to build schools or hospitals, or to do something constructive? The engineers had put up a sign that read, "Welcome to Iraq," with arrows pointing to the "Beach" and "Golf Course." So far, this still felt like training. The guns were firing for real, but the rounds were hitting downrange and out of sight.

I was talking with the battery captain when a breathless lieutenant came running up: "Sir, there are reports of chemicals on the battlefield."

My stomach dropped. I had managed to convince myself that Saddam would not use chemical weapons, and now I wasn't fully protected. I ran back to the tent, plopped down on the ground, and asked a soldier to help me lace up the rubber boots.

When the guns paused from firing, we loaded up and crossed into Iraq, a heavily armed carnival caravan, with packs, sleeping bags, boxes of food, and crates of water bottles lashed to the sides of the artillery and Humvees. The guns rolled north and fired all day, and at night they circled around like covered wagons. In the center of the protective ring was the TOC, or tactical operations center. I wasn't sure what happened inside the TOC, which was the brigade's classified nerve center, because it was off-limits to me.

The brigade was a pack of its own, and the soldiers pulled in tighter now that the hunt was on. I was on the outer ring, riding with the lower-ranking troops. I was free to interview soldiers and grabbed commanders if I needed official information for a story, but I didn't have access to the secrets inside the headquarters. A lot of what I did was to stand around and watch.

When we settled in for the night, my escort, whom the troops nicknamed "Pathfinder" because he was not great at finding his way, announced that in the morning he was taking me back to the rear. I was stunned because the ground war had just begun. I can't go back now, I pleaded, but he insisted. There was no way I was leaving, but I didn't think I could stay without an escort from Public Affairs.

I explained the situation to the brigade commander, Col. Morris J. Boyd, forty-seven. He said it was no big deal. I could stay with the brigade, even if my escort left. Out here, Colonel Boyd was the absolute boss. "There are two ways we could do it," he said. "I could brief you every day about our operations, and you could write your stories. Or I could read you in."

I thought it was a trick question, because option two sounded like unfiltered access to the brigade's operations and secrets. If he was going to read me in to the battle plan, I would be inside the brigade during combat. This was a dream of every reporter.

"The catch is you would have to stay for the duration," Boyd said, answering my unspoken question. "You would know too much to leave."

That did change my calculation. The expected length of the war and the anticipated casualties were highly classified, but it could take a couple of months to clear the Iraqis out of Kuwait. I had heard casualty estimates in the thousands for US troops. Everyone expected a few reporters to be killed. I didn't want to commit myself to such a long time, but it was a unique opportunity.

The other part of the deal was that Boyd's S-2, or intelligence officer, would read my stories for a security review. The brigade did not have a media person, so "The Deuce" would perform the task. I didn't have to think long about the ground rules. "I'm in," I said.

As Colonel Boyd was walking back to the TOC, I said, "Sir, I just want to tell you that I feel privileged to be here."

He came back and said, "You are getting to see something that not many people see. The sergeant major and I are going to quit after this one and go fishing. No more of this for us. We're going to leave it to the younger guys."

The camp was dark at night, except for the occasional sliver of light when someone opened the door of the TOC, which was an expandable trailer. The TOC operated all night, with people and information going in and out around the clock. We slept nearby on the open ground, and I was advised to bed down near a vehicle so I wouldn't be run over in the darkness. I put my sleeping bag next to Pathfinder's truck and tried to sleep. I had been on the ground for an hour when a soldier came over and stood above me.

"The colonel wants to know if you want to sit in on the meeting," he said.

I jumped up and followed him closely in the dark up the steps to the command trailer. He opened the door to the TOC, and the light blasted my eyes. It took a minute to recognize the brigade commander without his helmet. I was beginning to think it was part of his head. Colonel Boyd introduced me to about twenty of his young officers and sergeants, including one woman.

They stood in front of two large maps, one showing US positions and the other showing the Iraqis, right down to individual units. This was exactly what I had been trying to figure out since August. Here was the battle plan, and it was close to the one I had imagined. I kept thinking I was not supposed to see the map, but I couldn't keep my eyes off it. I remembered being thirteen and catching a look at a *Playboy* magazine.

"What kind of security are we going to have?" Colonel Boyd asked.

"Fifty-fifty, sir," one of the officers replied.

"What's 50–50?"

"Half of each section up and half asleep," was the answer.

"We need to run a sanity check on that," Colonel Boyd responded. "I'm not expecting a full, frontal attack tonight, but we've got to be on guard against a straggler coming in with a grenade who wants to do his bit for Allah. Let's have good security, but let them get some rest."

Capt. Bill Cain, the intelligence officer, briefed everyone on the disposition of Iraqi troops. I admired how he spoke of the Iraqis in an almost intimate way, as in, "He's thinking we are coming from the south." In a calm and measured way, Cain described two nearby Republican Guard units on the move. One appeared to be heading toward Basra and one toward Baghdad, but neither was moving to engage US forces.

Colonel Boyd said he wasn't interested in fighting over a piece of ground: this was a movement to contact, not a movement to territory. To me that meant they were planning to chase Saddam's elite Republican Guard and destroy it, not just drive it out of Kuwait. They spoke in a bewildering array of acronyms and jargon. Even after covering the military every day for a couple of years, I wasn't sure about FLOTs, MSRs, or phase lines. Like a lot of people at the Pentagon, I had spent more time worrying about budgets, Congress, and interservice rivalries than actually fighting a war.

After the meeting, I tried to get comfortable on my little piece of ground next to the truck. Pathfinder was inside the cab, already asleep. He was sick of me, and I wanted to stretch out and be by myself, so he slept inside the truck while I slept outside on the ground. I was excited about the war and my new access to the brigade leadership. I wasn't really afraid, but it was energizing. I liked the tunnel vision of war, the absolute focus on life and death. There was nothing to think about except fighting: no grocery shopping, no bills to pay, no politics, and no plotting and scheming. Even though I was just along for the ride, I liked being part of something big, something that mattered, something that would change the world.

I did worry about one thing: What if the soldiers I was with made a mistake or fired on the wrong target? What if they committed a war crime or an atrocity? Would I betray them and write the story, or betray my readers and not write it? For my own reasons, I wanted them to have a good war.

I drifted off to sleep only to wake with a start: I couldn't breathe and my eyes stung. Gas attack! I sat up coughing and looked around. All quiet in the camp. Nobody was racing for cover or putting on masks.

Then I realized I was sleeping under the tailpipe, and Pathfinder had started the engine. Blue exhaust, kept close to the ground by the cold night air, enveloped me. Furious, I struggled to get out of the army sleeping bag (labeled with extensive instructions for use, including, "How to make an emergency exit." Really). I expertly made the emergency exit and banged on the window, trying to reach through and hit Pathfinder in the head.

"What are you doing?" I yelled.

"I was cold," he replied, "so I turned on the heater."

I reinserted myself in the bag on the other side of the vehicle, away from the exhaust, and fell asleep.

Pathfinder was a good sport and left me with the brigade the next morning. I printed a story on my battery-powered printer and showed it to the intelligence officer, Captain Cain. The Deuce looked at it briefly and handed it back. After that, he didn't ask to read any of my stories. I asked Pathfinder to hand-deliver the story to the media pool office in the rear.

I was told to ride with John Woodley, the command sergeant major, and his driver Spc. Stan "Tex" Lenox, whose soothing drawl made me sleepy. Tex's dream was to return home and become a deputy sheriff in Argyle, Texas. ("No sir, they don't make any socks there.")

I felt safe with Tex, even when he drove us into a minefield. Actually, it was Colonel Boyd who drove us into the minefield, and he was the boss, so Tex followed. Colonel Boyd was buzzing all the time and could not be still.

Tired of standing around our camp, he jumped into his Humvee and told the driver to get moving. Tex tried to keep up, with Command Sergeant Major Woodley in the passenger seat and me in the back of our Humvee, known as the Ugly Mule.

We raced across the sand until Boyd's driver hit the brakes, hard, and Tex stopped right behind him. The two Humvees were bumper to bumper in the middle of the empty desert. I looked out the window and saw why we had stopped so suddenly: we had driven into a cluster of unexploded bomblets, possibly dropped from rockets we had fired in the days before the ground attack. The bomblets were small cylinders shaped like soup cans. I knew that bumping them could detonate the bomblets, and despite the diminutive name, they could kill us all.

We sat for a minute while the sergeant major and the colonel talked on the radio about what to do. Tex and I looked out the window at the ground. I was wearing a helmet and flak vest over my chemical suit, but right then I wasn't worried about protecting my chest or head. I moved over toward the middle of the Humvee to sit above the transmission, hoping to put a little more metal between the bomblets and my bottom. Now I understood the jokes about sitting on your helmet.

Woodley, the command sergeant major and the most senior enlisted man in the brigade, decided he would get out and guide us backwards and away from the bomblets. He was afraid to continue forward, and since we were in the rear vehicle, it made sense for us to back out first. Woodley led the way. He was forty-seven years old, most of those years spent in the army, and he was chesty and stern with a deep, gravelly voice. Nobody messed with him, and even Colonel Boyd treated him more like a peer than a subordinate.

He opened the door and stepped down onto the sand, one boot at a time. I didn't think of him as especially graceful, but he could have been a ballet dancer walking on his toes to get behind the Ugly Mule. He waved at Tex to drive straight back, directing him to follow the tracks we had made going in. Tex eased on the accelerator and backed us toward the sergeant major and out of danger. When the Ugly Mule was safe, Woodley performed the same maneuver with Colonel Boyd's Humvee.

One brush with death was not going to slow down Colonel Boyd. We were still zipping around the desert looking for action when a chaplain sped by in a Humvee flying a tall black flag with a white cross. The chaplain meant well, but he could have been a Crusader coming across the desert, with "Spiritual Maintenance Vehicle" painted on the windshield. Colonel Boyd roared over and made the chaplain take down the flag, explaining—well, yelling—that this was a war between armies, not religions.

On the morning of February 26, we were up at 4 a.m. It was so dark I couldn't find the Ugly Mule. I stumbled around on the sand, groggy and sick to my stomach because of the lack of sleep and an overload of junk food, dragging my gear and my computer, hoping I wouldn't be left behind when the brigade moved out. That would be dangerous, and worse, embarrassing.

Colonel Boyd snuck up on me in the blackness and I jumped. He was vibrating with enthusiasm, which I had learned was his normal state. "I remember what you said yesterday, and it was very astute, that there is a lot of movement and a lot of energy expended to get to this point," Boyd declaimed in his full briefing voice.

I was barely focused. I enjoyed military theory as much as the next guy, but not at 4 a.m.

He droned on, "but you've got to remember, that it all ends with putting steel on the target. We tend to focus on the inputs and forget what is important is the output . . ."

Go away, colonel.

By 10:30 a.m., we had traveled seventy-one miles. I heard commanders on the military radio order the troops to let the Iraqis withdraw if they were on foot but to shoot up the enemy vehicles. Loose columns of Iraqi prisoners walked by us going the opposite way toward Saudi Arabia. Their uniforms were filthy, and they had no equipment, not even a change of clothes. The smell of them hit me like a punch.

Colonel Boyd had ants in his pants again, and off we sped in search of action. I could hear the whine of tank engines, the rattle of tracks, and scattered machine-gun fire. There were deep, rumbling explosions in the distance when bombs hit the ground. We were in untracked desert, with no buildings, roads, or landmarks. There were no trees and little vegetation, just varieties of sand: soft as pudding, gravelly mix, and hard-packed.

We pulled up onto a dune next to an American tank, and a startled tanker looked down on us and said, "Sir, uh, there is contact just over this hill." That just made Colonel Boyd want to go closer, but he relented, and we drove back to the safety of the pack. The convoy headed deeper into Iraq.

At the next meeting in the TOC, one of the junior officers wanted an accounting of everyone's position on the battlefield for his planning. Colonel Boyd got mad: "We happen to be in the middle of a bloody firefight. We don't have time for that. You guys are going to get the basics right or one day you are going to get us all killed." Everybody looked at the floor until the storm passed.

We stopped for a few hours at night. Woodley dug a little pit in the sand for a fire and heated up a metal coffee pot. The coffee was delicious. In the deep darkness, we stood around the Ugly Mule, ate junk food, and watched a rocket raid chew up an Iraqi convoy.

Everyone was hidden in darkness until the raid began. The first rockets launched in a whoosh of white fire. Then there were little red bursts in the sky downrange, and the bomblets rained on the Iraqi convoy. When a bomblet found a vehicle it started a yellow fire that sparked up when it hit ammo or fuel. Soon there was a row of golden balls burning on the horizon. At the best explosions, the soldiers went ooohhh and aaahhh like the Fourth of July and yelled "hooah" and "Get some," until the sergeant major reminded them, with an Alabama drawl roughed up by too many Marlboros, "Hey, don't forget there are guys dying out there."

One of the younger officers, watching the convoy with night-vision goggles, said, "Fuck 'em." We laughed, but everyone knew what was happening. They tried to pretend it was the same as training—that was the emotional protection.

I fell into it, too. If I had tried to open myself to all that pain, I would have dissolved. It was easier and safer to take one step back and maintain my distance. My job required me to be open and sensitive to what was happening around me, but I had to protect myself emotionally if I were going to be out here for months. I was watching, I told myself, not participating. That was my job.

Taylor, the medic, talked to me that night about his job and the irony of being a medical person at war: "I'm in the business of saving lives, not taking them. But if it comes down to him or me, it's not going to be a coin toss."

As we continued to roll through Iraq on the morning of February 27, the soldiers' morale was high and we were moving fast. I bounced along in the rear of a vehicle, trying to take notes and listening to the back-and-forth on the military radio. Someone said, "See you in Basra," and asked, "Permission to stop for tail?" A more mature voice answered back: "Chatter is fine, but we've got a job to do."

There were unexploded US missiles in the sand, pointy noses buried like lawn darts, sharp fins in the air. They might have been duds, but maybe they were just waiting for a nudge to explode. We drove by Iraqi tanks with the turrets popped off as easily as caps off beer bottles. In one crater was a crumble of metal bits, as if the tank had been run through a grinder, forming a burnt metal nest for the chunky engine block. Armored personnel carriers burned and sizzled, shrunken bodies were charred and black. A helmet and uniform were spread on top of a greasy smear in the sand. Body parts. Blankets, helmets, boots, and scraps of paper blowing.

Our convoy stopped in front of an Iraqi bunker complex. Before we went closer, the commanders wanted to confirm no one was inside hiding. Just one Iraqi with an automatic weapon could kill a lot of people if we were close enough. The guns set up and eight howitzers pounded the bunker for fifteen minutes. The ground shook, and the guns spit yellow fire. In the daylight, the rounds leaving the barrels reminded me of golf balls heading down the fairway. The targets were not the luxury bunkers where Saddam and his generals took shelter. These were holes scratched in the dirt, covered with sheets of tin and draped with blankets, or simply metal culverts buried under the sand.

When we got closer, we found hundreds of defeated Iraqi troops waiting to surrender. At first, the US soldiers weren't sure how to react, glaring at the enemy because that's what they thought was expected. Then an American threw down a water bottle. Someone else threw down an MRE. The Iraqis were tired and hungry and must have been frightened about what was going to happen to them. Some did not even have boots, and their feet were covered with sores. They waved quiet thank-yous for the food and water.

Then one of the Iraqis gave a thumbs-up and said, "Bush Number One! Down Saddam!" It wasn't funny or even sad, but it was telling. Spc. William Raymond, twenty-one, of North Highlands, California, told me, "Yesterday I wanted to kill those guys. Today I just want to hug 'em."

The US soldiers swept through the bunkers looking for stragglers. Inside they found a metal box with a padlock. They got excited and wanted to break it open, hoping to find secret military documents or at least a cool souvenir, maybe a pistol. They checked the box for booby traps, and then pounded off the lock. One of them carefully opened the lid and found the treasure: two potatoes, probably the last food in the bunker. Soldiers picked up abandoned Iraqi gear, ammo, and other souvenirs. They grabbed a small plastic bag of Iraqi dog tags that had been sealed for safekeeping.

I used the time riding in the Humvee to write. I had to look ahead for a clear patch of desert to type, otherwise the bumps sent my computer flying off my lap. When I had a story written, I printed a hard copy on a battery-operated printer. Then when I saw people going to the rear, especially on a helicopter, I ran over and asked them to deliver it to the military press operation. Everybody was happy to help. One day the colonel let me use the brigade radio to dictate a story. The radio operator read a copy of my story to another operator at the edge of our radio's range. Then that operator read it to someone else, until the story was relayed to the press operation.

The sky was gray and dark, and I could see for miles across the unbroken desert, as featureless as the surface of the moon. Bolts of lightning came straight down on the plain. There was so much armor I imagined a herd of iron buffalo. The tanks chewed up big sand moguls that would have tipped over a car. A-10 attack jets, called Warthogs because of their blunt appearance, banked and rolled leisurely above us, the sound of their Gatling guns like the tearing of huge metal blankets. The convoy made a sharp right turn toward the final battle in Kuwait.

When we crossed the border, someone on the radio announced, "At 1643 hours on 27 February Thunder Brigade is in Kuwait." Just then flashes erupted to the right, bright lights that appeared to be strobes or cameras flashing. I thought, either some Iraqi is taking our picture, or he's trying to kill us. I was wearing my helmet and flak jacket but I noticed, as if for the first time, that the door of the Humvee was 1/4-inch plastic. The door would not have stopped an arrow, let alone an armor-piercing round. I didn't hear noise from the weapons firing at us, so I hoped the muzzle flashes were still out of range.

Then I heard thumping rotors overhead. Roaring up from the south, a US attack helicopter flew across the desert straight toward the shooting Iraqis. The helicopter was so low it looked like a dragonfly gliding above the sand. It dipped its nose and fired, sending out a string of white pearls of light that settled on the Iraqi armored vehicle and turned it into a ball of fire. No more shooting. The helicopter banked and turned away from us. The convoy moved on.

There was fighting all night, and then it stopped.

President Bush came on the radio at 5 a.m. on Thursday, February 28 to announce a pause in offensive operations. Everyone around me was shocked. We were just getting going and now it was time to stop? It was hard for the soldiers to understand what was happening. We had the Iraqis on the run, and we could have destroyed all their tanks and equipment. No one I saw wanted to kill more soldiers, but neither did they want them to escape back to Iraq with their weapons.

A few people thought we should march on Baghdad and dig out the root of the problem—Saddam—but the commanders explained the mission was to drive Iraq out of Kuwait, and then go home. There was not going to be an occupation of Kuwait, and no one I was with even hinted at occupying Iraq. Still, there was confusion and disappointment. A soldier told me, "I don't want my son to have to come back here and finish this thing. Let's do it."

There was no celebration of victory. The only cheer went up when we were told we could remove the chemical suits, which were lined with charcoal and had stained our skin black as coal miners. I had been sleeping in my suit and even my boots during the short nights. When I pulled down the zipper, the sour smell of my own body just about knocked me over. I cleaned up with a wet towel and wrote a story about the end of the war and the reluctance of the soldiers to stop so soon. I printed a copy and gave it to a general heading to the rear in a helicopter. I sent a backup version on the army teleprinter.

Colonel Boyd gathered his officers. He acknowledged that everyone was exhausted and that they should force the soldiers to sleep; then they all had to get haircuts. When we go home, Boyd told the officers, "We can say we played, we played big time." They had fired 9,144 rounds from the howitzers and 2,700 rockets. We spent the day searching for souvenirs, eating junk food, and watching the engineers blow up Iraqi vehicles with carefully set charges.

By the next day, I was convinced the war really had ended. I had not expected this kind of victory, and I had not expected it in only four days. We listened to civilian news broadcasts on a shortwave radio, and the reporters said the US troops arriving in Kuwait City were being greeted as heroes.

Out here the sand was blowing horizontally in a stinging, blinding veil. Driving was impossible, and even walking was dangerous because I couldn't see three feet. The sky at noon was dark as midnight because the retreating Iraqis had torched the oil fields, and inky clouds of smoke blocked the sun. We hunkered down under the black sky and whipping sand.

When the sandstorm cleared, I said good-bye and promised to send the brigade copies of my stories, which I had filed at least once a day. Bill Cain, the intelligence officer, confessed that I wasn't at all what he had imagined a reporter to be. It wasn't like in the movies, he said, where the reporters and the soldiers were going at each other all the time. Colonel Boyd presented me with a brigade coin, which was an honor. I understood that if someone from the brigade ever asked to see the coin, and I couldn't produce it, the drinks were on me.

I never was a member of their pack, but the brigade had let me run alongside for a few thrilling days during the hunt of their lives. I was proud to have been with them. The soldiers presented me with a Russian-style, Iraqi tanker's helmet as a souvenir, and one of the Iraqi dog tags they had found abandoned in the desert bunker.

I hitched a ride back to Saudi Arabia with some National Guardsmen in two Humvees. We stayed on a marked route through the desert to avoid hitting a mine or unexploded ordnance, and we left the headlights off so we would not attract fire. We pulled up suddenly at a cluster of tents. A dozen Arabs in fatigues came running at us, screaming commands and waving their weapons. We hit the brakes and my eyes went wide. The soldiers turned out to be friendly Egyptians. They bummed cigarettes and confirmed we were headed in the right direction.

We were in a tight little convoy when the vehicle ahead of us—the only thing I could see were the brake lights—vanished in the dark. We jumped out and ran forward until we saw the back end of the Humvee sticking up in the air, the rear wheels spinning. The front was jammed into a waist-high trench. I guessed the trench had been made by our allies the Syrians, because I remembered the sergeant major telling me, admiringly, "Those boys can dig."

No one was hurt badly, but everybody seemed paralyzed looking at the buried Humvee. What are we gonna do? I dunno, what do you wanna do? They went back and forth, and I was afraid we were going to spend all night there.

Someone wanted to light a flare. No, another one said, we might call in an air strike on ourselves. I just wanted to get home.

In this case, I wasn't going to be a passive observer. I rummaged around in the vehicles until I found an "entrenching tool" (in the army, it could never just be a shovel) and started hacking at the sand. Everybody watched me dig. "Isn't there another shovel?" I asked. Somebody started digging in the dark on the other side of the vehicle. Then silence. "I don't hear digging over there!" I yelled, sweating now and increasingly angry. Dig, dig. Silence. "I don't hear shoveling!" Dig, dig. We broke down the trench wall, used a cable to pull out the stuck vehicle, and rumbled south.

I needed a phone. I had not talked to the office since before the ground attack, and I wanted to check in. When we reached the Saudi border, I convinced the guys to stop at a hotel by promising to treat them all to phone calls home. They hadn't talked to their families in weeks. It was Friday afternoon in Washington, and my coworkers would be clearing their desks to head across the street to Stan's bar.

At a worn and dusty roadside motel, I explained to the clerk at the front desk that we just wanted to make a few phone calls, but I would happily pay for a room. I was excited to talk to the office. I wanted a friendly voice from home, a pat on the back for a job well done, and a cash bonus.

I dialed the number in Washington, and the editor on duty answered.

"Where have you been?" he demanded.

"Uh, Iraq and Kuwait?"

The editor did not think that was funny. "Why didn't you file?"

I held the phone to my ear, sick to my stomach. Only a couple of my stories had gotten through, the editor said, and they were days late, too stale to use. There was no record of what I had seen, no story, and therefore I had failed as a reporter in the most fundamental way.

I didn't say anything. I was disappointed but not crushed. I had experienced a war and had seen men at their best and at their worst. I was more mad than anything, mad at the military for not delivering my stories as they had promised and mad at myself for believing they would. I just wanted a hot meal, a shower, and a bed with sheets. I kept quiet, hoping the editor would forgive my failure. I asked him, "What should I do?"

"If you want to salvage anything," he said, "you better sit down and write the best story of your life."

After their calls home, the guys wanted to continue to the base camp, so we said good-bye. I got a room, ordered a pot of coffee, and started to write. I had a lot of material, too much for one newspaper story, so I told my own story of watching the artillery help win the war in one hundred hours. I worked fast because Friday night was not a good time to send out a long story; Saturday papers were thin. The sooner I got it in, the more likely it would be used. I wrote fast and easily—the experience was still fresh. I was happy writing, energized again.

The story recounted my time with the artillery brigade, the people I had met, how it felt sitting inside the howitzer during a raid, driving into the minefield, and watching the Iraqi convoy be destroyed. I described the fear and bravery of the soldiers, their quiet competence, and their nagging concern that the war had ended without getting Saddam.

I read the story one last time, hooked up the computer to the telephone in my room, and dialed. Nothing. I dialed again. Nothing. The connection wasn't working. I had to get through to Washington. Every minute of delay meant another paper that would not get my story in time to publish. I could picture the time zones across the continental United States as newspaper deadlines hit from east to west. I had to move fast because I would not get a second chance to make this right.

I took the computer down to the front desk and tried to explain the problem to the clerk. He just shrugged his shoulders to say how sorry he was.

"The room phone is not working," I said, my voice rising. "I need to use the switchboard."

"No, that is not possible," he said. "The room phones are for guests."

"But it's not working!"

"I am very sorry, sir."

I mumbled some kind of apology, put my head down and pushed my way behind the front desk near the switchboard. I dropped to my knees, pulled a screwdriver out of my bag, and removed the wall plate where the main phone lines were hidden.

"Sir! What are you doing? You cannot do that!"

"Sorry, I'm really sorry," I said, blocking the computer with my body. "I'll just be a minute."

Inside the wall, I found the connections and attached two alligator clips. I hit the code to dial Washington and heard the happy buzz and click when the two computers connected like old friends. I called to confirm that the story had arrived and answered questions from the desk. Then I treated myself to that hot meal, long shower, and a bed with sheets.

# 12

# A BABY, A BALLET, AND A BOOK

— ON HAPPINESS —

A week later I was on a flight home. Dale told me the only reaction to my final story was about the Iraqi dog tag I had been given as a souvenir. The way I had worded the story, some readers got the erroneous impression I had desecrated the body of an Iraqi soldier. The complaints came from US veterans who understood better than I did that a dog tag represented a real person and the link to his family.

Since my first day on the job, Dale had warned me that most errors started with a seemingly minor detail, because we carefully checked the big, controversial things. It was the little things that could trip you up, he always said. In this case, I should have been more precise in describing how I got the dog tag, or just left it out of the story. Dale apologized for not catching it, either.

The dog tag, with the tiny Arabic writing, made me uncomfortable anyway; at some unconscious level I felt its power. I mailed it to the International Committee of the Red Cross with a letter about how I had obtained it, and my sincere apologies. I asked them to please try to return it to the soldier's family.

Scripps Howard treated me like a returning hero and sent me to speak about my experiences in cities where we had newspapers, including Cincinnati, which also was the corporate headquarters. The host for my talk at the Queen City Club was Charles Scripps, a grandson of the company founder, and a kind and soft-spoken man. We talked about beer, astronomy, and just about everything except for the newspaper business. He thanked me for all I had done for the company, which seemed weird because I was the one grateful to the Scripps and Howard families for letting me run around the world for the previous decade.

The next day Bill Burleigh, the corporate boss who seven years before had approved my assignment to Mexico City, gave me a ride to the airport. That was the kind of gesture that stayed with me. He was many levels above me, but all he wanted to talk about was my future. I told him I loved being a reporter, and that I hoped to write books someday. Burleigh was full of encouragement and assured me I had more good things ahead.

Back at my cubicle in the Washington bureau, piled with yellowed, unread newspapers, reports from think tanks, news releases, receipts that I needed to submit for reimbursement, and boxes of old notebooks, I fell into a funk. My life felt like the pile on my desk: clogged with things that didn't matter. The whole Washington scene was depressing. I was drowning in the vacuous talk, rote political arguments, and petty disputes and intrigue that were the focus of capital life. When you met someone, they wanted to know your title to determine your worth. Even parties felt like work with drinks.

I had just witnessed more than one million people locked in the death grip of combat. The stakes were control of Middle East oil, which meant the entire world depended on the outcome. There was clarity and purpose covering the war. I didn't wish for another war, but I missed the stripped-down focus on something important and the feeling of being at the center of things. The camaraderie of reporters in the field had vanished, too, now that we were back in our offices. Soldiers often said they preferred to be deployed, and some struggled at home. Once you experienced life in the field—the danger but also the closeness with your comrades and the sense of mission—you wanted to go again. I needed something bigger.

"I might have a book idea for you." The caller was Bill Burleigh from corporate. I thought we had been making small talk about my future on the ride to the airport, but shortly after my visit he met a Gulf War vet with a story to tell. The soldier was an army doctor who had been shot down, badly wounded, and captured by the Iraqis.

When her helicopter crashed into pieces behind enemy lines, Maj. Rhonda Cornum was presumed killed in action. By the time the Red Cross found her alive with other POWs in Baghdad, the war was over and nobody paid much attention. CBS reporter Bob Simon and three members of his crew also had been captured by the Iraqis, and their release after the war was covered heavily in the media. But few people knew about this army doctor who also had been held prisoner.

I was in good with the women in Army Public Affairs, who appreciated my stories about women in combat in Panama and the Gulf War, so they vouched for me. Major Cornum and I spent a day together, but it took all my skills to get even the barest story out of her.

"It was not that big a deal," she said.

She had gone in to rescue a downed F-16 pilot, only to be shot down herself. Five soldiers on her rescue helicopter were killed in the crash, and Cornum—with both arms broken and a bullet in her back—was captured with two other soldiers and held prisoner. Sounded like a pretty good story to me.

"If you don't write it down, it didn't happen," I told her. When she reluctantly agreed to do a book, I interviewed Cornum, her family, and army colleagues, and I turned the whole thing into a story in her words, sort of like being a rewrite at City News. I worked on the manuscript every day from 5 a.m. until 9 a.m., when I went to my day job at the Washington bureau.

Cornum insisted my name be on the cover with hers. "If people don't like it," she joked, "I'm going to blame you."

When the first box of books arrived from the publisher, Maru hovered over me while I gingerly picked out the first copy. I gently opened the pages, starting from the covers and working toward the center, the way I had been taught in school to open a new book without breaking the spine.

"You did it, Pito!" Maru said, hugging me while I held the book, proud and relieved it was finished.

I was afraid to read the book in print, fearing it was not as good as it could be, but Cornum was happy, and the reviews were enthusiastic. The *New York Times* named *She Went to War* a "Notable Book of the Year," and just as importantly to me, it was assigned reading at some of the military training schools.

The book left less time for Maru, but she had started dancing again with Mexican friends. They practiced after work in church basements and sewed costumes by hand. She formed her own group, the Maru Montero Dance Company, and began to get bookings around Washington. Maru did everything all the way, and then pushed it harder. Soon she was performing at the Kennedy

Center and the White House and getting rave reviews in the *Washington Post,* which called her new company "magic."

A dance company for her and a book for me felt like enough to keep us busy, until Maru declared that we had to move to a house: "I'm not having a baby in an apartment." I don't remember discussing a baby, or that we needed a house to have one, but thankfully I just went along. I did insist that if we were going to upgrade from our little condo to a real house, it would have to be in the outer suburbs and priced below my absolute limit, because we still couldn't afford the city. The house Maru picked was, of course, way over my absolute limit and still urban enough to "walk to sushi."

I was quietly anxious about having a baby because of what I had experienced in Kuwait and Iraq. After the war I did a lot of reporting about a mysterious illness called Gulf War Syndrome, which had sickened thousands of vets. Soldiers I had been with complained of strange rashes, fatigue, and muscle aches. I felt fine, so far. I just hoped I hadn't damaged myself in some unseen way that would be passed on to our unborn child, among the generation called "Desert Stork" babies. Maru knew what she wanted and got pregnant as soon as we moved into our new house. The next summer we had a perfect, beautiful, and healthy baby we named Isabella.

I had read about tears of joy, but it always sounded like an oxymoron, or something that happened to other people. Tears meant fear or sorrow, not happiness. Maru was in the hospital bed resting from the birth. On her chest was the baby, swaddled in a blanket and wearing a little cap over her black hair. Maru handed Isabella up to me for the first time, and I felt I was taking a very large, warm burrito into my arms. I wasn't sure how to hold her, but once I got her cradled into my arms she looked up into my face. Her eyes were dark like her mother's, and I was overcome with emotion, with happiness and completeness, like something missing had been found. I sobbed tears of joy.

From that moment, the three of us were inseparable. I couldn't wait to get home after work to see Isabella. I got up early with her, so Maru could sleep before I went to the office. Some mornings I pretended I was covering a story on Capitol Hill, just to steal an extra hour with the baby. The three of us went to art exhibits, movies, and neighborhood parks. We took long walks every day through the summer and fall and into winter. At our favorite sushi restaurant, we put Isabella on a blanket under the table, where she slept happily through dinner.

No one had told me a child would change my life, not that I would have listened or understood. Nor did I realize how happy and fulfilled I could feel married to the right woman. Some of the meaning and purpose I had sought covering stories was being siphoned off to my new family, and I liked it. At the same time, I felt a sense of accomplishment publishing my first book, and it led to more writing offers. I also was proud of all Maru had accomplished with her dance company. Our lives had taken another interesting turn, once again with little forethought from me, and I felt my heart expand with love and possibility.

# 13

## RESCUE IN SOMALIA

—— ON ATTITUDE ——

Maru, our 4-month-old baby, and I were at my parents' house in Chicago for Isabella's baptism and first Christmas, when the call came from the desk. By now, my mom dreaded those calls, because it meant I was going some place dangerous. This time Dale had a destination that could not have been more frightening: Somalia.

By late 1992, the African country had broken down and people were starving. When the government collapsed, warring clans prevented food from getting to those who needed it. The images on television were horrific, and American politicians asked, why do we have this big military if we don't use it to help? President George H. W. Bush ordered US troops to beat back the warlords and deliver food to the hungry. Dale wanted me to be there to cover it.

Once again, I kissed Maru before leaving for the airport. But for the first time before going to war, I also kissed our child good-bye. So many times previously I had been able to switch off my gentler emotions to chase a story. This time my feelings and responsibility as a husband and father overwhelmed my professionalism as a reporter. I felt fear and dread, plus pain and guilt for leaving them. The story was the biggest in the world, but surely other reporters could cover it. I never had declined an assignment, however, and I wasn't going to now.

We stood together one final time at the door, the three of us. I had my arm around Maru, who was holding the baby. I tried to make Isabella smile up at me, even though my tears were falling on her blanket.

A few days later, I joined 169 Marines and their families in a parking lot at Camp Pendleton, California. Their commander, Lt. Col. Pete James, forty-two, called everyone in close one last time. "To the families, you have my pledge I'll do everything I can to bring every Marine home. Because they are dear to me. They are dear to me." There were hugs and tears and nervous laughter.

A little girl in pink barrettes, who was going to spend Christmas without her father, shouted over and over: "I don't like good-byes! I don't like good-byes!"

We made refueling stops in New York, Rome, and Cairo before landing in Mogadishu, the capital of Somalia. By the time we arrived, the chartered jet was littered with discarded newspapers and magazines and messy food trays, but the civilian flight attendants were pleased to be doing their part to help people in need. One of them told the Marines she was proud of them, and that "the Big Guy doesn't forget."

Jet-lagged and apprehensive about what was ahead, we shuffled down the steps off the plane and into Africa. A cool breeze blew in from the choppy waters of the Indian Ocean. The air was humid, and the terrain around the airport was covered with thick green vegetation. The natural surroundings were verdant and pristine, but everything made by humans was broken, toppled, or smashed. Rubbish sat in smoldering piles amid abandoned cars and aircraft engines, stripped of parts and wires. Hundreds of people watched us from just off the tarmac, more curious than threatening.

The only civilian among the Marines, I climbed up into the open rear of a five-ton truck. We sat on benches facing each other, our backs exposed to the street. The Marines carried their weapons, stocks down and barrels up, between their legs. They lugged seabags filled with clothes and supplies, including cases of industrial-strength bug spray labeled "Permethrin Arthropod Repellent." I had a knapsack for my computer and notebooks, plus an old parachute bag for clothes, snack food, a roll of toilet paper, a pack of baby wipes, and ski goggles for blowing sand.

The Marines were taking malaria pills and had received as many as ten injections to protect them from typhoid, cholera, plague, and hepatitis—not just the "A" variety, but also B, C, D, and E. They were warned about exotic health risks such as schistosomiasis, which was caused by a parasite that burrowed into human skin, and told not to eat or drink anything unless it was prepared by the US government. I had gone to an international travel center for my own shots, but my biggest worry during any rough travel was a common but debilitating stomach bug.

The health and environmental risks were bad enough, but then we rolled out of the airport into a lawless city. I had been to some tough places before, but none like Somalia. Dented cars swerved through pitted streets crowded with people. Horns honked and trucks rumbled past vendors selling trinkets and clothes. Stripped-down jeeps were mounted with heavy weapons, and even boys carried automatic rifles. Young men, lean and hungry and hiding their weapons just out of sight, stared at us from open doorways. Women in colorful wrap-around skirts stared, too. Small children laughed and shouted, "Americanos!"

Our truck stopped and started through the cratered streets. The buildings were crumbled, and not one window frame had glass. There was no paint that wasn't faded, and bullet holes pocked the walls. The entire city appeared to have been ground down, or blasted with gravel from a hose. Some of the younger Marines with me on the truck had never deployed before and had never been outside the United States; they just stared, mouths shut.

Then Somalis charged the truck. One of the younger Marines shouted: "Get back! Get back!" He pointed his weapon at them and they stopped.

I was less afraid of the crowd—they seemed excited to see us—than I was of the Marine shooting someone by mistake. If he did shoot, we would be swarmed. Most of the Marines appeared more overwhelmed than afraid. Back home we had seen starving children on television, so it was a relief to see people who looked relatively healthy. Still, the destruction was complete, and the need too great for anyone to fix quickly, even the United States Marine Corps. Tensely scanning the jostling crowd for threats, one of the Marines quietly spoke my own thoughts: "What the *fuck* are we doing here?"

We drove through the gates of the port, basically a vast parking lot with warehouses and berths for ships. Marines were pounding stakes into the hot sticky asphalt and raising tents. Enormous cargo ships were being unloaded. Guys with torches cut windows into the sides of empty shipping containers to convert them into offices and places to sleep. Everywhere there was the rumble of heavy machinery and the beep-beep of forklifts backing up.

An American flag snapped in the wind above the scarlet and gold flag of the Marine Corps.

One warehouse was filled with long rows of cots draped with green mosquito nets that shimmered in the breeze blowing off the ocean. The port—the entire country—no longer had electricity, running water, or sewage disposal. Marauding Somalis had pulled out the city's electrical grid to sell the copper wire. They had torn out and sold the pipes, the sinks, and the toilets, too. Before the Marines turned it into a dormitory, the warehouse had served as a giant communal toilet. A grader was needed to scrape the human waste off the floor. The smell, inside and out, was burning garbage and excrement.

In the morning, before the sun came up, a big, off-key voice sang the words to "That's Amore." The accent wasn't Italian; it was pure Tennessee. It wasn't in tune, either, but it was loud, very loud. Lieutenant Colonel James was up and ready to work. His Marines in the First Landing Support Battalion, wearing distinctive red patches on their uniforms to identify them as the lords of the port, were in charge of unloading the fast-arriving ships and planes carrying military equipment and food for the starving.

The home base of the Red Patchers—a cluster of tents and shipping containers under camouflage nets—was named Camp Bubba because Lieutenant Colonel James called everyone Bubba, as in, "What do those army bubbas want?" The ten women Marines with the battalion, known officially (and awkwardly) as WMs, were called "Bubbaresses." Soon Camp Bubba even had a regular newsletter known as "Rack Talk," filled with essential Marine lore such as "the five types of wounds" and the word-of-the-day.

James was most pleased to learn his guys had fixed a broken grader. He shouted at them—he was always shouting—"OUT-FUCKING-STANDING!" They were jazzed by the attention and praise. That made it even more uncomfortable when, in front of everyone, a Marine general lit into Lieutenant Colonel James for having stubble on his chin. I almost spoke up and said, "He hasn't shaved because he's been up all fucking night working. Sir." I held my tongue, and James did, too. He spent a good deal of energy trying to keep his mouth shut.

I rode along on missions to deliver food, and to disarm warlords, and then returned to the port to write. Like most people I knew in the business, I preferred reporting to writing, and I always felt a little deflated after I filed. The reporting was energizing—out there in the world learning new things—and then I forced all that energy into just five hundred words of copy. One second later the story was gone, and I was finished, spent.

The idle moments were not good for me. I was very aware that Christmas was coming, more aware than anytime since I had stopped believing in Santa Claus. Having a baby and a family at home sharpened the meaning of the holiday for me, and that was reflected in the stories I wrote. In truth, my obsession with Christmas was more about me than about the people I was covering. Muslim Somalis didn't celebrate Christmas, and many of the Marines had lost track of the holiday. The joke was that USMC stood for U Suckers Missed Christmas.

I considered myself lucky to be with the Marines, because my reporter friends were living in uncomfortable and unsafe conditions. A veteran of previous conflicts, Mike Hedges, had rented a house with other reporters, and they had hired their own drivers, cooks, and security. They invited me to their villa for lunch, which was the first locally prepared meal I had eaten. I was careful to try only the food that had been cooked, nothing fresh, and no water unless I saw the bottle. Those were the rules I always followed in less-developed parts of the world.

I had fun catching up with Hedges and the other reporters, including Larry Jolidon, a friend from El Salvador and the Gulf War. I felt at home with them, and it was safe to relax. We were competitors, that was part of it, but over a meal it was just laughs and war stories and nods of recognition. We traded gossip about people we knew, and horror stories about boneheaded editors back home.

My reporter friends and I never talked about politics as partisans, although we did share a disdain for most politicians in all countries. I now thought of journalism as something higher than politics, almost a religion, and war correspondents belonged to the most extreme and tight-knit order. This place was rough and scary, which made sitting around the table after a good meal with friends even more beautiful.

Hedges had the brains of a professor and the strength of a lumberjack, but he looked thin and drained. I knew they all had been knocked down by diarrhea. I also wondered how safe they were with rented security. If the guards could be hired by one side, there was a chance they could be hired by the other side. I was relieved, if maybe a little ashamed, when I returned before dark to the safety of the port and "my Marines."

Sticking close to the Marines was my assignment. My instructions from the desk were clear: write about the US troops. The editors told me not to worry about Somali politics, because our readers were going to care more about fellow Americans than suffering Africans. I didn't take this as racist or narrow-minded. Racism did taint some coverage, of course, but I would have gotten the same instructions if we had invaded France or Germany.

Every reporter learned from the first day that the closer a story was to home, the more carefully it would be read. For me, "local" meant the Marines, especially if I could find them from cities where we had newspapers. I sometimes yelled into a crowd of uniforms, "Anybody from Denver or Memphis? Abilene?" Quotes from them would be gold in the hometown newspapers.

People teased us about looking for the "local angle," but that was what our experience told us was valuable to readers. And by valuable I don't mean money. I didn't care about "selling papers" (because I didn't share in the profits), but I did want to be read.

Attached to one of my stories, I included this personal note to my editors: "Dear Desk: Your correspondent is sharing a Conex container with a snoring Marine first sergeant just a few feet from the harbor. Thank God for the breeze. The flies are bad, especially because they are tiny bombers loaded with disease that they drop on our food. There is no mess hall, so we eat MREs. I still cannot eat tuna casserole for breakfast (especially served cold in a green plastic bag), but I'm a big fan of crackers and peanut butter. That is good because the goal is to be constipated in order to stay out of the latrines. The smell is so strong that it creates gusts of wind. No showers yet, but you can get fairly clean with a canteen cup. Anyway, it's only been a week. I am trying to hook up with the landing at Kismayo. That may mean I will be out of touch for a few days, so don't worry if I don't call."

In addition to safety, another benefit of being with the Marines, which I kept to myself, was the ships in the port. I was having trouble finding a way to file my stories until one of the Marines suggested, "Why don't you use the phone on the ship?" A phone? Genius! He led me on board a huge civilian cargo ship, which was delivering military supplies, and introduced me to the radio operator named Harmon. Nobody but me called him Harmon. He and all the radio operators on ships were known as "Sparks." I didn't want Harmon to get in trouble, so I offered to call collect, but he waved his hand to say no problem.

He invited me to stay for dinner: thick juicy steak, baked potato, and corn-on-the-cob. The food was so good I was embarrassed to tell the Marines. Harmon, perhaps inspired by the odor radiating off my clothes, let me use the shower in his quarters. I also kept that to myself. I had one cold beer and just about fell asleep right there. I tumbled down the stairs, dragged my cot out of the shipping container to sleep in the fresh air, and didn't wake until the next morning.

I enjoyed special status with the military's elaborate press operation in Somalia because I covered the Pentagon. Familiarity was the first step in a trust-based relationship. The organization you represented mattered—the *New York Times* and the *Washington Post* were not going to be frozen out—but so did the character of the reporter. I liked the people I covered, and they knew I cared about getting the story right. I put in a lot of "face time" at the Pentagon, and kept my hair trimmed and shoes polished. I had respect for the uniform, and I didn't automatically assume people were lying to me. I wrote critical stories that occasionally made them pull out their hair—that was expected and honorable—but people knew I tried to be fair.

Too much familiarity, however, could lead to an occupational hazard of a beat called "going native." Reporters who identified more with the people they covered than with their readers needed to change beats. I saw this happen with foreign correspondents, but also with Pentagon reporters who fetishized weapons systems, and police reporters who refused to see brutality. Covering the Pentagon and other beats, I tried to keep my demeanor courteous and my attitude somewhere between skeptical and cynical.

Now, in the Pentagon hallway called Correspondents Corridor, my grinning mugshot was displayed with the other beat reporters who covered "the building." I was proud to belong to that group, and I sent a snapshot of the gallery to my parents. The little room called the Ernie Pyle Alcove now had deep meaning for me. The memorial honored Pyle and other reporters killed during World War II, including those from Scripps Howard newspapers and from the Scripps wire service, United Press. When I had first seen the portrait of Pyle years before, I felt only mild historical interest. Now, after spending so much time as the "Scripps Howard reporter" with troops in the field, I was constantly reminded of him. Pyle's fifty-year-old columns, which I read in collections my parents had found for me at used bookstores, did not feel dated. The combat he wrote about felt like what I had experienced, only worse. Before I went to Washington as a reporter, I had never heard of Ernie Pyle. Now I felt him everywhere.

Like Pyle before me, I had spent much of my time in the field with the army rather than the other services. So when I was told to go to Somalia, my first call was to Army Public Affairs. They were happy to help, but the army was deploying after the Marines and couldn't get me there soon enough. I understood, but I did plant a little seed of jealousy that I would be traveling with a rival service. Then I told the Marines that the army couldn't get me to the action on time, which just confirmed the army's lumbering stereotype. A couple of days later, I was on the way to Somalia with the Marines.

I had help understanding the Marines from Otto Kreisher, who covered the Pentagon for Copley News Service, part of a ninety-year-old family newspaper group similar to mine. Otto had been an enlisted Marine before becoming a commissioned officer and aviator in the navy. Like me, Otto had started as a cub reporter in Chicago, but he was more than a decade older, and his military experience gave him a unique perspective. Since World War II, fewer reporters were veterans, and sometimes the lack of military experience showed in our coverage. If anything, Otto's time in uniform made him tougher on the officer class, and he had little tolerance for incompetence or lying. He was tolerant of me, however, and my dumb questions about the Marines and the navy.

Otto wanted to join up with the amphibious landing in Kismayo, a port city about three hundred miles south of us. I went back and forth about whether to do it. What if fighting broke out in the capital and we were stuck on a ship? Also, I dreaded the hurry-up-and-wait pace of the field trips and the lack of control. On the other hand, what a great adventure. And there would be hot food on the ship, maybe a real shower. More seriously, there was the ghost of Ernie Pyle pushing me forward. I could not allow myself to stay in the rear.

Reporters were fighting over the few available seats for the flight to the Kismayo landing ship. I got into a tug-of-war over a seat with someone from NBC until David Bloom, a twenty-nine-year-old rising star at the network, stepped in. He was jovial and funny, always on. At first I thought it was an act, but the more time we spent together, I saw it was real. He was the opposite of me—he made me feel like a wallflower—and I really enjoyed him. I wanted to be more like he was, more outgoing and less fearful. There was room on the plane for everybody, Bloom declared, and I got a seat. We flew to the USS *Juneau* and joined 100 Belgian commandos and 224 US Marines for the landing the next day.

The ship's crew invited the visiting reporters to a steak dinner. The commanders were upbeat and relaxed, and to be honest, the whole thing felt a little staged. There was no compelling reason for the Marines to make an amphibious landing, other than because they could. It was good training, though, and the Marines were experts at keeping their image in the news.

"Our intention is to go ashore with a smile on our face," John Peterson, a navy captain and the commander of the task force, told us. "There always is some risk, so we will not go to shore unarmed."

After dinner, we were taken to bunks somewhere in a windowless room inside the ship. I never knew where we were below decks, so I followed Otto. The bunk beds—and the floor, ceiling, and walls—were freshly painted metal, and I felt enclosed inside a thick can. I cleaned up in the head and enjoyed the hot water, folded my pants, and got into bed wearing a t-shirt and underwear (for modesty and readiness).

Lying on my back staring at the metal ceiling, which was just inches from my nose, I fell asleep listening to the gentle rumble of the engines. Then I woke in a sweaty, fast-breathing panic, convinced the ceiling was pressing down on me. I jumped out of bed and landed with a thump on the metal floor. My hard landing woke Otto, who was sleeping just below me. He didn't laugh at my nightmare; he just told me to go back to sleep.

Reveille sounded at 3 a.m. and we struggled out of the racks. I packed my stuff, got coffee, and climbed down to the cavernous well deck. The engines of the tracked amphibious vehicles—called "hogs"—were idling, spewing a thick gray cloud of exhaust that floated above the men in the darkened belly of the ship. Marines, stripped to shorts and t-shirts and shiny with grease and sweat, spread their combat gear on poncho liners for one last check.

I was told to squeeze into Track #102 with fifteen Marines, weapons, food, and gear. We raced to get everything packed, we climbed in, the doors were closed and sealed, and then we sat. Just as on land, military life at sea was comprised of long periods of getting ready and waiting, and then bursts of heart-pounding excitement. A reporter's job, even back home, had a similar rhythm.

The air inside the closed vehicle was thick with diesel fumes and body odor. There were no windows, so I couldn't tell if our track was moving or just rolling with the ship. I felt mildly nauseated, over-tired, and a little anxious. A talkative Marine corporal named Charles Luke, who said he was twenty-two and from Farmington Hills, Michigan, tried to be nice. "Don't worry about rolling over because we will probably come up right. The bad thing is we'll be rolling around in here with ammo boxes and other stuff, so there'll be some broken bones."

Then I heard louder engine noises and metal grinding. I couldn't see it, but the ship's doors had opened, and our hog was on the move. We plunged into the ocean and bobbed a couple of times before the unwieldy craft stabilized, and we motored toward shore. I kept one hand on my gear and one hand clutching something solid so I wouldn't be tossed around.

The young Marines thunderously pounded their boots on the metal floor and roared the lyrics of a Queen song. The stomp-stomp-clap rhythm of the classic rock song was familiar from high school football, and it did feel like we were heading into a big game, only better armed.

Saltwater dripped on us from leaky seals, the water filling up around our feet. "If you have to puke, do it in your helmet so it doesn't plug up the drain holes," shouted Jason Davis, 22, a lance corporal from Ewing, Missouri.

"When we get to the beach our favorite people are going to be there," Davis told the men. I wasn't sure what he meant until he added, "Don't shoot any media personnel. As much as we'd like to shoot 'em, we can't. So don't." Again, this was not meant personally, and I never took it that way.

The next sound was a grinding, grating noise when the track rose out of the surf and onto the beach. Then we stopped, and the flat metal door in back was lowered to the sand. I looked at my watch and made a note: 6:30 a.m. Sunlight filled the chamber and the Marines scrambled out the back shouting, "To the right! To the right! Go to the right!" I jumped out, too, holding my helmet on my head with one hand and my notebook and gear with the other. I stuck close to the Marines, not sure what to expect.

The sand was white and fine where the Marines fanned out and hunkered in fighting positions behind grassy dunes. I fell onto the sand with them and tried to get my bearings. After the ship, then the darkness inside the track and the choppy sea, I was sick to my stomach and disoriented. The sun burned my eyes. A pair of fierce-looking Cobra attack helicopters, with shark teeth painted on the front, thumped overhead. Hovercraft loaded with jeeps, trucks, and heavy equipment roared toward the shore behind us in misty clouds of white sea spray. Farther out on the horizon were darkened silhouettes of the big ships. The scene was straight out of a recruiting video. It was glorious.

Two whistle blasts from the platoon leader ordered everyone to scramble back inside the vehicle. There was no opposition on this beach, so we were marching inland. I stood in the open top while we thundered down a dirt road, fishtailing through the sand. Grabbing both sides of the vehicle to keep from flying out, I looked over at the speedometer when we hit forty-six miles per hour, which felt closer to one hundred. Somalis came out to cheer, rhythmically clapping their hands and singing. The mood was more Rose Parade than armored assault, and people appeared welcoming. The Marines quickly accomplished their mission, and within hours relief planes were flying into the town.

Good news was waiting for me back in Mogadishu. I had made sure the army knew I was having fun with the Marines by asking the desk to fax my stories every day to the Pentagon. Sufficiently shamed, the army arranged for an extraordinary ride-along with the Ninth Psychological Operations Battalion from Fort Bragg, North Carolina. The psyops soldiers normally operated in secret, but the commander told me I could accompany a team to Baidoa—the infamous "City of Death"—and Bardera, two towns that had seen terrible hardship.

I was handed off to a young sergeant and a junior enlisted man. Their weapon of choice was a seven-hundred-watt amplifier and loudspeaker mounted on top of their Humvee. They had the usual weapons, too, but their mission was to convince the Somalis to cooperate rather than fight, and to use words instead of bullets. This was going to be a challenge, because the two soldiers had studied German as part of Cold War training for Europe and did not speak the local languages. They did have prerecorded messages in Somali, and they were in good spirits, excited about a road trip across a country as big as California, but with dirt roads and landmines. I wasn't sure how they felt about me tagging along, but they didn't have a choice.

Dale, my managing editor in Washington, always told me to imagine an interview as a first date. You wanted to use good manners and a light touch. I was going to be with these guys for a couple of days, so I started slowly to not spook them. Mostly in the field, I was the first journalist the soldiers had ever met in person. They all had opinions about "the media," but few had ever talked to a real reporter.

Joe, the sergeant, was a twenty-five-year-old Gulf War veteran, and we traded war stories. Jamie was twenty-two and had been on a mission to help Haitian refugees, which I also had covered, so we had a connection, too.

We packed up, I got comfortable in the back seat, and we pulled out with a convoy of Marines. Joe said to his partner, "We don't want to hit any mines out here. Let's shake out the mojo." They rattled wooden necklaces with charms of zebras and giraffes.

Joe turned in his seat to explain, "I'm covered on both bases. I've got a St. Christopher medal, too."

Jamie turned to show me his St. Michael.

They cranked up the Red Hot Chili Peppers on a boom box. When they checked in on the radio, I heard their call sign: "Psycho One."

I knew this was going to be a different kind of road trip.

Did they think the African charms and Christian saints were effective against landmines?

Joe turned back to me, solemnly nodded his head yes, and said, "That's powerful juju, sir."

Jamie loved to drive holding a microphone and lip-synching with the tapes recorded in Somali. People would be walking nearby, half-listening to the broadcast, assuming the speaker was a Somali man. Then they would cautiously look over at the Humvee and see the light-skinned, muscular American apparently speaking their language quite fluently.

"Greetings," boomed the voice in Somali. "We come in peace."

People stared, eyes wide and mouths open, and Jamie would grin and wave at them. Then the Somalis got the joke, laughed, and waved back. This always set Jamie and Joe guffawing and slapping the seats in pure pleasure. They rode through small villages like gregarious traveling salesmen hawking their wares, which, in this case, were peace and goodwill.

Our first rest stop after many hours was an abandoned Soviet-built air base outside Baidoa. The base resembled a ghost town hit by a tornado, cluttered with the remains of jets and rusted radars amid the broken buildings.

I tried dozing in the parked Humvee, but the sun's rays through the open turret felt intensified, so I was like a bug being fried with a magnifying glass. I climbed out and tied my poncho to the door to make a little tent, but then I was sitting in an airless, plastic bag. My body was so dirty that when I scratched the back of my neck, my fingernails filled with gunk that looked like rubbings from an eraser. A fresh baby wipe felt cool on my burned face. My clothes smelled musty and were never quite dry.

Hygiene and normally private matters were regular topics of discussion. The Marines we were accompanying talked about whore baths and how to clean between your butt cheeks. A sergeant suggested we line a tent with plastic so everyone could pleasure themselves. "You'd need oven mitts to go in there," he said, and the guys all laughed.

Not known for their modesty, the Marines had constructed a toilet from a fifty-gallon drum cut in half and placed in the open between two busy dirt roads. I took one look at the latrine and decided to hold it as long as I could, possibly until I got back to Washington.

While I was contemplating the toilet, a lieutenant colonel approached and asked who I was.

Reporter, I said, offering my hand.

He turned abruptly and walked away, in a rare display of rudeness.

I was told there was only one other reporter in the convoy, a Brit, and the many reporters left behind in Mogadishu were not happy.

A young Marine intelligence officer, the S-2, said the Brit probably wasn't even a reporter, more likely undercover for MI6, British intelligence. He told me, "I figure you must be a real reporter because otherwise you wouldn't have given me the name of some news service I've never heard of."

"That's cold, Two," I said. He was a smart young guy, Tufts grad. I smiled and added, "I can't help it if you are so ignorant of American history that you don't know Scripps Howard was started in 1878, founded United Press, and sent Ernie Pyle to cover World War II."

He laughed. Whatever.

We stood in the sun for hours as 3,200 Marines loaded their gear. Then we stood some more while the vehicles were lined up in a convoy. People were grabbing full water bottles to drink and empties for urine. That was a bad sign: it meant we weren't going to stop during the road march. I was okay peeing in a bottle, which in a moving vehicle was trickier than it sounded, even for a guy.

My bigger worry was that I had not pooped, and I would feel better if I did. I didn't want the convoy to leave without me, however, because that would have been worse than being a little backed up. I knew there would be no warning when we got the order to start driving. The rhythm was always the same: Hurry up. Wait. Go! Go! Go! I did not want to use that tin-can latrine. Should I go to the bathroom now or wait? Probably I should wait. Well, now maybe it's going to be awhile before we leave. If I just went nearby . . .

I grabbed a roll of toilet paper and a shovel and shuffled off away from the vehicles. There wasn't a single tree or even a bush higher than my knees, just flat, scruffy desert. I was not especially modest at this point, but I had the best results pooping in private. Better not to walk too far from the convoy, however, so after a few hundred feet I scratched away some dirt, dropped my pants and squatted over the hole.

As soon as I did, engines turned over and rumbled. Heavy, metal doors slammed shut. Then more engines started. I glanced up over the tiny bush I was trying to hide behind. People were running around the vehicles, throwing stuff inside and taking their seats. Blue exhaust smoke filled the air. Of course. Now they were in a big hurry to leave.

A voice yelled above the convoy noise, "Hey reporter dude! Let's go!"

I buried my meager deposit in the sand and ran back to the vehicle, buckling my pants along the way, clutching the roll of toilet paper under my arm and trying not to bang myself in the head with the shovel. This apparently was very funny to everyone but me. "Fuck you guys," was my clever retort. I got back to the jeep, splashed some water on my hands and wiped them on my pants, below the knees. We pulled out of Baidoa. Next stop, Bardera.

The road was just a gravel strip carved through bushes as tough as steel wool and armed with thorns that could pop a tire. The convoy passed miles and miles of shoulder-high sorghum and small villages filled with delicately crafted, acorn-shaped, thatched huts. Hundreds of Somalis turned out to cheer and wave, staring at the Marines as if they had landed from a different planet.

Every hour or so, either Joe or Jamie would say, "It's not hot. It's *Africa* hot!" And then laugh hysterically. It was funny the first three or four times.

We were traveling into the bush and back in time. The cities we left behind had been built by Somalis, and then destroyed by them. The primordial African countryside was almost unchanged by human hands. We drove by women working the ground with short wooden hoes that forced them to bend deeply. Other women led donkeys carrying jugs of water or bundles of firewood. When the road was smooth enough to write, I took notes about this beautiful, ancient place, and I imagined myself far away from my own world.

Until I saw a woman carrying a baby in a shawl tied on her back. That was how Mexican women carried their babies, and from there my mind jumped to Maru and Isabella and the chubby rings of fat around her legs, and how she got slippery as a seal in the tub. These babies were not so fortunate. And suddenly they weren't so far away.

That night we stopped at the airport outside Bardera. The commanders wanted word of our arrival to get around, so there would be no surprises and plenty of time for tempers to cool. There was no real enemy other than the societal breakdown that prevented food from getting where it was needed. The world could have sent an international police force instead of warriors, but maybe it was the Marines' potential for great violence that kept Somalis from resisting.

We climbed stiffly out of the vehicles after the long ride. I guzzled a bottle of water, so chlorinated it tasted like a warm swimming pool. After nine hours of bouncing and engine noise, the quiet and stillness were welcome. The dust-coated Marines seemed to have traveled inside a giant vacuum cleaner bag. The ones who rode up top appeared to be wearing pancake makeup.

Exhausted, I tried to sleep that night in the back of the Humvee. It got cold after dark, and I kept waking to add more layers of clothing, until I was wearing everything I carried. The next morning we rolled into Bardera. Children were the first to greet us, running alongside the vehicles, shrieking with laughter and clutching at the rags that fell off their nearly naked bodies. They were so thin they seemed to be all knees and elbows. "Okay! Okay!" the kids shouted happily, laughing delightedly when the Marines spoke to them.

Most people seemed pleased, relieved, or at least curious to see the troops. A few Somali men, however, lurked in the shadows of darkened shacks, staring angrily without making a sound. Many of them were armed, and if just one of them started shooting at us, the whole place would blow.

Further along, we saw people on the ground. They must have been trying to walk to safety or to food, and then collapsed on the roadside. They were hungry, so thin they looked like stick figures. Men and women were too weary to stand, lying on the filthy dust and so weak they ignored the swollen flies that buzzed around their heads and landed on their dripping noses. Their eyes, even those of the youngest children, were wet and dark, shiny, and unfocused. Medics helped those they could.

We were ordered not to give people food without medical supervision because it could overwhelm their weakened bodies. I just watched and took notes and did not help anyone. It was all too much. Parts of me shut down just then, like a circuit breaker during a power surge. The first thing to go was my curiosity, then empathy. I was overwhelmed and in shock. I did not like the feeling.

My big concern, as always, was filing the story. I turned my notes into a feature about Christmas Eve and another story about the road trip. Late in the afternoon, I noticed a portable antenna atop a burned-out building. That looked promising, so I made my way there. There were a handful of Marines camped on the dirty floor of the building, which like everything else was torn apart and trashed. In the middle of the floor was a familiar pair of silver metal suitcases: satellite phone.

I knocked on the busted doorframe and introduced myself. I explained I had stories written, but if I couldn't transmit them soon, the shelf life would expire and they would be worthless. The Marines were friendly and didn't see a problem helping me do my job.

I knew how to work the phone, so I dialed the office computer and filed the stories. I called a second number to confirm that the desk could read the words without any garble. I also asked my editors to call the families of my escorts, Jamie and Joe, to tell them their soldiers were fine and Merry Christmas to all. I hung up and sat back, relaxed, knowing I had fed the beast.

By the time I got my stories in, it was getting dark fast. The Marines kept flashlights and cigarette lighters low to avoid attracting attention or drawing fire. Everybody was in his own private world. Some were smoking, dozing, or talking quietly. At least one kept an eye on the street, but the evening was still. There was random gunfire, but it didn't sound close or threatening. The Marines didn't pay much attention to me.

I slid closer to the phone. No one seemed to notice. I opened my computer and called up the story I had just filed. I cupped a flashlight to shield the light, and dialed a number I knew by heart. The phone rang about three times before someone picked up and said, "Hello."

"Hi mom, it's me."

"I'm holding your baby!" my mother gushed, thrilled to hear from me but far more excited to have Isabella in her arms. I pictured the family sitting in the living room, the baby in my mom's lap and my stepfather nearby. My brothers would be there with their wives and children. I knew the Christmas tree was decorated and piled with presents.

My mother gave Maru the phone and we talked in Spanish. My mom never appreciated us speaking Spanish because she feared we were talking about her (and sometimes we were), but Maru and I had fallen in love in Spanish, and it was the only way to have any privacy or intimacy.

"Are you okay?" I asked.

"No," she said, in that weak, choked voice that meant, I am going to cry and I want you to take care of me. I didn't hear that voice very often, but only when she was at the end of her strength. Her first sign of anger or upset was to be cold or distant. Then she would lash out. Only when she had exhausted those stages did she show weakness. She had to be far gone or she would not let me see fear. I was worried now. I needed her to be strong so I could stay strong.

I tried a joke, and that got a small laugh. I told her how I scammed the call, and the Marines were right next to me but didn't know what I was saying. "I've got the screen of my computer up and I'm pretending to dictate my story."

She laughed again.

I told her I missed her. I could feel the tears just behind my eyes.

"Kiss my baby for me," I said. "Merry Christmas, too. I have to go. I love you."

I clicked off the connection and packed up my computer.

One of the Marines looked over and asked, "Did you get your story in?"

"Yes, thanks," I said, and then burst into tears, big heaving sobs. "Everything's fine," I blubbered, trying to compose myself.

They looked up but didn't say anything. Crying was another of those private things that happened with your battle buddies. Nobody judged me or even seemed surprised. They didn't know me, and I wasn't wearing the uniform, but I was there on the ground with them. I wiped my eyes and laughed a little. I made a joke about my story being emotionally powerful. I was embarrassed, but I felt better after draining the tension. I didn't cry often, but when I did, the relief was complete.

In the darkness, I saw flashes of white teeth smiling. I thanked them again, grabbed my gear, and groped my way back to the Humvee.

Jamie and Joe were waiting for me with a Christmas gift. We were parked along a dirt road near soldiers from the French Foreign Legion. They were hard-looking guys who had spent some serious, unpleasant time in Africa. The Legionnaires were sleeping on the ground alongside their vehicles, and they were admiring the simple, folding cots used by the Americans.

The Legionnaires were traveling light—no cots and no tents—but the one advantage they had over us was food. This was a French force, after all, and they weren't going into battle with cold tuna casserole in a plastic pouch. There was some trading—nobody would tell me the details—and the boys presented me with my Christmas gift: a genuine French field ration.

As excited as kids unwrapping a present under the tree, we tailgated at the back of the Humvee and tried to figure out how to prepare the food. The ingredients were more elaborate than an MRE and included a small heat tab to warm the main course. Oh yeah, this field ration had actual courses. The little cube burned very hot, and we used it to warm some kind of meat in a savory sauce. There was a small bottle of wine. We shared the food and passed the wine. We toasted each other, Christmas, our families.

The stars came up and filled the black sky all the way to the horizon. The night cooled off, and we nestled into the Humvee to sleep. I thought about my baby. Jamie and Joe probably were tired of hearing about her, but they didn't make me shut up. I missed Maru, but I was glad she was with my family and not alone tonight. I said goodnight to the boys. It turned out to be a nice Christmas.

After the road trip, I was ready to go home. In fact, I had been ready to go home after the first week in Somalia. One morning, like all the previous mornings, I filled a canteen cup with cold water from a tank called a water bull and bent over to shave using the side mirror on a Humvee. I would not have bothered to shave, except I was with the Marines, and felt I should observe the dress code. Wearing only boxer shorts, I splashed my face and hair and lathered up with shampoo. Somalis stood on a ridge looking down at us with the curiosity of visitors at the zoo. I didn't care anymore. I was careful not to use too much water, but I really needed a bath. I wasn't sure about water etiquette. How much was one person allowed to use? I washed off most of the soap and dried my hair with a towel. I felt better clean.

Then I rinsed the soapy canteen cup and filled it with hot water. I mixed in the powdered contents of four packets: hot chocolate, instant coffee, creamer, and sugar. It was warm and sweet. This was breakfast, again.

That was the moment I realized I knew all about deployments, and I had seen enough. The survival tips I picked up in Central American conflicts, the invasion of Panama, and the Gulf War had paid off, but there was nothing more I wanted to learn. I had done all of this before, and I didn't want to do it again.

Somalia felt different from other places I had worked because I was more conscious of the danger. I didn't know a noun from a verb in the local languages, I didn't know my way around, and I wasn't sure who the bad guys were. I got the feeling it didn't matter to them that I was a reporter and not a combatant. Nor did they care that the Americans were trying to help. Just as we didn't know much about them, they didn't know much about us.

The human suffering was, paradoxically, too vast to take in and too sharp to ignore. I had a long visit under a shady tree with a renowned and learned Somali poet, and even he was at a loss to explain what had happened to his country. There were so many people in pain that I resisted seeing them, yet a single baby's cry pierced my heart. For my own safety, I tried to look away. I knew intellectually that our stories in the media focused the world's attention on helping Somalia, but I did not like how helpless and distant I felt emotionally.

I was older now, too, going on thirty-six. When I covered cops in Chicago and Border Patrol agents in El Paso, the officers were older than I was. The youngest soldiers in Somalia could have been my own kids.

I missed Maru and felt guilty for being absent during so much of Isabella's first year. She was born the day Hurricane Andrew tore into Florida, and I had to take a quick trip there to cover the cleanup. Now I had missed her first

Christmas and baptism to be in Somalia. Maru and my parents went ahead with the ceremony, with my brother and his wife serving as godparents. I tried not to think about them, except when Maru or Bella forced their way into my thoughts.

I remembered one of the lessons from Rhonda Cornum, the POW from Iraq. She told me that when she was captured, she had placed her daughter and husband in the "family drawer" and kept it closed until she was released. When I was in Somalia, I tried to keep my family drawer closed, but it felt wrong: shouldn't I feel some pain for leaving my wife and baby? I had been absent during so many milestones in Isabella's life, big and small, that never would be repeated. Was I betraying her and Maru if I deliberately kept them apart from me?

Flying in a Black Hawk helicopter across the hot sands of Somalia, enjoying the rush of speed, I realized in an instant that it was all too dangerous. As a husband and father, I shouldn't be doing this, I thought. I loved flying fast and hugging the ground, what the pilots called nap-of-the-earth, but I was being selfish and putting my career and ambition ahead of the people who needed me. Was it possible to do this job well and raise a family? I wasn't sure anymore. I was certain that if something happened to me, and I left behind my wife and baby, I would be punished for eternity.

I had to get out of this place.

# 14

# ANYWHERE BUT SOMALIA

—— ON THE VALUE OF A STORY ——

I was so ready to escape Somalia, even for a day, that I drove to the Bardera airfield with Bart Gellman and Dayna Smith from the *Washington Post* with a single goal: get on the first plane out, no matter the destination. Anywhere but Somalia. We spotted a British C-130 and walked out to talk to the crew, who were laughing and playing badminton around the transport plane. I wondered for a minute if they were mature enough to fly. Sure, they said, hop on board. We're heading to Mombasa.

We landed in neighboring Kenya and took a taxi to a resort hotel. The place was deserted, either because of the season or the war next door in Somalia. We sipped cold Tusker beers on the beach and watched camels walking in the sand. I swam in the ocean, took a hot shower, and enjoyed a good meal. The next day I flew back to Somalia. I felt better after the short holiday, but I had made a decision.

I called the office and told them I was ready to come home. The story was over, I said, and I was just babysitting.

Not so fast, the desk responded. President Bush was going to visit the troops in Somalia, and I should stay to cover him. I protested that it was just going to be a photo op. The desk insisted. End of discussion.

I was stunned and then angry. I kicked myself for having saved all my vacation until the end of the year to spend time with the baby. We weren't allowed to carry over vacation into the following year, so now I would lose the days I had stockpiled. No way I would give up my time. And I didn't want extra pay instead of days off; I wanted the time back. Fighting the desk was futile. The only thing I could do was work hard and rub their noses in it. They wanted me to stay, so I would write the hell out of it.

On the first day of 1993, President Bush told the hundreds of troops gathered before him at the airport in Mogadishu: "You ought to be very, very proud of the way it's begun."

Then Bush, a combat veteran himself, switched gears. He knew what the troops wanted to know. "That's great," the president said about the humanitarian mission. "But how long?"

The soldiers, sailors, and airmen cheered. The Marines barked and whooped.

"I wish I knew the answer," Bush said. Groans rose up from the baked, dusty crowd. "I do know it's not an open-ended commitment," Bush offered. More cheers, but not as loud.

The president boarded his plane to fly back to Washington, leaving the Marines to wonder how long they would be in Somalia.

Five minutes after the desk cleared my final story about the president's visit, I was packed and ready to leave. Actually getting out of Somalia would take a lot longer.

During the final days in Africa, I moved slowly and deliberately. I didn't volunteer for anything stupid. Getting hurt at that point would have been like finishing a marathon only to break an ankle in the parking lot. More to the point, I remembered that my predecessor Ernie Pyle was killed just before the end of World War II. Somehow it seemed worse to die in the final moments of a dangerous assignment.

I had done the calculation many times before: How much risk was a story worth? Every good editor—the ones who had been in the field—always told me the same thing: "No story is worth dying for." Still, a good story was worth some risk. The question was, how much and for how long?

When I ran toward burning buildings in Chicago or drove down mined roads in Central America, I was too excited and maybe too young to be afraid. When I waded into street protests and riots, I was convinced my reporter's notebook was a shield. In exposing corrupt foreign governments, I figured my blue American passport was a get-out-of-jail card. Now I knew I never had been as safe as I had once assumed.

Some of the novelty was gone, too. I had written thousands of stories from thirty countries, so many datelines that they blurred together. When I was on vacation with my parents in Chicago, I realized my family had little interest in things that obsessed me, such as Nicaragua's foreign policy or whether the United States really was capable of fighting two wars simultaneously. My childhood friends, the ones who were not journalists, definitely did not believe any story was worth dying for.

Most importantly, I had a new family to love and protect. A few years earlier, I had nothing waiting for me at home except an empty apartment, and the story was everything. I used to be thrilled to parachute into a new place, the more risky the better because it meant a bigger story. Now the balance had shifted. I remembered the editor who had warned me long ago that every correspondent reached a moment when "your legs go." Maybe that day had arrived for me.

The Marines in Somalia were not allowed the luxury of these philosophical debates about risk versus reward, or even less about work-life balance. They could not refuse to go outside the gates on a mission.

And the Marines were better off than the Somalis, many of whom were homeless refugees without food or medical care. All of them faced danger and uncertainty. This was the most extreme example of my being in a tough place but not *of* the place, and being safer than the people I covered. I felt bad leaving my Marines in Somalia, and awful for the Somalis whose suffering continued, but not so bad I was willing to stay another minute.

Lieutenant Colonel James called everybody in for a little ceremony and presented me with a Red Patch souvenir: a piece of cardboard, decorated with a strip of red tape, and signed with good wishes from the entire battalion. I was pleased and wrapped the gift carefully in a shirt to protect it in my bag. James shook my hand and put me in a Humvee for the airport.

My Marines were in charge of unloading all incoming aircraft, so they had easy access to the airport, but the flights themselves were controlled by air force personnel, referred to as "airedales," but not to their faces.

The Marine gunnery sergeant who drove me to the airport had a lot of authority at Camp Bubba, but the air force had decreed that reporters could fly only on certain days on certain flights. I wasn't sure how soon I could get on a plane. Perhaps the service rivalries I sometimes used to my advantage would now work against me.

I walked inside the terminal and talked my way into the control room. Sure enough, the air force guy in charge started listing all the reasons I could not possibly get on a flight that day, or even that week.

Lieutenant Colonel James showed up at the terminal a few hours later and asked why I was still in country. When I explained that the air force wouldn't allow me on a plane, he let off a string of cusswords that made me feel better. Then he marched me in and ordered the air force guy to put me on the next departing Marine aircraft.

The air force guy, a master sergeant, was outranked, and more importantly, he was outmanned. But he wasn't going to give up without laying down a few obstacles. The reporter can go, the air force guy said, but he needs a Marine escort.

Lieutenant Colonel James looked around the room, found a fellow lieutenant colonel and "volunteered" him to be my escort. Fine. All set. But when the next aircraft was ready, there wasn't an extra seat for me. My escort apologized and left me behind.

I watched the plane fly away, and sat back down on the cracked plastic chair in what used to be the airport lounge. The air force master sergeant came over, grinning. "Every time you try to make an end run like that, it just makes it more complicated," he said.

"I apologize," I said. "I'm just desperate to leave." I was trying to be nice because I needed this guy on my side.

While this was happening, a Northwest Airlines 747 taxied by the window. It must have been a charter that had brought in fresh troops, the same way I had arrived. When that plane left Somalia, I wanted to be on it.

I went out to the flight line and yelled at Lance, one of my Marines, waving my arms to get his attention. He was only fifty feet away but couldn't hear me over the engine noise. There was a red line painted on the ground that unauthorized people were not to cross, mostly for safety reasons. I put my toes on the line and shouted louder. Nothing.

I was afraid the plane would leave without me, so I ran back inside and told the air force master sergeant there was no reason I couldn't jump on that 747. Another air force guy agreed, which just set off the first guy.

"I'm sick of the media going anywhere they want, running around stealing our MREs and walking into our tents whenever they want," the master sergeant said. "If he goes across that red line, I'll have him arrested."

Back on the tarmac, a Humvee rolled up, and the Marine driving shouted, "Pete! Are you still here?"

"I need to ask about that jet," I said, pointing to the Northwest plane.

"Hop in," the Marine said.

"No, I already got yelled at. Go out there with Lance and see if you can ask the crew on the 747 if they will take me. Please. I don't care where they're going as long as it is out of this fucking place."

"Roger that."

The Marine drove over and huddled with Lance. Then they climbed the rolling stairway up to the jet. I watched a flight attendant come to the door and talk with the Marines. Then the Marines drove back to me, my toes still on the red line.

Lance said, "They're only going to Cairo." I looked back toward the control tower, and then out at the plane. Lance read my mind. "Just get down low in back and I'll drive the long way around so they can't see you from the tower."

I got on the floor behind the front seats, and we drove out to the blind side of the jet. When we got there, I couldn't see the control tower, so I figured they couldn't see me. I crawled out of the Humvee and ran up the steps. The engines were off, and the door was open for ventilation. A flight attendant in a blue skirt and white blouse met me at the doorway. For having traveled a full day with a planeload of soldiers, she looked very put together.

"I've got to get out of here," I said. "Please take me, please. I'll buy a first class ticket, whatever you need. I want to go home. Take me home."

"Come with me," she said.

We climbed the spiral staircase to the flight deck, and the captain came out to take a look at me. I explained that the air force guys were making it impossible for me to leave, but I couldn't stay in this place for another day. "I'll buy a ticket," I said.

"Do you have a valid passport?"

I almost didn't register the question because it was so easy to answer, and it sounded like he was going to take me. "Yes, sir."

"Would you mind showing me?"

I handed him my passport.

"We're only going as far as Cairo," he said.

"Cairo is great," I said. "I can get a commercial flight home from there."

"What about that Marine who came up here asking about you?"

"Lance? I saw that guy get promoted. A field promotion," I said.

"He must be doing a good job," the captain said.

"They all are doing a good job," I said.

The pilot looked at me again. Then he said, "Take any seat."

The plane had been ridden hard from Fort Drum in New York. There were blankets and pillows on the floor, food left on trays and papers and magazines on the seats. Four hundred soldiers had been dropped off, and now it was just the flight attendants for the return flight.

I cleaned off an aisle seat and buckled my seat belt. I was afraid to sit near the window because the master sergeant might see me. He could drag me off the plane just to make himself feel better. I was tense waiting for the doors to close. I wanted to hear the engines start.

Instead, I heard heavy treads coming up the metal stairs. Shit. The captain walked to the open door and blocked it with his body. I couldn't see anything except his back, but I could hear him clearly.

A voice from the stairs said, "Sir, you know you are not allowed to take passengers out of here."

"Yes, I know," the captain said.

It was quiet for a moment. Then I heard boots going back down the stairs. The door closed. The engines turned over and we taxied down the runway. I didn't relax until I felt the landing gear go up inside the plane.

Once in the air, a flight attendant named Pamela told me there was a change in plans. This plane would stop in Cairo, but the Egyptians would not let civilians—me—transfer to another flight. Instead, a fresh crew would fly the plane empty to Philadelphia, and I could ride along.

That's perfect, I said, even better. "I've got a new baby waiting for me at home," I said.

"I'll bet you are ready for a long hot shower and a good meal," Pamela said, bringing me a cold beer and fluffing my pillow before settling into the seat next to me. She was smart and funny, and we talked while I ate. Neither of us mentioned that I also was going home to my wife. She looked and smelled so good that I was one smile away from proposing something incredibly stupid. Was I a complete idiot? I blamed it on Somalia.

When we landed in Philadelphia, Pamela and the other flight attendants formed a scrum to hide me from immigration and smuggled me through a back door into the terminal. I thanked them again and bought a ticket for the quick flight to Washington.

# 15

# HOME FOR GOOD

—— ON LEARNING FROM MISTAKES ——

After Somalia, I opened the door into a changed home. There were baby toys on the floor, milk bottles in the refrigerator, and new jackets, hats, and mittens, all in miniature. Maru and Isabella had developed their own routine without me. I was relieved to be home, but I had moved too fast from one environment where I was supposed to behave a certain way into another environment where the expectations were totally different. Stress, jet lag, and lack of sleep made me exhausted. I was too tired to hold up any defenses, and my emotions were exposed. I felt hypersensitive, as though my feelings were sunburned.

Isabella didn't care, and she was happy to see me. Maru was happy too, but expectant, waiting for me to do something. I didn't see that she wanted something from me; I was too tired. We were planning to visit my parents in Florida, but right away Maru started telling me she was too busy with the dance company. I should take the baby and see my parents without her, she suggested. The thought filled me with dread. My mom would worry something was wrong with our marriage, I didn't have the skill or the energy to handle the baby by myself, and I wanted to be with Maru.

I tried to breathe and remember she had gone through a big disruption, too. She had traveled with Isabella for Christmas in Chicago and had been doing everything at home without any help. She didn't have any experience with babies, either. She was tired, too.

Please, I said, come with me to Florida. I don't want to go back to work yet, my mom needs to see me, and we can have some time together.

Okay, Pito, she said.

I loved her like crazy.

I couldn't stay awake in Florida. Every time I sat down I fell asleep. I slept in a chair, on the couch, in the car.

"What's wrong with you?" my mother asked, concerned that I wasn't well.

"I'm just tired," I said.

Every night I dreamed of Somalia. I was with the Marines, and I needed to go on a mission. The commander said it would not be possible. But I had to go. The frustration was almost a physical barrier. At once I understood that expression about banging your head against a wall. The dreams were about being trapped, which was how I felt in Somalia. I wrote about the dreams in my journal. The notes were just for me, but this was the kind of writing I enjoyed. Dale said I could write something more personal about Somalia for the wire, but it didn't feel right to use so much suffering to satisfy my need to be creative.

Another editor, calling with judgmental disappointment in his voice, asked why I had written so much about the Marines and not about average Somalis. He either didn't know that was my assignment, or he had forgotten. I squeezed the phone in frustration but did not respond.

Washington had moved on. US troops were still arriving in Africa, but Somalia was old news. The desk told me people in the office were asking why I wasn't in Iraq, which was being bombed again. Or, since I was in Florida, I could run over to Central Command in Tampa to cover the Iraq story from there.

I felt myself tighten up. If someone had ordered me back into trouble when I finally was on vacation with my parents, my wife, and my new baby, I would have quit. But then what would I do? There was nothing that interested me except journalism. I could not be without a job because our savings would last only a couple of months. Now with the baby, we also needed the health insurance and the life insurance.

As it turned out, the desk kindly looked the other way to let me keep my vacation days, and then some. Their only assignment: enjoy the time off.

I started to relax. Every morning I picked up the *New York Times* and the *Miami Herald*. My parents took the *Wall Street Journal* and the *Sun-Sentinel* from Fort Lauderdale. Some days I also grabbed the *Palm Beach Post* or the *New York Post.* I loved the newspapers, all of them, each in its own way, like old friends. I knew the writers and photographers, and I knew the work behind the stories. I saw why the editors chose certain photos and how they played them. To me, a newspaper was no longer just a beautiful if imperfect portrait of the world on a single day, but now it was deeply engaging on many levels, the way a well-crafted building was appreciated by a seasoned architect.

I wanted to work for an elite organization like the *Wall Street Journal* or the *New York Times,* but I no longer was sure I was willing to make the personal sacrifice. When I was in Mexico, the *Times* correspondent was Rich Meislin, an elegant writer. I teased him about having a car and driver. He said, "Sure, you give your life to the *Times,* and they give you a car." He wasn't being funny.

I envied the impact he had, though. When he wrote something, it made things happen, even moved the stock market. I was not likely to move the market, but on the other hand, I didn't have the pressure of that responsibility. I also didn't have millions of people picking over my every word, ready to pounce on some error or perceived bias.

I had the luxury of saying no to assignments, not always, but when it really mattered. My workplace was caring compared with the cutthroat environment at some news shops. I relished the freedom to travel and pick my own stories. A reporter friend from Mexico, who had been to our wedding, knew me well and was in the life himself, once gently but firmly chided me for daring to complain about my work. "If you're unhappy, *hermano,* it's not the job, it's you." I knew he was right.

More than ever, I hungered to learn new things and to write about them, but at my own pace. Maybe now was the time to leave daily journalism to write books.

In Florida, my new daughter happily pulled me away from thoughts of work. Isabella wasn't interested in my ideas for books—she still chewed her books. The days were perfect, blue skies and warm sun. I couldn't bear to visit the beach; the heat and sand flashed me back to Iraq and Somalia, but I happily stood in the cool water of the pool. Maru handed me the baby, and I held Isabella in her red and white bathing suit, floating in front of me like a bobber. We slipped water wings onto her arms and soon she was splashing around, laughing and shrieking with pleasure.

One night we were relaxing after a day at the pool, and Isabella suddenly started to scream. Not just crying, but screaming. I ran for her, but she would not be consoled. I passed her to her mother. Still she didn't stop crying. Maru talked to her, asked her what was wrong. Isabella didn't speak yet, but Maru's voice usually helped. This time, she kept bawling.

My mind raced back over what had happened that day. The pool. An ear infection. Oh my God, and we were flying home on a plane soon. We would have to cancel the trip. What if her hearing were permanently damaged?

Then Maru flipped Isabella over and rubbed her back. I didn't know a baby could burp so loudly, but when she did, she stopped crying and fell contentedly asleep. False alarm. But I knew right then I was going to worry about my daughter for the rest of my life.

Maru worked on the dance company while we were in Florida. I didn't want to work at all. I was happy to nap with Isabella on my chest, drooling a puddle on my shirt. Maru walked through new choreography, coached her dancers over the phone, and tried to raise money. She wanted to invite Madonna to do a performance together. I thought that was a longshot.

"Why do you doubt me?" she demanded, feelings hurt.

Damn. I had stepped in it again.

I proposed the three of us drive to Miami Beach for an art deco fair. I knew Maru would appreciate getting away on an adventure. The day was hot, and Isabella was sweaty and squirmy until we hit the pool. The art deco was nice, though, and it reminded us of our old neighborhood in Mexico City.

We stopped by the post office to mail the letters I had written to foundations asking to support the dance company. And one invitation to Madonna.

"Thank you, Pito," Maru said.

I just smiled.

"We are so very happy," Maru said. "Do you think something is going to happen to us?"

"Something bad?"

"Something really bad," she said, nodding her head because she knew for sure it was coming.

"You sound like your mother," I said.

"My mother was right about a lot of things."

Nothing bad happened on that trip, nothing that made us suffer the way we both thought maybe was inevitable. Would we be punished for having so much good fortune? For having meaningful work, and each other, and now this perfect child? When life was too good was when you were struck down. Still, nothing bad happened. We had to make do with worrying about the unknowable future.

I did a few more overseas reporting trips, including three weeks in China and a month visiting four countries in South America to cover the drug war, but I was traveling less. I knew I had done my last foreign reporting when I didn't want to cover the 1994 guerrilla conflict in southern Mexico, which should have been a good story for me because I knew Mexico and I knew war. I was positive the "uprising" wasn't going anywhere, however, and I just didn't have the interest or the energy. In my college days, I would have rooted for the rebels. Now I saw their leaders as clueless intellectuals dangerously acting out a romantic fantasy.

Another reason for my reluctance to travel to war zones was our family's financial security. We had a son, Lucas, almost three years after Isabella was born. When I tried to get extra life insurance in case something happened to me, every company turned me down unless I provided a letter from my employer saying I no longer would be sent on combat assignments.

My boss Dan was not happy: "Are you nuts? You finally figure out something you're good at and you don't want to do it anymore!" He had four kids of his own, though, so he wrote the letter, and I got the insurance.

Dan didn't know what to do with me. I think he considered me unrealized potential. I had done all I ever dreamed of as a reporter, but he expected more. When the number-three person in the Washington bureau, the news editor, was promoted to run one of our papers in California, Dan wondered if I would be interested in the job. I never had considered going into management. The idea of sitting in an office chained to a computer sounded like prison, but I was bored and needed a new challenge. I also knew there would be a pay raise and more regular hours.

Maru said the decision was mine alone. I had tried to help her around the house, especially after Isabella and then Lucas were born, but Maru carried most of the work and responsibility for the children, even while she was running the dance company full-time. My older male bosses urged me to solve the problem by spending "quality time" at home when I wasn't traveling, but I knew the family needed quantity time.

Isabella was one of those kids who was a miniature adult, and we took her everywhere. Lucas was built like a bag of cement and had only one speed: full. He was so energetic and loud in the mornings, I hustled him outside to let Maru sleep. Many years later our lovely neighbor across the street admitted that she called Lucas the neighborhood alarm clock because his playful yelling woke her every morning. Lucas was ready for anything, and I wanted to be there for him and Isabella, so the kids were a good reason to take the management job.

My old friend John from El Paso already had taken a desk job with AP photos, and he said being an editor wasn't as bad as he had feared. Dale and others in the bureau were happy for me and thought it was the right career move.

One person would be relieved if I stopped traveling: my mother. The problem wasn't so much the travel as the destinations. When protesting French farmers blocked the roads to Paris with their tractors, I half-jokingly lobbied to cover the "conflict" (and take Maru along). I couldn't convince the desk to send us, however.

After listing the pros and cons—on an American Airlines cocktail napkin during a flight to somewhere—I accepted the editing job with a burst of energy and enthusiasm for work. I always had assumed I would be a reporter forever, but I did not regret going on the desk. I missed the travel and the clarity of a single consuming story, but I was happy to spend the nights at home with my family. Instead of taking pride only in the stories I wrote, I felt ownership of the one hundred stories and photos we provided every day to hundreds of papers around the globe. I imagined the wire itself flowing through my veins and into the world for millions of people to see.

For the first time, I was working indoors every day and sitting in a comfy chair (at the Pentagon they called it "flying a desk"), but the pace could be fierce. I saw myself like an air-traffic controller: bringing in raw copy, sending out the finished stories, and trying not to allow—or make—a critical error.

I also was excited to dig into the business side of news, because in 1996 we could see the nascent internet was going to change newspapers and our jobs, but we didn't know how. We built our first website and created email addresses for the staff.

I was happily awake and engaged at work. Once again, my career had taken an unexpected turn to the right place, with little direction from me.

As part of my new position, I flew to the corporate headquarters to visit Bill Burleigh, the man who had sent me to Mexico, come up with my first book idea, and become the chief executive of the entire company.

I confidently told Bill I could handle the journalism part of my new job—it wasn't that difficult—but now I was fascinated by the economics of news. I had big hopes for making money with the news wire and launching innovative media products, especially digital ones. I thought he would be pleased, but he frowned and was silent for a minute. Then he said, "I've seen a lot of good editors ruined by the business side." I tried to remember his well-meaning caution the first time I actually spoke the words "maximizing shareholder value."

And I didn't really get the journalism, either, or how to be a good leader. In a single promotion, I had leapt over the fifty reporters and editors in the Washington bureau who had raised me from a cub. Now I was supposed to be their boss. As usual in the news business, no one formally taught me anything about how to do my new job. I was a good reporter, so my bosses assumed I would be a good editor, which—as all of us had witnessed many times—was not necessarily true.

One of the first stories I edited was by the veteran White House reporter Ann McFeatters. Ann was technically now under my supervision, but she had the experience and the clout to do whatever she wanted.

Her story, written on deadline, was not clear to me. I tried to improve the story, especially what I considered the tortured lede, and sent it on the wire. A few minutes later she was standing behind me, and I could feel the anger coming off her like heat. I swiveled around in my chair to face her.

"In twenty-four years of journalism," she said in a voice deliberately loud enough to rattle the entire newsroom, "I've never seen a story edited so poorly. You made it absolutely wrong, and we've got to send out a correction right now."

"The story was not clear," I snapped back, "or I would not have made it wrong." My defensiveness did not help. She was right. If I had just asked her before assuming I knew what she meant, I would have avoided making a mistake under her byline.

Corrections were embarrassing, but the only thing worse was an error that went uncorrected. Every second mattered when an error had moved on the wire, because editors would be putting the story into their papers. We were petrified a paper would print one of our errors and make us all look bad to readers. Our credibility was like blood: if too much spilled, we would die. I quickly wrote the correction myself and sent it.

That night I talked to Maru about what had happened. I had known since being a cub reporter that making mistakes was how we learned, but I felt awful about my careless editing and my graceless behavior as a rookie manager. Maru made me feel worse by reminding me that Ann had a leadership role in the office beyond her title or mine. More importantly, Maru said, Ann and her husband, Dale, had been good to us since the moment I joined the bureau. They even had me over for Thanksgiving dinner one year when I was alone in Washington. Their home on a leafy street, filled with books and three children, was the model for how I wanted us to live.

The next morning, I went to see Ann at her desk. Humbled, I apologized for making her story wrong and promised to check with her the next time before making significant changes to a story. Then I asked for her help learning to run the bureau.

She agreed—emphatically—that I needed help.

# 16

## EPILOGUE

—— ON JOURNALISM ——

By 2003, a decade after covering my last gunfight on foreign soil, I had become the old guy at a desk deciding which reporters would go to war.

My boss for fifteen years, the venerable Dan Thomasson, had retired under company policy at age sixty-five. He was not ready to stop working, but he chose me to succeed him as Washington bureau chief and editor of a global news service. I did not always take his advice on how to run things, which was infuriating to him, but he didn't realize how much of his spirit and teaching already were part of me. Most of his guidance proved to be wise, even when I wasn't ready to hear it.

The United States was preparing for a second war with Iraq's Saddam Hussein, the same leader I had seen in action in 1991. This time the US president was George W. Bush, the son of the man who had led the first war against Saddam. I remembered the frustrated soldier during the first war who had told me he didn't want his son going back to finish the job. His fear had come true.

I wanted to return to Iraq myself, but there was too much to manage in Washington. Also, I would miss our daughter, Isabella, ten, and our son, Lucas, who was seven. If Saddam didn't get me this time, I thought, Maru would kill me. That's what I told myself, anyway.

Some of our reporters had been in combat, including the invasion of Afghanistan two years earlier, but others never had covered anything more dangerous than a hearing on Capitol Hill, so we prepared them with the proper equipment and vaccinations. I delivered the speech about "no story being worth dying for," but just in case, I promised they would have life insurance in a combat zone. We got satellite phones because, as I reminded them a dozen times, the story was worthless until they filed.

Our Washington bureau now served more than newspapers, so the dozen men and women headed to the war zone also were expected to file for television and online, with words, photos, video, and continuous updates on social media. This made more work for the reporters but enabled them to share their experiences with an unlimited global audience.

When I had slept on the same sandy ground during the first war with Iraq, I didn't have a camera or a phone, and the internet did not exist. Since most of my career had been with a wire service, however, I always had reported in real time and around the clock.

The team's coverage of the invasion was excellent, but later in the conflict a writer and photographer from one of our papers were injured while riding in a military vehicle that was hit by a roadside bomb. I felt sick, worried for our guys and their families. I had been shot at, teargassed, and chased by thugs, but never got a scratch. After a series of calls, we were convinced the two colleagues were not hurt badly, but they were shaken.

I advised their editor to order them home immediately, but to let them stay in Iraq if they insisted. The contradictory guidance was calculated. I knew from experience they would forever regret leaving too soon, but if they needed to come home, they could blame the boss. They finished their assignment and returned safely.

During the fourteen years I was a bureau chief and news media executive, my greatest challenges were about money and technology rather than breaking news or foreign wars. My most important job was to help quality news coverage survive and prosper in the digital age. As our once secure newspaper business (aka monopoly) fragmented, I desperately chased new revenue, cut spending, and lashed the staff with inane corporate euphemisms such as "doing more with less."

Fortunately, Scripps had diversified into cable television, and despite the grumbling of some old-timers, we adapted the Washington bureau to support our rapidly growing channels HGTV and Food Network. I helped launch another lifestyle cable channel, developed magazines and websites, and experimented with business models for digital news. With a more diverse staff (and Maru and our kids as the focus group), we created magazines in Spanish for the growing Latino market.

The Washington bureau put top priority on breaking investigative stories, and we led multimedia reporting teams with Scripps newspapers and television stations, covering everything from Sudden Infant Death Syndrome and unsolved homicides to cruelty at animal shelters. I was most proud to carry on the bureau's tradition of training (paid) interns, and I helped raise hundreds of cubs of my own.

Personally, my politics had moved to the boring middle, partly because I was older and partly because my views changed with experience. I sometimes wondered what might have happened if I had been a college radical in a country less tolerant than ours. In some of the places I covered, the wrong poster in a dorm room could have gotten me in trouble, or even killed. Many of the places I had worked, especially Mexico, the Middle East, and Africa, had grown far more dangerous for reporters.

I long ago had lost my passion for strident activism or partisanship of any kind. I had political opinions, but they were not fervent, and it was important professionally to keep them to myself. My own mother complained she didn't know who I voted for. My view of partisan politics was the same as that of good soldiers or judges or police officers: yes, politics was important, but I had a job to do no matter who was in power.

The one belief I was passionate and vocal about was that with good information, people would make the right decisions. I was less interested in telling people what they should do than in telling them what they should know. Sometimes covering the news felt remote—that we were observing the world rather than changing it—but it always felt meaningful.

Even when newspapers were closing or laying off reporters, I never stopped being grateful I found journalism. I felt satisfaction mastering a craft and purpose in the work. Looking back at the very first big fire I covered on that cold day in Chicago, it seems odd even to me that my response was not to help the injured but to take notes. At that moment, I felt I was doing what I was supposed to do: my job. My story is about finding the news, both as an occupation and as a calling. I always marveled that I got to explore the world and write about it. And they paid me.

I was fortunate that older people had opened doors for me, the same way Maru was lucky to have been discovered as a dancer. We both stumbled into careers that allowed us to grow into ourselves and live happy, productive lives. We shared the same hope for our own kids, whatever jobs they chose.

As the newspaper industry declined, however, my job was not as enjoyable, and by 2012 I had laid off more people than I ever had hired. Things were only going to get worse. Maybe now was the time to return to writing, which is what I had set out to do after college. It had been years since I had written anything except memos and corporate presentations. My boss snidely called me the "Minister of Propaganda" because of my adulatory reports about the Washington bureau to the corporate office, obviously intended to protect our jobs from budget cuts.

Also, this life was not what Maru had signed on for. I had promised we would go to Washington for two years; now we had stayed almost twenty-five. Her dance group—expanded to three companies, with kids, teens, and adults— had become the premiere Latin dance organization in Washington, but the stress was exhausting, and we didn't have time for each other. We always talked about doing more together, about traveling, or even teaming up on a business. Instead, I went to the bureau early and stayed late. When I got home at night, she turned over the kids and went to rehearsals or performances.

Years before, I had promised her to retire when I reached fifty-five, which was the magic age when my pension and benefits would be secure and the kids would be grown. Back when I made the promise, my fifty-fifth birthday seemed far in the future, and I figured that by then I would be walking with a cane and happy to slow down. The day came too soon, and I wasn't ready. I tried denial, negotiating, and rationalizing, but I had made a promise and I knew it was time. Reluctantly, I said good-bye to colleagues and the company that had given me so much.

In 2013, I set off on a new adventure, once again, not sure exactly where I was headed.

———

Forty years after I started as a cub reporter, the pace of change in the news media feels faster than ever. In my lifetime, the TV networks shocked everybody when they doubled the length of the nightly national news—from a mere fifteen minutes to thirty minutes. Few imagined TV news around the clock, or entire networks presenting current events, or that a "public service" like news would be so profitable. The tone of television news changed, too, from traditional broadcasters playing it straight to more "personality" and then outright opinion, partisanship, and shouting matches.

The means to cover the news improved dramatically. Cell phones and portable, wireless gear meant correspondents didn't need to carry dimes for pay phones or worry as much how to file text, photos, and video.

The reporters covering the news changed, too. Enrollment at journalism schools flipped from mostly male students to mostly female. A few (but not enough) women, African Americans, Latinos, and Asian Americans became leaders in mostly white male newsrooms. The modest demographic changes were part of a healthy redefinition of which stories should be covered, how they could be told, and who should tell them.

Newsroom culture evolved with the times. My grandparents, both newspaper reporters, remembered newsrooms filled with crude talk, cigarette smoke, and booze, but the stories in the newspapers themselves were puritanical and prudish. Later, because of real concern about sexual harassment in the workplace, reporters no longer were allowed to trade jokes in the newsroom about oral sex, but they could describe oral sex—and anything else—in the paper and on television.

Then the internet blew up everything. The power of a few people (including me) to set the news agenda was shattered. The old editors no longer could decide who was a journalist, what was a story, or what was fair commentary. Politicians and businesses could speak directly to news consumers without going through journalists as gatekeepers. Citizens could talk back to the media and to each other. Enabled and emboldened by anonymity online, the tone of political discourse grew more vicious.

The information network was always "on," meaning there was no more news cycle with deadlines and built-in pauses, just round-the-clock, unfiltered information. The faster pace and increased competition reduced the time to check facts and frame stories, and the news agenda could be set by a random, ten-second video from somebody's cell phone.

More information did not always mean more wisdom. My generation was taught not to believe everything we read. My children had to be skeptical of unlimited sources of information. Even photos and videos—once the definition of unfiltered truth—could be misleading or lies. It was as if a tornado had hit the Library of Congress, knocking the covers off books and scattering the pages. There was more stuff but less sense.

Some of this change was positive for readers: consumers had easier access to more news from more places than ever in history. The challenge was sorting through the propaganda, bias, and lies to find news that was accurate. When individual stories were freed from context and shared online, it was harder to judge the reliability of the original source.

Even with this greater volume of stories, traditional news providers could not sustain the revenue that had allowed us to cover entire cities or even the world. It wasn't that news companies failed to act; it was that we did not come up with strategies to make money when our products (news and advertising, especially classifieds) suddenly were free and ubiquitous. In the same way, the internet gave listeners more music in more places for less money, while the music providers—artists and record companies—struggled to survive.

The "crisis" in media and the collapse of local newspapers is a business problem more than a journalism problem. We once had a lock on advertising and news delivery, and now we don't. Investment has not kept up with new technologies, as evidenced by the amateurish and clunky digital operations at many local newspapers and TV stations. Newspaper revenue and employment are half what they were only a dozen years ago.

Underneath the job cuts and uncertainty, however, the journalism mission has not changed. The basic challenge still is to make sense of reality and to share that reality with others. Getting the facts *right*—asking for the middle initial like they taught at City News—and telling the stories quickly, accurately, and fairly, remain the goals. Journalism has never been complicated to do; it's just difficult to do well.

The highest form of journalism—investigative reporting—is more vigorous and less restrained than ever. Today, just as when I started, the most important work is not "covering" what everyone can see but exposing things that are hidden, either because of ignorance or because someone is trying to hide them.

Reporters still need to develop sources by building trust and relationships. Then they must tap those sources to understand and explain what others cannot see. This means discovering and exposing hidden patterns, truths, and secrets. The talent and courage necessary to uncover investigative stories are not different because of the internet.

Most importantly, journalists must strive to remember and protect our highest values. Technology is changing all professions, from medicine to law to education. Still, we expect our doctors, lawyers, and teachers to maintain rigorous standards of excellence and integrity. The same should be true for journalists.

The disconnect between journalists and our audience is not new. We've long spent too much time covering things people don't care about, and often from a point of view they don't share. A simple example is how reporters talk about the government "losing" money from tax cuts, instead of how people will keep more of the money they earn. This is a form of bias, but it is so common that most people take it for granted.

Good reporters pride themselves on keeping their personal views out of their coverage, but it takes effort. The night Bill Clinton was declared the victor in the 1996 presidential race, some people working in my newsroom clapped and cheered. I was appalled and spoke sharply to them. It didn't matter whom they supported in the privacy of the voting booth—many of us wore "I Voted" stickers to work—but they knew better than to share their opinions in the newsroom. I was deeply embarrassed because interns working that night saw something so unprofessional.

The complaints about bias are a product of declining trust. Reporters never have been especially popular, and even when I started, polls on trustworthiness ranked us below doctors and police officers. The distrust has grown, and today's readers have more ways of being heard, which is why the complaints about coverage seem louder. While we consider ourselves part of the solution to the nation's problems, many readers and viewers see us as part of the problem.

President Donald Trump did not create the distrust of the media, but he figured out how to exploit it. He didn't invent "fake news," but he's got a talent for labeling things he doesn't like. And he's right that some media people are on a seek-and-destroy mission against him personally as well as his policies. Only two of the nation's top one hundred newspapers endorsed Trump in 2016. Just for the record, 93 percent of US newspapers endorsed Richard Nixon in 1972. Two years later Nixon resigned.

Reporters should be less worried about President Trump than about the people who elected him in 2016. To many of the 63 million voters who wanted Trump to shake up the system, we in the media were part of that corrupt and unfair system. Add to that number the Hillary Clinton voters who thought reporters were unfair to her and gave Trump too much uncritical coverage. Then there are the millions who didn't vote at all—a bigger number than those who voted for either Trump or Clinton—who are impervious to our calls to "civic duty." How did so many citizens come to view us as the opposition, and how do we convince them we are on their side?

To earn trust, our driving principles should be speed, accuracy, and fairness. Journalists must be fast because competition makes us better. Accuracy is the minimal requirement for real news. But even if we are fast and accurate, only fairness will earn the long-term confidence of the people who count on us.

Are we meeting our own standards of speed, accuracy, or fairness?

Technology allows reporters to be faster than ever, but most old-fashioned scoops don't last because they are quickly matched by competitors, and most readers don't know or care who broke what story. Reporters know, however, and scoops are a measure of skill, even if keeping track matters mostly to us. We should focus more on being first with truly original reporting, rather than being first to reveal what some politician is going to say in a speech that night.

Good reporters want to be accurate, but there is a temptation to be first rather than right, especially when bad information can be "updated," which also is a nice way of saying corrected. The pressure to update stories constantly on multiple platforms means less time to report and check facts. A positive development is that accuracy is easier to measure now because stories are instantly visible to all, and "fact checker" has become a growing job category in journalism.

Fairness is the hardest goal to measure and achieve. If fairness is in the eyes of the beholder, we are failing miserably on both the right and left. Even by our own professional standards, we should be concerned by the vitriol of the coverage, the smirking and eye-rolling of TV reporters, and the angry frustrations that boil over into our reporting and social media. The current political climate is bringing out the best and the worst in journalism, which makes it harder for the many reporters trying to be fair.

We can start by practicing what we preach to others about honesty and transparency. Honesty in our work is important to the people we cover and to our audience. We should talk publicly about how we get stories, the ground rules for interviews, the sources and documents that support our conclusions, and why we publish and broadcast what we do. We must try harder to get information on the record. When we have an opinion, it should be based on verified facts, well argued and free from outside influence. And can we please separate news and commentary?

Journalists have to break their own stories, not follow the pack. They have to see things for themselves in the real world, because if you are reading something on a screen, you've already been beat. When you approach a story or a source, be insistent but courteous, skeptical but not cynical. The most important news-gathering tool is still the question. Ask questions from the point of view of the people watching your story, not the people you are covering. Then really listen to the answers. In the current polarized environment, we have to be extra vigilant against appearing partisan, even in our questions.

Pause before you file, especially on deadline. Ask someone to look over your shoulder, even when you are "only" posting on social media and not doing a "real" story. People rightly judge us by the quality of our work, including on social media, which is why everybody needs an editor.

I'm restating these basic rules because the only way to win trust is to earn it. Too many people think we are biased, and they are not all wrong. This problem goes far beyond the current occupant of the White House and affects media around the world, not just in the United States. We are married to our audience in the sense that we can't survive without them. It's time to listen to them and then restate our vows of accuracy and fairness.

Real journalists do not create "fake news," which is deliberately false reporting or carelessly false reporting that is not corrected. Fake news also occurs when ideological blinders and personal opinion distort reality, sometimes intentionally and sometimes unconsciously. Fake news is not simply making a mistake. Everybody makes mistakes, but real reporters correct them.

There was no golden age of news in the past, however. In many ways, journalism is more professional than ever. When American newspapers were young, they were filled with lies, rumors, fake news, and political manipulation. It is true that when I started, reporters knew more than they put in the paper, and today people are quick to publish or share more than they really know. Again, this is about values—fairness and accuracy—and not about the internet or the nature of social media. Technology is not to blame when we cheat on our values, but it can be an enabler.

The journalism business will figure out a way to prosper because quality news has enduring worth to individuals and society. Reliable coverage might even be more valuable now because false information circulates so easily and is manipulated by political operatives, scammers, and governments.

Good journalists still make a product people want, but we have to figure out how to get paid during the difficult transition to a new business model. The news industry will not become nonprofit, because it won't generate enough money for real scale. Nor will journalism be government-run, because of American history. That leaves a market-based, profit-oriented news media, or some combination of business models, which would be beneficial to all because of the variety and competition among news organizations.

I spent my career trying to resist predicting the future, so I'm not going to predict the future of the news business, but every enterprise requires a growing stream of revenue. Advertising, the traditional funder of news, has declined for many news organizations, and readers and viewers are not paying enough as subscribers to cover the gap. Maybe there is a third way beyond advertising and subscriptions. I am positive that any winning business strategy will be built on the values of honesty and integrity.

For young people attracted to a career in journalism, money always has been secondary to the calling, which was fine when we had a monopoly but a disaster when the business model collapsed. Young reporters—even those who can't add and subtract very well—must learn the business of news as well as the craft of journalism. If you are starting a news career, you could end up working for a company that doesn't even exist today. And you could be the one who creates that new company. I hope you do.

We know the right values—speed, accuracy, and fairness—and we know the difference between real news and fake news. Rapidly improving technology allows us to report and distribute real news instantly from anywhere to everyone. Journalists need to embrace the newest technologies, recommit to our highest values, and develop business models that will pay for quality news coverage.

If we play it right, the combination of new digital tools and universal connectivity—powered by old-school news values—could make this the beginning of a real golden age of journalism.

———

These days I only read newspapers and don't write for them. Like many of you, I occasionally want to throw the remote control at the TV news or threaten to delete my social media accounts. I'm truly happy to have more time with Maru, and we are proud of the adults our children have become.

But sometimes friends ask me, "Do you miss being a reporter?"

Every single day.

# 17

# WHERE ARE THEY NOW?

## —— IN ORDER OF APPEARANCE ——

**Theo Stamos**—My first trainer at City News traded journalism for law and was elected the Commonwealth's Attorney for Arlington County and the City of Falls Church, Virginia, near Washington, DC. One of her recent summer interns was my son, Lucas, meaning Theo taught journalism to me and law to my son.

**City News Bureau of Chicago**—The business model failed (but never the journalism), and the office closed. Editor **Paul Zimbrakos** took his teaching skills to Loyola University Chicago. Alumni include *New York Times* columnist **David Brooks,** former digital czar at NPR and the *New York Times* **Kinsey Wilson,** and investigative reporter **Seymour Hersh.** My two City News friends who went out west and helped get me the job in El Paso have a daughter, **Kate Linthicum,** who is a *Los Angeles Times* correspondent in Mexico, based just a few blocks from where Maru and I lived.

**Lynn Sweet**—The courthouse reporter who schooled me by scooping me became the *Chicago Sun-Times* bureau chief in Washington, a familiar face on TV news and president of the Gridiron Club, the oldest (and most fun) journalism organization in the capital.

*Chicago Tribune*—I never did get to work for my hometown paper, but when the *Trib* went through massive cuts and couldn't afford its rent, I invited the entire Washington bureau to share office space with the Scripps bureau, a mutually beneficial move, even though we were competitors.

**David Axelrod**—The former *Tribune* political reporter became chief strategist for a young senator from Illinois, **Barack Obama,** and helped get him to the White House.

*El Paso Herald-Post*—My first newspaper closed in 1997. Editors **Harry Moskos** and **Tim Gallagher** went on to run bigger papers. Photographer **Ruben Ramirez** became a TV journalist and then chief photographer at "the other paper." Reporter **Joe Olvera** ran for mayor before dying at seventy-one. My friend **John Hopper** retired after a distinguished career at the Associated Press. John's daughter, **Jessica Hopper,** got the journalism gene from her mother and her father and is a respected music writer and editor.

**Scripps Howard**—The company now called E. W. Scripps spun off the cable networks HGTV, Food Network, and Travel Channel, and then sold all of the newspapers. The news service closed after I retired. The vibrant Scripps Washington bureau is more than one hundred years old, covering news for local television stations and digital news organizations. The managing editor, **Dale McFeatters,** retired as chief editorial writer, and the former White House reporter, **Ann McFeatters,** still writes a column.

**The Mophead**—Several years ago, US criminal charges against **Gilberto Ontiveros** were dismissed without prejudice, meaning they could be filed again. I never saw him after our jailhouse interview, although I confess I did not look very hard.

**Alejandro**—My friend and driver in El Salvador was murdered. His brother blamed it on Alejandro's work with me and other US reporters. I've changed his name at the family's request.

**Dan Thomasson**—My Scripps Howard mentor and boss wrote a weekly column until he died at eighty-four. Friends often asked, Did Dan ever mellow? No.

**Linda Bray**—The military police captain's historic role in the invasion of Panama led to congressional proposals to lift the ban on women in combat, but it took twenty-three years, when most combat jobs were opened to females.

**Pete Williams**—The Pentagon spokesman, who fixed my passport to let me cover the Gulf War, returned to journalism as an excellent reporter for NBC.

**John King**—From a Gulf War "pencil," King got his own show covering politics on CNN.

**Adel al-Jubeir**—Our young Saudi handler during the first war with Iraq became his country's ambassador to Washington and then Foreign Minister.

**Katie Couric**—I failed to convince the talk show host to let me help write her memoir, but she did fine without me. She has been an award-winning reporter and host on all three of the traditional television networks and now runs her own media company.

**Rhonda Cornum**—The army doctor I worked with on her POW memoir became a brigadier general and a senior medical officer in the army, with a special interest in training soldiers to be mentally resilient to combat stress.

**Desert Storm Veterans**—I was honored to be invited to the twenty-fifth Gulf War reunion by the VII Corps commander, **Gen. (Ret.) Fred Franks.** One of the leaders of the vets' charitable organization was **Stan Lenox,** who drove me into (and out of) a minefield. Years later, my experience with the artillery brigade would become one of the models for putting reporters with troops in combat, now called embedding.

**Red Patchers**—"My Marines" of the First Landing Support Battalion built an orphanage in Somalia before returning home to California. Nine months after I left Somalia, eighteen American soldiers were killed and seventy-three were injured in a battle that was portrayed in the book and film *Black Hawk Down*. The incident led to the US withdrawal from Somalia.

**David Bloom**—My Somalia friend from NBC died in 2003 while covering the second war with Iraq. He was thirty-nine.

**Barton Gellman**—After our escape from Somalia, the best-selling author and reporter broke stories and worked on projects that won three Pulitzer Prizes. He helped introduce the world to Edward Snowden, who revealed secret US government surveillance programs.

**Maru Montero**—The dance company continues to perform beautifully after more than twenty-five years. Maru restored a little house in Mexico City, so our family can be at home in both countries. Our daughter **Isabella,** twenty-seven, and son **Lucas,** twenty-four, both graduated from college and are working. Neither has more than a passing interest in journalism or dance.

**Julie Morley**—My mother says she loves me. (I checked it out.) My step-father, **Robert B. Morley,** died in 1999, and my four stepbrothers and I grew into "real" brothers.

After I became bureau chief, I was curious about the journalism careers of my mother's late parents, **Ann** and **Art Moore.** They had died before I became a journalist, but many years later I discovered their story in company records that were in my Washington office all along. Searching through old Scripps magazines, I learned that my grandparents had started together in the 1920s at papers in San Diego and then San Francisco, both owned by Scripps Howard. I could not have felt more proud that we worked for the same outfit.

# 18

# LESSONS

—— ON WHAT I LEARNED ——

Speed-Accuracy-Fairness

Better to be right than first

Better to be fair than right

Honesty above all

Facts first, opinion to follow

Sources are everything

Sources can be wrong

Documents are your friends

There is no news in the office

Break your own stories

Be skeptical but not cynical

Ask, and then really listen to the answer

Stand with your audience

Everybody needs an editor

Master the business of news, not only the craft of journalism

Good values plus smart technology equal great journalism

# INDEX